About Island Press

Island Press is the only nonprofit organization in the United States whose principal purpose is the publication of books on environmental issues and natural resource management. We provide solutions-oriented information to professionals, public officials, business and community leaders, and concerned citizens who are shaping responses to environmental problems.

In 2001, Island Press celebrates its seventeenth anniversary as the leading provider of timely and practical books that take a multidisciplinary approach to critical environmental concerns. Our growing list of titles reflects our commitment to bringing the best of an expanding body of literature to the environmental community throughout North America and the world.

Support for Island Press is provided by The Bullitt Foundation, The Mary Flagler Cary Charitable Trust, The Nathan Cummings Foundation, Geraldine R. Dodge Foundation, Doris Duke Charitable Foundation, The Charles Engelhard Foundation, The Ford Foundation, The George Gund Foundation, The Vira I. Heinz Endowment, The William and Flora Hewlett Foundation, W. Alton Jones Foundation, The John D. and Catherine T. MacArthur Foundation, The Andrew W. Mellon Foundation, The Charles Stewart Mott Foundation, The Curtis and Edith Munson Foundation, National Fish and Wildlife Foundation, The New-Land Foundation, Oak Foundation, The Overbrook Foundation, The David and Lucile Packard Foundation, The Pew Charitable Trusts, Rockefeller Brothers Fund, The Winslow Foundation, and other generous donors.

This Sovereign Land

This Sovereign Land

A New Vision for Governing the West

DANIEL KEMMIS

ISLAND PRESS

Washington ♦ Covelo ♦ London

ISLAND PRESS is a trademark of
The Center for Resource Economics.

Library of Congress Cataloging-in-Publication Data
Kemmis, Daniel, 1945–
This sovereign land : a new vision for governing the West /
Daniel Kemmis.
p.   cm.
Includes bibliographical references and index.
ISBN 1-55963-842-7 (cloth)
1. Public Lands—West. (U.S.) 2. Public lands—West (U.S.)—
Management. 3. Land use, Rural—Environmental aspects—West
(U.S.)—Management. 4. Conservation of natural resources—West
(U.S.)—Management. 5. Environmental policy—West (U.S.)
6. State rights. 7. Federal-state controversies. 8. West (U.S.)—
Politics and government. I. Title.
HD243.W38 K46 2001
333.1'0978—dc21   2001002093

Printed on recycled, acid-free paper

British-Cataloguing-in-Publication Data available.

Manufactured in the United States of America
2   4   6   8   9   7   5   3   1

To my students

Contents

Preface

Two long-standing personal passions account for this book. One is my lifelong love for politics, and the other is the way I feel about the American West. Over the years, I have come to know that behind my fascination with politics lies a sometimes mysterious but apparently unshakable faith in democracy—in the capacity of people to solve their problems and realize their potential together. This democratic faith makes me a democrat with a small "d," but this portion of my identity shades imperceptibly into my being also a loyal big "D" partisan Democrat. Meanwhile, my second commanding loyalty—the deep affection I feel for the West—is rooted in a strong emotional response to its magnificent landscapes and their power to shape and sustain the ecosystems that have evolved on and with those landscapes. Humans are part of those ecosystems, and so are their evolving politics. It is with the power of the West to shape its politics that my two passions intersect. What this all adds up to is that this book is the work of a westerner, an environmentalist, and a democrat who is also a confirmed Democrat.

It is from this particular blend of perspectives that I describe here, as honestly as I know how, what I see the West making of itself. What I see is a very powerful, inspiring, hard, and demanding set of western landscapes having created over time a people so fundamentally defined by those places that they must

finally—must soon now—claim sovereignty over their homeland. So the westerner and the democrat in me has long been
convinced, and because of this I have found myself more and
more often dissenting from my Democrat and environmentalist
friends. So deep are some of the disagreements that I have often
doubted whether I was actually seeing what I thought I saw in
the West. Those disagreements and doubts made this a particularly hard book to write. But in the end, leaving the door open
to the possibility that I might just have it wrong, I have tried my
best to convey my understanding of where the West has been
and where it is going.

I believe that westerners, claimed by and committed to their
place, have finally come to the borders of a political maturity
that will enable them to take responsibility for the place that
made them westerners. And I believe that these commanding
landscapes—these sovereign landscapes—will be best served by
a people at last allowed to be sovereign over their homeland.

It is precisely as a democrat and an environmentalist that I
am convinced the West is now ready to be in charge of the West,
and that this can happen only through a gradual, thoughtfully
conceived, and carefully executed transfer of responsibility for
most of the public lands in the West. I do not mean privatization
any more than I mean turning the land over to the states. What
I do mean will take a book to tell. By the end of the book, I
expect many of my friends, colleagues, and neighbors to disagree with me still. Those disagreements and debates may eventually lead me to different conclusions from the ones expressed
here. But of this, at least, I am certain: the West has finally
matured enough to do justice to the open discussion this book
invites.

Acknowledgments

I am indebted to the William and Flora Hewlett Foundation for supporting both the researching and the writing of this book. As with every other individual and organization named here, the Hewlett Foundation is not accountable for what I have written. Most especially Michael Fischer is not, but he most especially deserves my gratitude for unflinchingly encouraging the development of unorthodox ideas.

The Center for the Rocky Mountain West at the University of Montana provided the institutional support for this effort, but it was the Center's people who provided the real support. Thanks to Joey Bernal, Paul Galasso, Susan Gibb, Tara Gunter, David Highness, Patty Hixson, Amy Inman, Greg Lakes, Doug Lawrence, Lori Lustig, Celeste River, Anne Robinson, and Carolyn Schultz for the teamwork it takes to do this kind of work. Special thanks to T. J. Abbenhaus for work on the maps and to Susan Fox for some superb pinch-hitting.

Jeannie Thompson provided more kinds of help than I even know about, but I do know how faithfully she guarded my morning writing time.

The best part of a regional studies center is the intellectual stimulation it provides. My colleagues Bill Farr and Larry Swanson have kept me as honest as they could, and my ongoing debate with Pat Williams about public land issues has been as helpful as it is stimulating.

This book wore out more than its share of research assistants, leaving me the advantage of getting to know more than my share of very fine young thinkers and writers. Thanks to Molly Kramer for getting us started; to Emily Miller for overwintering the book so productively; to Caitlin DeSilvey for pulling it all together; and to Ari LeVaux and James Lainsbury for bringing it home.

I appreciate the support and patience of all my colleagues in the Western Charter Project and most especially the many stimulating and clarifying conversations with Jim Butcher, Terry Minger, and Priscilla Salant.

Less frequent but deeply influential conversations are also echoed in this book. I recall especially talks with Terry Tempest Williams, Benjamin Barber, Chris Carlson, Bill Hornby, Patricia Limerick, Ed Marston, Luther Propst, Rosemary Romero, Charles Wilkinson, Donald Worster, and Monty Zeller.

Closer to home, I've had the advantage of working with Don Snow and Sarah Van de Wetering, Gerald Mueller, Jim Burchfield, Tom Petersen, Matt McKinney, Hank Fischer, Tom France, and Greg Schildwachter, all of whom have shared freely their experiences with and ideas about collaboration to deepen my own.

From within the land management agencies, I've benefited particularly from conversations with Dave Williams and Peggy Harwood, Cynthia Manning, Hal Salwasser and Orville Daniels, Gloria Flora and Ruth McWilliams.

Marc Jaffe believed in this book before anyone else did. Carl Brandt was next, and he became more than an agent to me, which perhaps is part of being a good agent. At Island Press, Jennifer Alt and Cecilia González provided excellent assistance; Barbara Youngblood and Pat Harris were outstanding, and Barbara Dean's skill as an editor is the invisible presence in this volume.

Finally, thanks to Sam, Abe, John, and Deva for your unswerving faithfulness.

The Lay of the Land

The American West has long been viewed, by its residents and by others, as standing apart from the rest of the United States. Since the early days of America's history, the West's distinguishing characteristics and its relationship to the rest of the country have been subjects of analysis, celebration, misunderstanding, and conflict.

This book focuses on the interior West, also known as the Rocky Mountain West, a region that is bordered by but does not include the Great Plains to the east and the Pacific Coast region to the west. Wallace Stegner described the region in relation to its neighbors in terms that fit well with the perspective of this book:

> So—the West that we are talking about comprises a dry core of eight public-lands states—Arizona, Colorado, Idaho, Montana, Nevada, New Mexico, Utah, and Wyoming—plus two marginal areas. The first of these is the western part of the Dakotas, Nebraska, Kansas, Oklahoma, and Texas, authentically dry but with only minimal public lands. The second is the West Coast—Washington, Oregon, and California—

with extensive arid lands but with well-watered coastal strips and also many rivers.[1]

Stegner might have added that the coastal states also have a substantial amount of public land, as does Alaska. For that reason, the "dry core" must be prepared at least to make political alliance with the Pacific states over public land issues and with the prairie states over a broader range of rural issues. For some purposes, then, both the Plains and the coast are part of the West, as is Alaska, and in some instances this book will treat them as such. But the core of the West, particularly the West whose issues occupy this book, is a region dominated by these features: mountainous terrain, aridity, and public lands.

If any one feature sets the West apart from the rest of the country, it is the power and presence of its landscape. The West is about land, and about the relationship of people to land. No other region comes close to the West's expansiveness of landscape in proportion to the number of its people, as figure 1 illustrates. But that relatively low population density is only one dimension of the dominance of land and landscape in the region. Land is ubiquitous in every dimension of western life. Ask people why they live in the West and the answer will most often have to do with landscape, far more often than would be the case in any other region. Attend ten public meetings in the West and see how many more of them involve land than would similar meetings anywhere else.

This dominance of land and landscape makes its presence felt in public policy, largely because so much of the West is publicly or tribally owned. In fact, if you map America's public lands, you have essentially mapped the West, as figure 2 shows. More than 90 percent of all federal land is found in Alaska and the eleven westernmost states of the lower forty-eight—Montana, Idaho, Wyoming, Colorado, Utah, Arizona, New Mexico, Nevada, Cal-

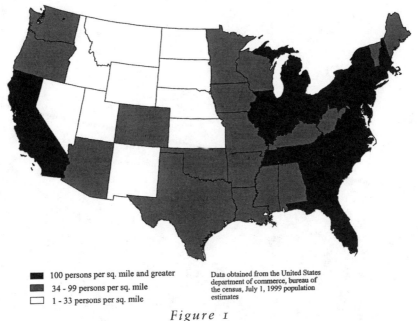

Data obtained from the United States department of commerce, bureau of the census, July 1, 1999 population estimates

■ 100 persons per sq. mile and greater
■ 34 - 99 persons per sq. mile
☐ 1 - 33 persons per sq. mile

Figure 1
Population Density by State

ifornia, Oregon, and Washington. These federal holdings are so vast that they dominate not only the geography but also the politics of the West. Geographically, the Forest Service and the Bureau of Land Management (BLM) alone own more than 411 million of the roughly 1.2 billion acres that make up Alaska and the eleven lower western states—about 34 percent of the total land area. Nationally owned lands take up an astounding 83 percent of Nevada's total land base, more than 60 percent of Idaho's and Utah's, and more than 45 percent of the land base in four other western states. These lands are owned by the national government and run by its agencies in Washington, D.C. The BLM, the Forest Service, and increasingly the U.S. Fish and Wildlife Service and National Marine Fisheries Service have been given primary responsibility for managing these vast western acreages.

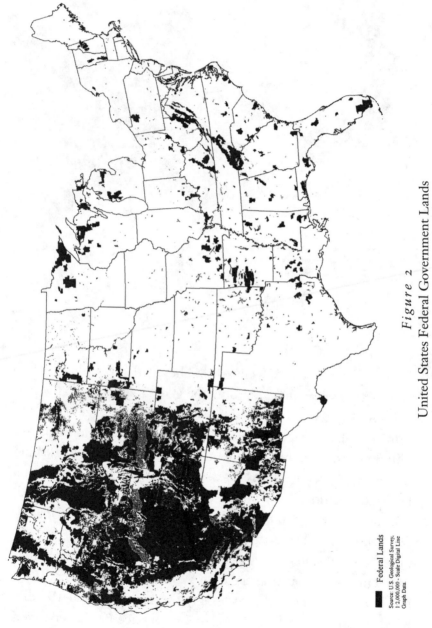

■ Federal Lands

Source: U.S. Geological Survey,
1:2,000,000 - Scale Digital Line
Graph Data.

Figure 2
United States Federal Government Lands

The West is also Indian country, as figure 3 demonstrates. Indian tribes govern roughly one-fifth of the interior West, and as devolution comes to their lands, they control them with less and less federal interference. More than 1 million Indians live in the eleven lower western states, roughly half of them on reservations. Arizona contains the largest percentage of Indian land, with roughly one-third of the state covered by reservations. The largest western reservations are the size of some eastern states, and they are governed at a very high level of complexity and sophistication. Forty reservations maintain their own fish and wildlife operations, for example; twenty-five are members of the Council of Energy Resource Tribes; and thirty offer and regulate casino gambling.[2]

As figure 4 shows at a glance, by the 1990s the interior West had become (and was expected to continue to be) the country's fastest-growing region. In terms of percentage of change in population, the five fastest-growing states in the 1990s were all located in the interior West.[3] Nevada, Arizona, Colorado, Utah, and Idaho ranked first through fifth, respectively, in percentage of population increase during that decade. New Mexico ranked twelfth and Montana twentieth, with Wyoming trailing the regional pack as the country's thirty-second fastest-growing state. The regional growth affected both city and countryside. Between 1990 and 1998, the region's metropolitan areas grew by 25 percent and its rural areas by 18 percent, both rates significantly higher than elsewhere in the United States.[4] The relentless wave of migration into the mountains puts steadily increasing pressure on all western land, including public land. It also creates growing challenges in terms of regional identity as relative newcomers, less familiar than old-timers with the region and its traditions, become a more dominant force in the West.

Despite the increasingly diverse demographics of the West,

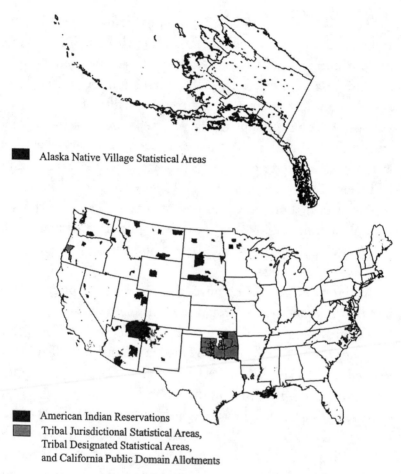

Alaska Native Village Statistical Areas

American Indian Reservations
Tribal Jurisdictional Statistical Areas,
Tribal Designated Statistical Areas,
and California Public Domain Allotments

Figure 3
Tribal Lands in the United States

by the end of the twentieth century the political geography of
the region had become remarkably homogeneous. Whereas
much was made in the 1990s of the southern domination of the
Republican Party, far less attention was paid to the fact that
Republicans exercised even more solid control over the interior
West. The maps of districts of the U.S. House of Representatives and of governorships shown in figures 5 and 6 tell that part

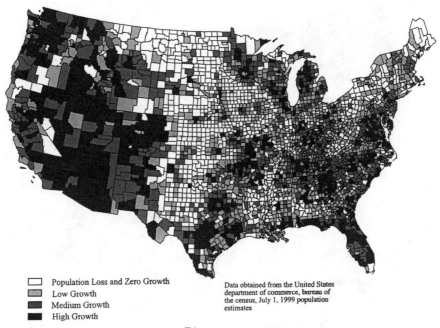

Population Loss and Zero Growth
Low Growth
Medium Growth
High Growth

Data obtained from the United States
department of commerce, bureau of
the census, July 1, 1999 population
estimates

Figure 4
United States County Population Growth and Decline, 1990–1999

of the regional story very clearly. Following the 2000 elections, three-quarters of the congressional districts in the interior West were held by Republicans. The story with governorships was even more telling. There were Democratic governors in Missouri and Iowa and in the Pacific Coast states, but none—not one—in the giant, 1,200-mile-wide swath in between.

These statistics and maps present a snapshot of the West at the turn of the twenty-first century, capturing some of the features that set the region apart from the rest of the country. But this is a snapshot of a rapidly changing region. Some of the maps may already be outdated by the time this book is published, and others soon after. In fact, what this book predicts is that the map of the West will be substantially redrawn in the coming decades—including the map of the public lands. Such a degree

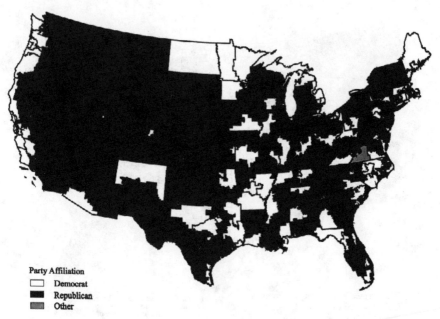

Party Affiliation
☐ Democrat
■ Republican
▪ Other

Figure 5
Congressional Districts, 107th Congress

of change can be frightening, and the West sometimes seems nearly paralyzed by the currents sweeping through and around it. But the West has always prided itself on its ingenuity and adaptiveness. The following chapters are offered in that spirit, as a fresh way of understanding where the West has been so that it can more intelligently decide where it should be headed.

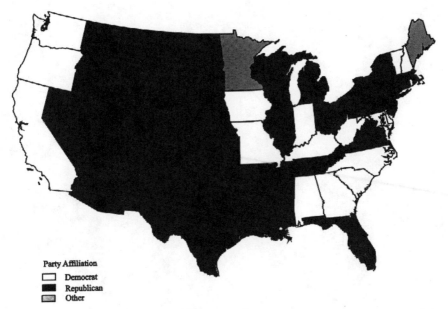

Figure 6
Party Affliations of Governors, January 2001

The
Lost Trail

"A big wild country just perfect for big wild critters
like bears and loggers."
—People for the West

Mandated by the Endangered Species Act of 1973 to increase the
number of grizzly bears in the northern Rocky Mountains, the
U.S. Fish and Wildlife Service in the 1980s identified the Selway-
Bitterroot region of Idaho and Montana as one of the few remaining areas big enough and wild enough to sustain a viable population of the wide-ranging, civilization-averse animals. In July 1997,
the agency released its draft environmental impact statement
(EIS) on grizzly bear restoration in the Selway-Bitterroot ecosystem, giving initial preference to a proposal called the Citizen
Management Alternative, which had been drafted by a coalition of
conservationists, timber producers, and labor unions. Under this
approach, the governors of the two states would appoint a team of
citizens to monitor and manage an initially small but then steadily
growing population of grizzlies in the Selway-Bitterroot.

Public hearings were duly scheduled on the draft EIS in Salmon, Idaho, and in Hamilton and Missoula, Montana. Among the hundreds of people who showed up to testify, only a handful supported the Citizen Management Alternative. Instead, the bulk of the testimony came alternately from those who opposed the presence of bears in the mountains under any conditions and those who supported wilderness-like protection for most of the northern Rockies, under the theory that with enough habitat free of roads and logging, the bears could and would take care of themselves. The "no bears" people were dead set against that approach for two reasons. First, it clearly aimed to stop or sharply curtail logging throughout the region, putting even more pressure on the already beleaguered timber-dependent communities in both states. The second threat was even more visceral: it came from the bears themselves. Many threatened and endangered species (think of the northern spotted owl) have themselves come to be seen as threatening to resource-based industries and communities, but few of those species actually eat people. Sometimes grizzlies do, but even when they do not, they scare the daylights out of folks. Not for nothing is this species named *Ursus arctos horribilis.*

Between the threats of bodily and economic harm, the grizzly reintroduction issue was tailor-made for the politics of fear, and the gears of that politics were duly and instantly engaged. As soon as the Fish and Wildlife Service released the draft EIS, Republican senators Larry Craig of Idaho and Conrad Burns of Montana, declaring that the national government was forcing grizzlies on an unwilling populace, persuaded the Senate Appropriations Committee to add a rider to an appropriation bill preventing any reintroduction of the bears, pending further study on "population viability."[1] The real intent, well understood in all quarters, was to put pressure on the Fish and Wildlife Service to keep bears out of the Bitterroot Mountains. Senator Burns' often-repeated question throughout this phase of the controversy, clearly intended to help the agency see the light, was, "What part of 'No' don't the feds understand?"[2]

While conservatives attempted in this way to prevent by federal action any federal action at all, several environmental groups were rousing equally powerful emotions on behalf of the bear by supporting a full-scale invocation of the Endangered Species Act through what they called the Conservation Biology Alternative. At its heart lay habitat.

Glacier and Yellowstone National Parks are the best-known homes of grizzlies in the lower forty-eight states, in part because of news stories of periodic grizzly attacks on sleeping or hiking tourists. But there is also inhabited grizzly country adjacent to the two parks, most notably next to Glacier, with Waterton-Glacier International Peace Park to the north feeding grizzlies into Glacier from the well-populated habitat of the Canadian Rockies, and the Bob Marshall Wilderness and Flathead Indian Reservation extending Glacier's grizzly habitat southward. To the west, the protected wilderness of the Cabinet Mountains provides another link to the Canadian Rockies.

It was these sizable but scattered pockets and chains of grizzly habitat that underlay the Conservation Biology Alternative in the Selway-Bitterroot. The great dream of conservationists in the northern Rockies had long been to create a continuous chain of linked wildlands through the mountains, "from Yellowstone to the Yukon," as a recent recurrence of this dream has begun to put it. The grizzly is the central, indicator species by which the success of this strategy has always been intended to be measured. If the grizzly can travel (or, more important, meet and mate with other grizzlies) from Yellowstone National Park to the Yukon Territory, the ecosystem will be essentially whole. And if not, then not.

Within that picture, the Selway-Bitterroot is an indispensable link, but it will be able to provide the linkage only if logging is sharply reduced and further road building halted in most of the national forests in the greater northern Rockies ecosystem. For years, the Alliance for the Wild Rockies had pursued this goal by drafting a bill to create the Northern Rockies Ecosystem Protection Act (NREPA) and repeatedly persuading eastern representatives to introduce it in Congress. For the same number of years, Montana and Idaho congressional delegations, responding primarily to timber companies, sawmill workers, and timber-dependent communities, had made sure NREPA never emerged from any committee. Then, as the Fish and Wildlife Service ground its administrative way through its mandate to expand grizzly populations, the Alliance for the Wild Rockies saw a chance to achieve its grand objective without congressional action. The Conservation Biology Alternative for grizzly bear recovery was wilderness by way of endangered species protection; it was NREPA in administrative clothing. And, of course, its opponents, including Senators Burns and Craig, knew it.

What was surprising about the grizzly controversy, though, was that the senators and the rest of the "no bears" contingent paid no attention to the "make it all wilderness" people, who paid them just as little attention in return. Instead, both sides concentrated their opposition on the Citizen Management Alternative. Conservatives opposed it because it would bring bears into the Selway-Bitterroot; environmentalists, because it did not protect enough wilderness and because it took management of the bears out of federal hands and turned it over to Montanans and Idahoans. In both cases, the issue was about territory and, finally, about sovereignty over that territory. If you turn a forest over to bears, you automatically reduce human dominion over that forest. With grizzlies around, humans cannot walk or sleep as sovereignly in the woods as they had before, and given the bears' legal status as a threatened species, they cannot cut as many trees or build as many roads either. These fears of losing control over the forests were matched from the other end of the political spectrum by the environmentalists' fear that if locals were allowed to begin managing western forests, the big federal stick of environmental protection would be splintered. From this perspective, the aggressive exercise of national sovereignty appeared crucial to protection of the bear.

In the end, it is only in terms of sovereignty that either the grizzly story or the larger story it is part of—the story of the West—can sort itself out. There is only one way to have grizzlies in these mountains, and that is on the grizzlies' own terms. Or, rather, on the grizzlies' and the mountains' shared terms. Across eons, the terrain shaped the bear, grew it, strengthened it, taught it the habits that could make it sovereign over that terrain. It was the landscape that made it into what western essayist and fiction writer William Kittredge once called "the damned old gorgeous, terrible grizzly bear."[3] Now it cannot be anything else; either the grizzly is there on its own sovereign terms or it is not there at all. Those who are sentimental about the bear are welcome to their sentiments, but the bear will not be governed by them.

This is roughly how the West itself must now be understood. Whatever the feelings nonwesterners have about the region—whatever affections, whatever myths—the only way to take care of the West now is to give it the room it needs to take care of itself. If the West is to be the West that people care so deeply about, it will have to do it on its own sovereign terms.

This book is an effort to tell the story of that emerging regional sovereignty before it happens. By its nature, then, this telling of the story is speculative, just as one can only speculate about the paths the Bitterroot grizzlies will choose to follow if they are allowed and encouraged to come into the region. Much of the controversy over the various alternatives in the environmental impact statement turned on the inherent uncertainty and inescapable speculation about where, under various conditions, the grizzlies will go and what they will do on their way there. The grizzlies' paths simply cannot be predicted, yet their "possibility space" occupies a certain more or less definitive range determined by the nature of the animal and the lay of the land. Much the same is true about the way the story of grizzly reintroduction might itself unfold, and the way the larger story of the West will unfold through dozens of smaller stories like that of the Selway-Bitterroot.

There are maybe three or four genuinely plausible paths the grizzly story might now follow. Each of those paths is itself part of its own larger story, some of it already told, some of it waiting to continue to happen—or not. These stories as they have unfolded over the past century or so are the story of the West itself, and the way they unfold from this point on will be the future of the West. This book traces out one possible (I believe likely) future for the region, given the lay of the land and the nature of its inhabitants. In a nutshell, it says that the West will figure out how to be in charge of the West. Specifically, and most frighteningly to many who love the place, the West will achieve regional control over most of the public lands now controlled by the national government—and over all the elements of the larger ecosystems of which those public lands are such an important part. The West will be in charge of grizzlies and grizzly habitat, of salmon and their rivers, of mining in the mountains and grazing on the grasslands. The West will be genuinely sovereign over itself, as Ukraine is now sovereign and as Wales is becoming sovereign. Most important, within the normal limits of human frailty, the West will do a good job with its sovereignty. First, though, westerners from across the political spectrum will have to (and in fact will) agree on a western agenda—a common vision of what the region should be and how it will realize itself.

On the face of it, this is not a very likely turn for the story of the West to take. To understand why that might happen—why in fact it is likely to happen—we have to understand how this unexpected path emerges out of the more familiar paths, the ones already so clearly marked out, the ones people followed so readily and comfortably into the grizzly reintroduction hearings. Take the Conservation Biology Alternative, for example. This approach, using the full force of the Endangered Species Act to create de facto wilderness, follows the path laid out by the northern spotted owl in the old-growth forests of the Pacific Northwest. Some species cannot be reliably protected without preserving very substantial reaches of their native habitat. So, by federal administrative decree or federal court action or some combination of the two, wild country gains the protection of the national government from most forms of human alteration.

But the bigger story this path traces is not restricted to endangered species issues. This kind of invocation of national power in western landscapes also rides other mounts, as it did in 1996 in southeastern Utah when President Bill Clinton created the Grand Staircase–Escalante National Monument, protecting by administrative decree 1.7 million acres of the Colorado Plateau from an impending coal mine. This path of national command and control is, in other words, fairly well traveled, its twists and turns well understood, and it might well be traveled again in the case of the Bitterroot grizzlies. In fact, this path reaches back to the creation of the Montana and Idaho national forests themselves. Most of the national forests that proponents of the Conservation Biology Alternative would close by administrative action to future development—the Bitterroot, Lolo, Flathead, and Nez Perce National Forests—were themselves created by just such action in the famous Theodore Roosevelt–Gifford Pinchot "midnight reserves" of March 1 and 2, 1907. That story is retold in a later chapter of this book; for now, it is enough to know that for a century, the West has walked and walked again this path of Washington-based decisions about western landscapes.

On the other hand, the West has also walked the "cut the hell out of it" path (or, in this case, road) plenty of times. Westerners know that terrain; they could do the same in the Bitterroots with their eyes closed. They can keep bears out of there very, very easily, just as they can destroy almost anything with no thought at all. That Old West–style resource extraction path has its own century-long history, with enough force behind it to propel it well into the next century. It certainly has enough force to clear-cut many another Idaho mountainside, ensuring in the process that no Yellowstone grizzly will ever meet and mate with a Glacier grizzly.

So the West has at least two old stories now, both well established in its history and political culture, both bringing the full force of their momentum into the grizzly reintroduction issue— and, in various ways but finally always the same way, into every other public land or natural resource issue in the West. Every time, the question is, Which path shall we follow? And almost every time now, there is some third choice, such as the Citizen Management Alternative, that the proponents of the two well-worn strategies resist with equal fury—a third alternative that they sometimes, in one place or another, manage to squelch, but only to see it reappear in the next drainage over. Some new path, or some lost trail.

The eastern boundary of the proposed grizzly bear recovery area was U.S. Highway 93, running south from Missoula, Montana, through Salmon to Challis, Idaho. The road forks at Lost Trail Pass on the state line, with Highway 93 continuing on into Idaho and Montana's State Highway 43 bending back east and immediately crossing another pass (Chief Joseph) before winding down into Big Hole Valley, where Chief Joseph himself had repelled the forces of Colonel John Gibbon in 1877. It was up at the top, where Lost Trail Pass and Chief Joseph Pass stand so confusingly adjacent to each other, that many a traveler, including those who surveyed the state line, managed to get lost. South of those two passes, Idaho and Montana are themselves delineated by the Continental Divide; north of that point, because the surveyors were thrown off by the confusing topography, the state line meanders off on the ridge of a lesser divide. It is up there, on that false divide, that the grizzly issue is playing itself out. The unfolding story of grizzly reintroduction is a classic case of the dividing line between the two Wests—the one that has been and the one that might be—creating the region's destiny at last. Like the Bitterroots themselves, this dividing line can be more than a little confusing; it can leave you wondering exactly which side of the divide you are actually on at any given moment.

Today, every time some new western issue such as grizzly reintroduction makes its way toward a decision, some of the old, battle-scarred veterans, who have walked these trails and fought these battles over and over again, begin to ask themselves whether there might not be another way through these mountains. Take the loggers in the Selway-Bitterroot, for example. Yes, they have done all right on their old trail, and yes, they might manage, with the help of eagerly sympathetic U.S. senators, to coerce the Fish and Wildlife Service into forgetting about bringing grizzlies back into the woods. Then they could bid on more Forest Service timber sales, build more roads, clear-cut a few more of those big mountainsides down on either side of Lost Trail Pass. But following that old trail would be guaranteed to provoke an endangered species legal appeal, buttressed by all the accumulated below-cost timber sale ammunition in the environmentalists' arsenal. Because of all this, the "no bears" path is now a very risky route to take. A cagey grizzly encountering that substantial a risk in the woods would find some other way to go.

It is precisely that kind of caginess that led to the creation of the Citizen Management Alternative and is leading, step by step, to the creation of a West sovereign over itself. Start with the smaller issue; stay for now with the preferred alternative for grizzly restoration. It was the brainchild of the unlikeliest imaginable combination of battle-scarred westerners. Tom France had spent his working life on environmental causes, using his legal training to obstruct unwanted developments in wild country as aggressively as he used his rugged frame to power the ball forward on the field for the Missoula All-Maggots Rugby Club. At the Missoula field office of the National Wildlife Federation, he had learned as much as anyone about how to use federal power in environmental disputes. He knew that path, and he would have been a natural to lead the march down it on behalf of the grizzly. But he also knew the risks of that high-stakes game, including the very substantial risk of losing a winner-take-all endangered species battle—of losing, and seeing as a consequence increased logging and roading, with no gains and in fact real losses for the grizzly. He began to wonder whether there might be another road, and he, along with Hank Fischer, the Northern Rockies representative of Defenders of Wildlife, decided to ask that question of some of their oldest enemies.

Seth Diamond, Montana representative of the Intermountain Forest Industry Association, was a key player in France and Fischer's vision of bringing together environmentalists, labor unions, and the timber industry in the unlikely coalition that would eventually produce the Citizen Management Alternative. Diamond, trained as an anthropologist and a wildlife biologist, was already known for work he had done on grizzly bear restoration in both Idaho and Montana during an earlier phase of his career. He had previously worked for the Forest Service, where he had pioneered programs such as the Beartree Challenge, a timber-cutting project that aimed to improve grizzly habitat. As a result, the U.S. Department of Agriculture had awarded him its highest honor for developing an innovative project that utilized new technology to harvest timber in a way that favored grizzly bears. When he went to work for the timber industry, he brought with him all the resourcefulness, tenaciousness, and just plain ability to get what he wanted to which his old Forest Service colleagues had become accustomed, and with which they now had to contend in this formidable advocate for the industry.

In 1996, Diamond died in a plane crash in the Yaak-Cabinet Mountains area on his way to a meeting to discuss grizzly bear management. His obituary in the *Missoulian* noted his gift for building bridges, "helping people with polarized viewpoints find common ground."[4] Before his death, Diamond had talked about his work on the Selway-Bitterroot grizzly issue: "I never looked at the timber industry and grizzlies as being at odds," he said. "It was procedures and policies that were blocking things. What sold Hank and Tom to the folks I represent was that they made it clear they wouldn't use the grizzly to create a land-management agenda."[5] In other words, if they could stay focused on the grizzly and what it needed, they just might find a way to get bears into the woods while still getting logs into sawmills.

France and Fischer also approached Phil Church, president of United Paperworkers International Union Local 712 in Lewiston, Idaho, to talk to him about bears. Church had not become president of his local union by being an environmentalist. His job was taking care of his people, and he made sure France and the others knew it. But he had to weigh the risks of a forest closed to all logging because of full federal endangered species protection against the benefit to his workers of a "no bears" approach. Asked later about his decision to get involved in drafting the Citizen Management Alternative, Church remarked: "I can honestly say that we would not have gotten involved except for concern about our jobs. We bridged the gaps and created a situation where industry, organized labor and environmentalists could work on an issue for the benefit of everybody."[6]

Seth Diamond and Phil Church, like Tom France and Hank Fischer, knew every inch of their favorite paths through timber politics. If anyone could have ramrodded the "just say no to bears" response to the EIS, it would have been Diamond and Church. But in fact, when the hearings were held on the draft EIS, Diamond's replacement at the Intermountain Forest Industry Association, Greg Schildwachter, was there with Church, and the two of them stood alongside France and Fischer to testify in favor of the Citizen Management Alternative, which in fact they had, over many months of hard bargaining, written together.

One immediate consequence of this unexpected partnership was a spreading confusion among all the partners' old allies. "Which side are you on here, anyway?" became the unspoken subtext of not only the hearings themselves but also a steady stream of letters to Montana and Idaho newspaper editors. The confusion became glaringly public in the case of People for the West, a conservative (some would say redneck) organization funded primarily by resource extraction industries and widely identified with the "wise use" movement. As the grizzly issue gained visibility, the "just say no" side was suddenly thrown into disarray by an article in People for the West's newsletter supporting the Citizen Management Alternative. Calling the Selway-Bitterroot "big wild country just perfect for big wild critters like bears and loggers," the article made a hardheaded assessment of the politics of the situation: "The reality in Congress, in the courts, and in the administration is that 'no bears' ain't going to happen." Pragmatically, then, the article argued, People for the West should adopt the only genuinely western alternative—and doing so could help get the feds out of the northern forests. "If this actually worked under local auspices, we could marginalize Washington, D.C. and all the lobbyists," the article concluded.[7]

Asked by a reporter for his reaction to this right-flank endorsement of the Citizen Management Alternative, Tom France did an admirable job of not gloating—and for good reason.[8] Many of his old environmental allies were already questioning the purity of his "green" credentials; the fact that People for the West supported his position seemed simply to confirm his treason. But if France and the other environmentalists who wrote the Citizen Management Alternative found their loyalty in doubt, it was nothing compared with the pressure brought to bear on the errant forces within People for the West. One could practically hear from Missoula the shouting in Salmon, and what was being shouted was, again, "Which side are you on here, anyway?" Within days, the answer came back: People for the West was against bears. That article had been one person's opinion. He was sorry. No bears, no way.[9]

This effort to avoid defections was challenging to both sides, and to help their people stay on the right side of the divide, both sides planted rhetorical signs along the trail. The slogans had everything to do with sovereignty: human versus bear sovereignty, national versus western sovereignty. On the right, the mantra with which political correctness could generally be enforced was a simple one, playing directly on people's fears: "No bears." Or, in Senator Burns' formulation combining anti-bear and anti-Washington sentiment, "What part of 'No' don't the feds understand?" Whichever slogan was deployed on any given occasion, the message was your basic "No!"

On the other end of the political spectrum, the rallying cry did not come down to a single syllable, but it did center on its own *N*-word. This position was summed up by a group of environmentalists in a letter to the chief of the Forest Service. Alarmed by the stated willingness of several Forest Service officials to support the Citizen Management Alternative, these environmental leaders reminded the chief that "the Forest Service is managing National—capital 'N'—not local, forests."[10] This underscored capitalization of national sovereignty elegantly captured an argument so often repeated that it is known, almost word for word, by most westerners. It goes like this: "These are national forests (or grasslands). They do not belong to the people who live in or on or near them; they belong to all the people of the United States. A citizen of New Jersey (for some reason it's always New Jersey—perhaps always the same citizen) has as much right to say how these forests are managed as does a Montanan who lives right next to them."

This is a clear position and one firmly rooted in law. These *are* national forests; they *are* governed by national legislation, as are the millions of acres of western territory under the jurisdiction of the BLM. Legally, national sovereignty over vast tracts of the West is a simple fact of life. But in fact, things are not that simple, and no amount of sloganeering will ever again make them that simple. Consider one or two more stories.

Two weeks after the environmentalists sent the Forest Service chief their letter reminding him which side of the sovereignty divide *he* was on, the Forest Service itself issued a news release announcing an early-retirement buyout of 170 Forest Service employees in Montana and Idaho.[11] Almost none of these senior employees would be replaced because this buyout was part of an ongoing reduction in agency staffing driven by the bipartisan commitment to balance the federal budget. These might be capital *N* national forests, legally subject to national sovereignty, but the capital *N* national government exercising that sovereignty had fewer and fewer resources with which to assert its jurisdiction or fulfill its obligations. This, too, was part of a larger story, which had once been told as the story of "the bear in the woods." It begins far away from the northern forests.

The 1984 presidential election had been in part a referendum on Ronald Reagan's foreign policy. Having publicly identified the Soviet Union as the Evil Empire, Reagan had pursued an aggressive policy of military one-upmanship, deploying a breathtakingly costly new generation of tactical nuclear weapons in Europe and aiming to develop the order-of-magnitude more costly Strategic Defense Initiative, or Star Wars program. The cost of this policy contributed far more than any other factor to the historically unprecedented expansion of the national debt during the Reagan presidency. To keep Americans content with this aggressive mortgaging of their children's futures, the administration had to give its policy the strongest possible emotional appeal. The Evil Empire rhetoric was a start, but the quintessential moment in this drama may have been the deployment of the "bear in the woods" television advertisement during Reagan's 1984 re-election campaign.

Never mentioning the Soviet Union by name, the ad followed a grizzly through the woods, using the skills of the highest-priced media talent available to create a truly terrifying image of what it means "if there is a bear in the woods." If there is a bear in the woods, you had better be fully prepared for it. In fact, if there is a bear in the woods, you had better get rid of it, because these woods are not big enough for both of us.

The Soviet bear is gone, but America's national debt certainly is not, and throughout the 1990s the mortgage payments were reaching more deeply each year into every non-entitlement program of the national government. The 170 induced retirements in the Forest Service's Northern Region were just one more step in an ongoing reduction in force. The Northern Region's reduction was driven in part by a shrinking budget. Between 1992 and 1998, the budget for the Northern Region, standardized to the value of the dollar in the year 2000, dropped from $283 million to $234 million, a decline of 17.5 percent over six years.[12] The effect on the ground was that Washington was losing its grip on the West.

There comes a time in the life of any far-reaching empire when the imperial writ no longer runs with the requisite authority to its more remote provinces. In A.D. 409, the Roman Empire lost its authority over the British Isles in that way, and in 1947, the writ of the British Empire ceased to run to India. In 1990, the Russian Empire bowed to the assertion of Ukrainian sovereignty as Moscow lost its grip on that sovereign land.

The story of the American West has been substantially the story of empire, in that particularly American form called manifest destiny. The next stage of western history can be understood in part as a chapter in the age-old story of the withdrawal of imperial sovereignty from places the empire can no longer manage. But history teaches that the mere weakening of imperial vigor rarely leads to a new form of sovereignty unless those seeking relief from imperial dominance have created within themselves a steadily expanding capacity for self-government. What is happening now in the American West is a combination of these two strands. The steady reductions in force in federal land management agencies are occurring at the same time that thousands of westerners are doing what Tom France and Seth Diamond did in the Selway-Bitterroot: figuring out how to make it work themselves.

One of the more impassioned responses to their work came in the form of a letter to the editor of one of Montana's daily newspapers, the *Missoulian*, invoking once again the "these are national forests" argument and then carrying the argument one step further. Locally devised solutions such as the Citizen Management Alternative or the dozens of similar efforts springing up around the West, this writer warned, would "drive a stake in the heart of democracy."[13] What the writer meant by democracy was specifically national democracy. What belongs to all the people should be governed by all the people, and to give a few people in one place a special voice is inherently undemocratic. But this comes across as an increasingly hollow argument to more and more westerners. When they work hard together to solve problems the prevailing system cannot solve, it seems to them that what they are doing *is* democracy, not in a textbook sense, perhaps, or a legalistic sense, but in a lived, grounded, "of this place" sense. When they compare their experience—the experience of joining with former adversaries to solve very tough problems—against the frustrating bureaucratic procedures of a national government that simply no longer seems to work very well, they conclude that their approach is the genuinely democratic one. Beyond that, they think—with good reason—that their genuine, on-the-ground caring for ecosystems may in the long run prove them to be the most effective environmentalists. And increasingly they believe that in taking charge of their own places and solving their own problems, what they are doing is closer to the deep-running mainstream of American history than is either of the old paths of their detractors. Theirs is the Lost Trail leading all the way back to the Declaration of Independence, perhaps the most democratic document in history, signed by people who had finally decided that the old system simply no longer worked.

Everywhere you go in the West, on almost every issue you encounter you now find the same dynamics that were so palpable in the grizzly debate. Almost always there is someone invoking capital *N* national command and control and someone else just saying no to any form of control, and in the middle of it all is an increasingly compelling recourse to what almost no one is yet ready to recognize as the early stages of an emergent form of sovereignty. In the broadest terms, the picture that emerges is of the West taking charge of the West. What that means, from the outset, is that capital *N* national domination of the region and its landscape will be relentlessly challenged and steadily diminished. Put that way, the story line might be expected to move in the direction so long advocated by western conservatives— toward states' rights, and especially toward state (or private) control of federal lands in the West. But that is not the West's path.

The long history of those conservative efforts to westernize or at least denationalize control of the West will certainly feed into the next chapter of the region's history—as will the long history of national control. But the next episode will be something different from either of those stories. To understand what is about to happen, we have to follow the trails of those two stories, keeping alert to where both of them start to go wrong, start to become, in fact, myths of the West and therefore incapable of showing the region into its own future. Somewhere along those trails—somewhere between the two of them—the region is beginning to find itself, gather itself, tell and live its own story: the story not of a mythical West but of a sovereign, self-determining West.

Chapter 2

Imperial Origins

"The imperialism is peculiarly, even uniquely, our own kind, but the dispatch of the Lewis and Clark expedition was an act of imperial policy."
—Bernard De Voto

"The unity of our empire hangs on the decision of this day."
—Senator William H. Seward

"I hesitate to think what might happen to the forest service if in the course of human events it should lose the services of the genius [Gifford Pinchot] from whose imperial imagination this stupendous federal structure has issued like Minerva from the brow of Jove."
—A western congressional representative

If the West is ever to "outlive its origins,"[1] as Wallace Stegner put it, westerners must understand as clearly as possible the main strands of those origins. In particular, they must revisit that peculiarly American brand of imperialism called manifest destiny, which played such a significant role in shaping the West of today. This chapter looks closely at two United States presidents—Thomas Jefferson and Theodore Roosevelt—who helped define the West and set in motion so many of the trends and themes that made the West the distinct and all too often conflicted region it is. For our purposes, the greatest similarity between these two very different men had to do with the substantial influence of their presidencies on the history of the West. But there are other similarities. Neither man's western policies can be understood, for example, apart from his powerful imperial ambitions. But even though both men may justly be termed imperialists, both were complex individuals displaying traits revered by those who might find nothing to revere in their imperialist tendencies. One of those traits shared by both men was a love of nature.

Among all the presidents, Jefferson and Roosevelt were by far the most avid naturalists. Either of them could readily have pursued a career in natural science. On the surface, these men's fascination with, and care and concern for, the natural world seems utterly distinct from their imperialistic policies. But a close look at the lives and careers of Jefferson and Roosevelt reveals an intertwining of these themes in ways that affect the world to this day. In fact, the story of western expansion can be told, in significant part, as a progression from the policies of Thomas Jefferson, imperial naturalist, to those of Theodore Roosevelt, imperial conservationist.

Start with one biographer's description of Jefferson the naturalist:

> President of the American Philosophical Society . . . ,
> Jefferson had for thirty-five years continued his amateur scientific studies, filling volumes of ledgers with

notes on weather and the change of seasons, the blooming of the first spring flowers, of minerals and medicinal springs, of migrating birds and the bones of extinct animals, of all these interests concentrating most on observing plant life. There was no distance between his private studies and his public offices. . . .

At the President's House in Washington, he was often seen working with flowers and plants; a pet mockingbird entertained him as he plied his garden and carpenter's tools or, seated at his drafting board, pored over maps and charts. And he sometimes stole away on secret solitary expeditions up the Potomac and into surrounding hills and woods. Wrote Mrs. [Samuel Harrison] Smith [wife of the editor of the *Washington National Intelligencer*] in her diary, "Not a plant from the lowliest weed to the loftiest tree escaped his notice. . . . He would [get off his horse and] climb rocks or wade through swamps to obtain any plant he discovered or desired and seldom returned from these excursions without a variety of specimens."[2]

Jefferson the naturalist began to shade over into Jefferson the imperialist in the way his fascination with natural phenomena pervaded the conception and execution of the Lewis and Clark Expedition. In preparation for the expedition, he sent Meriwether Lewis to Philadelphia to study with the most eminent botanists, zoologists, and paleontologists of the day, and his instructions for the expedition directed Lewis to take detailed notes on the biological, topographic, and hydrologic systems of the West. He asked Lewis to study, among other things,

the soil & face of the country, it's growth & vegetable productions; especially those not of the U.S.
the animals of the country generally, & especially

those not known in the U.S.

the remains and accounts of any which may be deemed rare or extinct;

the mineral productions of every kind; but more particularly metals, limestone, pit coal & saltpetre; salines & mineral waters, noting the temperature of the last, & such circumstances as may indicate their character.

Volcanic appearances.

climate, as characterized by the thermometer, by the proportion of rainy, cloudy & clear days, by lightening, hail, snow, ice, by the access & recess of frost, by the winds prevailing at different seasons, the dates at which particular plants put forth or lose their flowers, or leaf, times of appearance of particular birds, reptiles or insects.[3]

For Jefferson, child of the Enlightenment as he was, such encyclopedic scientific research would have been reason enough to commission a Corps of Discovery. But he could never have mobilized the political support for such an expedition without giving Congress compelling geopolitical reasons for knowing some very specific things about the continent. The geopolitics were the ultimate driving force behind the expedition, both for Congress and for Jefferson himself. But the scientific research, highly valuable in its own right and deeply fascinating to Jefferson, would prove a useful adjunct to the imperial thrust of the expedition. What Jefferson did, in a secret message to Congress, was frame the expedition as a commercial enterprise aimed at securing American access to or hegemony over the Pacific fur trade. He hinted to Congress that the appropriation bill should deflect the suspicions of Spain and Britain by officially referring to the venture as a literary (i.e., scientific) expedition.

At the heart of Jefferson's western geopolitics lay the search for the "height of land"—the assumed point at which the headwaters of the Missouri and Columbia Rivers, and perhaps with luck even of the Saskatchewan River, the Colorado River, or the Rio Grande, lay within easy portage of one another. Here, Jefferson's scientific and geopolitical interests were indistinguishable. The concept of the continental "height of land" came from an eighteenth-century hypothesis about how all the earth's continents were constructed, and Jefferson would have been interested in discovering the North American height of land simply to prove the hypothesis. But as the leader of a commercially aggressive new nation, he was also acutely aware that if the height of land existed, it would be the point of easiest portage between the Pacific slope and the Mississippi River drainage. Jefferson the geopolitician knew that whoever controlled that portage would control the Pacific fur trade and, by that token, probably would eventually control the Pacific coast. Jefferson saw himself engaged with British Canada in a continental game of King of the Mountain. The Rocky Mountains (which Jefferson called the Stony Mountains) were not considered valuable in themselves; rather, they were seen as valuable only as the strategic headwaters of the great continental rivers. Where those rivers lay closest together was both unknown and crucially significant. It was a question Jefferson the scientist could ask with genuine eagerness, an eagerness only heightened and sharpened by the fact that the answer was also of the greatest geopolitical significance. Imperialism and science fit together perfectly: the imperial urge gave Congress an incentive to pay for the expedition, and the scientific questions Jefferson was so intent on answering gave the perfect cover for Meriwether Lewis and William Clark should they encounter Spanish or British forces inimical to their covert imperial purpose.

Jefferson the naturalist and Jefferson the imperialist were manifestly present in the instructions to Lewis. But the scientific part of Jefferson's instructions—his requirement that Lewis study soils, plants, and animals—was clearly subordinate to what Jefferson called "the object of your mission":

> The object of your mission is to explore the Missouri river, & such principal stream of it, as, by it's course and communication with the waters of the Pacific ocean, whether the Columbia, Oregon, Colorado or any other river may offer the most direct & practicable water communication across this continent for the purposes of commerce.[4]

For the purposes of commerce, yes, but that commerce could not be secured without political dominion—without the establishment of American sovereignty. This was the imperial motivation that was so thoroughly cloaked in commercial and scientific justification. Later American generations have often been willingly enough confused by the subterfuge, preferring to think of the expedition in more exalted terms than those of empire building, even though westerners such as Bernard De Voto have tried to disabuse them. "The imperialism is peculiarly, even uniquely, our own kind," De Voto wrote in *The Course of Empire*, "but the dispatch of the Lewis and Clark expedition was an act of imperial policy."[5] American imperialism was "peculiarly, even uniquely, our own kind" because Americans chose to experience and describe it as manifest destiny—something they had no choice but to pursue—rather than as self-willed empire building. And in fact, this way of framing the imperial urge gave it a staying power it might otherwise have lacked. When the hopeful myth of the easy portage was finally laid to rest by news of the endless, rugged, steep, very nearly impassable terrain Lewis and Clark discovered and experienced in the Rockies, Jefferson's inheritors saw that even in spite of the topography, if America possessed the crucial passes across the mountains, it could send enough settlers into Oregon and California to make American-ization of the coast inevitable—to make it a matter of destiny.

Jefferson was endowed with an almost limitless capacity to tolerate ambiguity—to allow contradictions to exist within and around him until the time came for their resolution. For some ambiguities the time did not, could not, come within Jefferson's lifetime, as in the case of slavery. Even today, the Jefferson who owned slaves and the Jefferson who proclaimed that "all men are created equal" is held accountable for contradictions within America itself, contradictions that his own large and complex being all too fully personified. It is tempting to speculate that the excruciating headaches Jefferson endured throughout his life were really America's headaches, which sooner or later Americans would have to live through and work out as a people. If that were so, the current conflicts in and over the West—the West that Jefferson took such pains to acquire and to explore—might be seen as another Jeffersonian headache, like the headache of slavery, this one also arising from a deep contradiction and taking decades, even centuries, to work its way toward resolution.

The fact is that Jefferson the "height of land" imperialist was always fundamentally at odds with another Jefferson: the decentralist, localist, agrarian democrat. The two met in the West. A particular strain of small-landowner agrarianism had been a crucial ingredient of Jefferson's democratic theory long before he purchased Louisiana. Jefferson was convinced that the only society that could be truly democratic—truly self-governing—was one in which small farms and independent farmers predominated. No small part of Jefferson's interest in the West had to do with his conviction that westward expansion would enable America to remain forever an agrarian and therefore a democratic nation. In 1787, Jefferson had expressed his democratic faith in a letter to James Madison: "This reliance [on the people] cannot deceive us, as long as we remain virtuous, and I think we shall be so, as long as agriculture is our principal object, which will be the case, while there remains vacant lands in any part of America."[6]

But could this actually work? Could the conditions for democracy be created through an essentially imperialist policy? Never in history had democracy and empire coexisted for more than the blink of a historical eye, and America would be no exception. Yet Jefferson seems to have had no choice but to launch both strands of this contradiction into the American West and to leave his beloved posterity the headache of working out the tension. Americans are still working it out. Most of this book is devoted to digging into the contradiction and then trying to discover a conceptual "height of land" from which some new perspective might offer itself. For now, let us follow the "course of empire" to its next plateau.

◆ ◆ ◆

Jefferson himself rarely used openly imperial language, but in the decades between his death and the coming of the Civil War, America began to experiment with new ways of describing its westward expansion. By the 1840s, both the British in Oregon and the Mexicans to the south and west had become galling limitations on what Americans had come to see as their manifest destiny to rule the continent. The term had a nicer ring than *empire*, but manifest destiny's imperial musculature was never quite obscured by its lyrical sheathing. Occasionally, the imperialism was unsheathed altogether. During the debate over admission of California as a state in 1850 following its "purchase" from a recently vanquished Mexico, for example, Senator William H. Seward told the U.S. Senate that "the unity of our empire hangs on the decision of this day."

That one sentence of Seward's spoke volumes about America,

about its recent history and its looming future—and about the West. By calling post–Mexican War America an empire, Seward spoke a naked truth that most Americans preferred to dress up in ringing terms such as *manifest destiny*. But what did Seward mean by saying that the future of this new empire "hangs on the decision of this day"? The legislation to admit California to the Union (as a free state) was one key element of the very complex Compromise of 1850—the last real glimmer of hope to hold the Union together against the centrifugal force of the slavery controversy. But contrary to the way Americans now choose to tell the story, it was not slavery alone that threatened "the unity of our empire." It was empire building itself that precipitated the crisis. And it was all about the West.

In fact, though we now think of the Civil War as a battle between two regions—North and South—it was really a third region—the West—that brought the conflict to a head. The North and South had worked out a rough but fairly stable accommodation that might have held for a very long time had it not been for America's expansion westward. It was not the question of slavery itself but of slavery extending into the western territories that finally became irresolvable; it was the combination of slavery and empire that finally brought on the Civil War.

Beginning in 1848, when the signing of the Treaty of Guadalupe Hidalgo secured America's openly imperial acquisition of vast new territories from Mexico, a decade of steadily escalating tension commenced over the extension of slavery into those and other western territories. The Wilmot Proviso, proposed as an amendment to the bill that funded the treaty, sought to prohibit the extension of slavery into all territories acquired from Mexico. The amendment was narrowly defeated in the U.S. Senate, but the issue remained bitterly unresolved, and for the next twelve years, through the Compromise of 1850, the Kansas-Nebraska Act, and countless other policy experiments and innovations, leaders on both sides of the Mason-Dixon Line worked tirelessly to resolve the conflict that westward expansion had brought so explosively to the surface.

This, then, was what Seward meant when he said in 1850 that "the unity of our empire hangs on the decision of this day." He meant that if California was not admitted as a free state, as a key anti-slavery element of the Compromise of 1850, the Union—which was now so clearly an empire—would not survive. The West had become the empire's key to holding North and South together. But it was not the key to that alone. The Wilmot Proviso mattered so much because settlers were already streaming into the West—both the West acquired by Jefferson from France in 1803 and the West acquired from Mexico in 1848. This was Jefferson's agrarian democratic dream rolling across the prairie, carrying the Jeffersonian headache over slavery into Bloody Kansas and who knew where next.

The significance of the 1850s to the later (and to this day still unfolding) story of the West is taken up again in chapter 7. For now, we can return to Jefferson's dream of a constantly expanding number of small farmers pushing the frontier westward and keeping democracy alive in their wake. Even the Civil War would not stanch this Jeffersonian flood. With passage of the Homestead Act in 1862, Jeffersonian agrarianism became a fundamental part of the Law of the West.

The Homestead Act offered 160 acres of land for free to any head of family or single person over twenty-one years of age who was a citizen of the United States. Railroads, eager to capitalize on the westward migration, spearheaded the onslaught of land seekers, bringing trainloads of homesteaders into the heart of the western frontier. In the wake of the Homestead Act came the Timber Culture Act of 1873, which allowed a settler to gain title to an additional quarter section (160 acres) of land in exchange for planting it with trees and fostering their growth for ten years. Finally, the Desert Land Act of 1877 was specifically designed to encourage settlement of the arid and semi-arid regions of the West, including the territories and states of Arizona, California, the Dakotas, Idaho, Montana, Nevada, New Mexico, Oregon, Utah, Washington, and Wyoming. The act allowed anyone to purchase 640 acres of land for twenty-five cents per acre if the land was irrigated within three years of filing. A farmer or rancher could receive title to the land anytime within the three-year period on proof of compliance with the law and payment of one additional dollar per acre.

What is so easily overlooked now is that the Homestead Act, the Timber Culture Act, and the Desert Land Act were nothing more or less than a massive, deliberate, concerted program for privatizing public-domain lands in the name of Jeffersonian democracy. What is also generally overlooked is that within a few years of their passage, all of the homestead acts were criticized by western explorer and policy analyst John Wesley Powell as bad public policy for the arid West. That story is told in chapter 8. Here, it is sufficient to note that Powell was utterly ignored, and the homestead acts were allowed fundamentally and often disastrously to shape the settling of the West. But as the nineteenth century neared its end, a new set of policies, involving a fundamental departure from the homestead acts and based on a very un-Jeffersonian theory of democracy, were brought to bear on the region. At the center of this change in western policies stood another man who was both imperialist and naturalist. Theodore Roosevelt was unlike Thomas Jefferson in many ways—in fact, he abhorred Jefferson's politics—but his fascination with nature was thoroughly reminiscent of Jefferson's. Listen to Roosevelt describe an outing during his college days:

> I shot several cross bills in the woods. . . . A woodcock was shot near Paul Smiths; none of the inhabitants knew what it was, or had ever seen another. The

blackbirds we saw were not the Scolecophagus but the females of Quisqualus purpureus. I found several colonies of this bird widely separated from one another, and shot both male and female specimens.[7]

So enamored of nature was the young Roosevelt that he nearly made a career of it. "When I entered college," he wrote in his autobiography, "I was devoted to out-of-doors natural history, and my ambition was to be a scientific man of the Audubon, or Wilson, or Baird, or Coues type."[8] During his first year of college, his father gave him permission to become a "scientific man" as long as he thoroughly committed himself to it. "I fully intended to make science my life-work," Roosevelt later recalled. "I did not, for the simple reasons that at that time Harvard, and I suppose other colleges, utterly ignored the possibilities of the faunal naturalist, the outdoor naturalist and observer of nature. They treated biology as purely a science of the laboratory and microscope."[9] Roosevelt, already wholly committed to what he would famously champion as "the vigorous life," could no more be confined to a laboratory than could a bull moose. He needed nature itself, in all its ruggedness, under his feet and in his nostrils, and he eventually needed more of it than the eastern seaboard could give him.

Like Jefferson, Roosevelt would eventually follow his love of nature westward. Roosevelt, however, would not need to send others to explore the region but would live out his western romanticism personally in his ranching and hunting adventures in the North Dakota Badlands and the Rocky Mountains. A few years later, having come to love the ruggedness of the West during his ranching phase, it was to the West that Roosevelt primarily looked for the recruits who would become his Rough Riders and follow him to fame on Cuba's San Juan Hill. Roosevelt's role in the Spanish-American War was both highly visible and politically advantageous. His volunteer cavalry unit, consisting of an unlikely mix of western cowboys and a fair number of adventure-seeking Ivy Leaguers, followed Roosevelt on his truly courageous charge up San Juan Hill in the face of bitter resistance from the Spanish defenders. This bold foray was perfectly suited (some critics would say designed and packaged) for the "yellow journalism" of the day. It firmly established Roosevelt's reputation as a rugged, assertive, and blatantly flag-waving leader. Roosevelt rode this sudden fame into the New York governor's mansion and then, in rapid succession, into the vice presidency and, on William McKinley's assassination, the White House. Throughout Roosevelt's rapid rise, and indeed for the rest of his life, the Rough Riders continued to adore him for his heroism in Cuba. Indeed, some of them followed him to the White House, colorfully demonstrating the contrasting sides of Roosevelt's personality. It would not be much of an exaggeration to equate Roosevelt's hospitality to the Rough Riders with a contemporary president inviting a contingent of the Hells Angels to sleep in the Lincoln Bedroom. As biographer Edmund Morris recounted:

> One of today's newspapers complains about the President's habit of inviting "thugs and assassins of Idaho and Montana to be his guests at the White House," but Roosevelt has never been able to turn away the friends of his youth. Shortly after he received the presidency the word went out that "The cowboy bunch can come in whenever they want to." When a doorkeeper mistakenly refused admission to one leathery customer, the President was indignant. "The next time they don't let you in, Sylvane, you just shoot through the windows."[10]

The eyebrows raised by the Rough Riders' presence in the White House were simply one visible manifestation of a deep ideological conflict with which Roosevelt never came to terms: a deep-seated tension between his celebration of western heroism and self-determination on one hand and the pursuit of an imperialist agenda in the West (if not against the West) on the other. It was his imperialist policy that would eventually turn the West against most of what Roosevelt stood for. And it is this unresolved conflict the West inherited from Theodore Roosevelt that, as we shall see in later chapters, lies at the heart of the identity crisis that currently plagues the region.

The contradictions that pervaded Roosevelt's western policies may be easier to understand if we first touch lightly on the way they played out elsewhere. Take the Panama Canal, for instance. Roosevelt was immensely proud of the remarkable engineering feat the canal represented, but he could not be quite as proud of the engineering of the treaty that allowed for its construction. When an earlier canal treaty with Colombia was rejected by the senate of that sovereign nation, Roosevelt covertly supported the coup by which the northern portion of Colombia seceded and set up its own country, Panama, which then proved obligingly eager to enter into Roosevelt's treaty. When Roosevelt asked his attorney general, Philander Knox, to explain to the cabinet the legal underpinnings of the administration's role in the coup, Knox laughingly replied, "No, Mr. President, if I were you I would not have any taint of legality about it."[11] The ribbing escalated when Roosevelt asked another cabinet member, Secretary of State Elihu Root, whether he thought Roosevelt had succeeded in answering the charges of the administration's anti-imperialist critics. Root responded: "You certainly have, Mr. President. You have shown that you were accused of seduction and you have conclusively proved that you were guilty of rape."[12]

Roosevelt could enjoy this kind of inner-circle badinage over the rough edges of his imperial foreign policy, but a flurry of stinging public criticisms led him to justify himself by means of a comparison to the steadfast Abraham Lincoln, who was often misunderstood but stuck to his guns no matter what anyone said. That Lincoln was also a rather notorious anti-secessionist who might have strained at the way Panama was created did not mar the comparison for Roosevelt. As one of his biographers noted:

> A more apt parallel than Lincoln would have been Thomas Jefferson at the time of the Louisiana Purchase. Of course, Roosevelt, detesting Jefferson, would never have drawn the parallel, but apt it was. Jefferson's Federalist critics had threatened to make trouble over the treaty with France, but in the end they couldn't bring themselves to reject such an obvious bargain.[13]

Nor, in the end, could the critics of Roosevelt's Panama policy "bring themselves to reject such an obvious bargain," and so the American presence expanded to a new quarter, as it had (with barely a taint of legality) in 1803. Roosevelt may have "detested" Jefferson, but the two men, whose presidencies lay exactly a century apart, had more in common than Roosevelt might have wanted to admit. What united them above all was their expansion of American dominion. Our interest here is in how this ultimately affected the West, but in Roosevelt's case it is easier to understand that influence against the backdrop of his broader imperialist pursuits. Consider one further, more far-flung installment in the nation's new imperial policy that was playing out at the same time as the Panama episode. This particular vignette involved someone who would play a central role in Roosevelt's western policy.

In 1902, Gifford Pinchot received a letter from an old friend, Captain George Ahern, asking if he could come to the Philippines to help Ahern organize a bureau of forestry for the islands along the lines of the U.S. Bureau of Forestry, which Pinchot had headed since 1898. Under doctor's orders to slow down, the hard-driving Pinchot decided to accept the invitation and make a leisurely passage through Europe and thence to Shanghai via the Trans-Siberian Railroad (checking out Russian forests on the way). Arriving at last in the Philippines, Pinchot immediately struck up a friendship with the governor-general, William Howard Taft, who had been sent a few years earlier by President McKinley to administer the American "protectorate" over these distant islands that the Spanish-American War had brought under U.S. domination. Taft supplied Pinchot with a 1,400-ton navy gunboat, from the decks of which he and Captain Ahern proceeded to inspect the Philippine forests.

Pinchot kept McKinley's successor, Roosevelt, informed of his findings in a series of letters, filling him in not only on forestry issues but also on the general status of the protectorate, which had fallen into American hands through a war that Roosevelt had done everything in his power to bring about. It was Roosevelt who as assistant secretary of the navy had sent the gunboats, under Admiral George Dewey's command, to Manila, where they had done their work well and expeditiously, driving Spain from the Philippines and creating the American protectorate whose forests Pinchot would inspect four years later from the decks of one of those same gunboats. The people of the Philippines, who had expected to become self-governing once the Spanish were gone, were less than appreciative of their protected status, especially since it was clear that they were now largely being protected from themselves. Before long, Roosevelt's Rough Riders and thousands of other westerners would come to feel much the same way about the American government, especially about that part of it directed by Gifford Pinchot when he became the first chief of the Forest Service.[14]

Westerners' resentment of Pinchot and Roosevelt's western legacy is so deeply and lastingly embedded in the marrow of western politics that it is impossible to understand fully the current choices the West faces without understanding at least a little about the policy roots of the Roosevelt-Pinchot legacy. For that, we must return briefly to the Homestead Act.

The conservation movement with which Pinchot and Roosevelt are so strongly associated in historical memory was a radical departure from that deep and deeply cherished strain of American democratic thought and practice exemplified by the homesteading phenomenon. Eastern cattle barons, lumber pirates, and mining interests had become adept at securing title to lands in the public domain, often by manipulating people who could have claimed the land as bona fide homesteaders. In the 1870s, instead of supporting the privatization of the public domain that homesteading constituted, certain progressive thinkers and actors began developing a contrary strain of public policy. As early as 1870, the fledgling conservation movement set out to prevent corporate interests from abusing the homesteading laws that were intended to settle the frontier with independent farmers. With the 1872 creation of Yellowstone National Park, the federal government established a precedent for "reserving" public ownership of large tracts of western land. The conservation movement had succeeded in its effort to protect one unique portion of the western landscape, but only at the cost of shutting would-be settlers out of potential homesteading property. Neither those homesteaders nor their progeny would forget this act of exclusion or the others that followed it, and the corporate interests whose abuses of the homesteading laws had largely brought on this new era in federal land policy would not hesitate to stir up at every turn outrage over the "lockout."

In 1891, after two decades of pressure from the conservation movement and an increasingly educated public, Congress granted the president the sweeping power to reserve certain tracts of the public domain from homesteading and other forms of privatization. Presidents Benjamin Harrison, Grover Cleveland, and William McKinley all exercised this power, most dramatically Cleveland in his "Washington's Birthday reserves" of 1897, when, ten days before the end of his second administration, he set aside 21 million acres with one stroke of the pen.

Roosevelt's legacy as a conservationist rests largely on his continuation and enlargement of this tradition of creating forest reserves. As he later wrote in his autobiography, "There was saved for public use in the National Forests more Government timberland during the seven and a half years prior to March 4, 1909 [that is, during his tenure as president] than during all previous and succeeding years put together."[15] Roosevelt had every right to be proud of that legacy, and every succeeding generation owes him and Pinchot a debt of gratitude for maintaining a public domain of such magnificent proportions. By creating the Forest Service and putting it under the vigorous leadership of Pinchot, Roosevelt ensured that there would be some national policing capacity to restrain and contain the timber companies, who by law could still cut trees on public land whether they had succeeded in privatizing the land or not.

The most extensive and memorable of the Roosevelt-Pinchot reservations were the "midnight reserves" of 1907. The high drama of this episode encapsulates all the major forces of the history of the public lands. One strand of the drama involved the conservation movement—that particular element of Progressivism that sought to defend the long-term public interest in resources against the short-term profit motives of resource extraction enterprises. Keeping the land in the public domain was a key ingredient of this policy; another was the new level of regulation of whatever private uses were permitted on the public land.

These private uses and private users presented the other major strand of the drama of the midnight reserves. The forests surrounding the Great Lakes had begun to play out, and the timber companies that had denuded Michigan and Wisconsin were turning toward Washington and Oregon, seeking wealth in the untouched forests of the Pacific Northwest. Earlier, in 1905, when Roosevelt set aside a batch of forested acres, those private interests had decided it was time to put a stop to these seemingly endless reservations of forests from the possibility of privatization. Oregon's Senator Charles W. Fulton attached an amendment to the agricultural appropriation bill of 1907 terminating the president's authority to reserve any further forestland in the states of Washington, Oregon, Idaho, Montana, Wyoming, and Colorado.

Now Roosevelt and Pinchot were confronted with a serious dilemma. They did not want that amendment to become law. But Roosevelt had to sign the appropriation bill, if only because it authorized Pinchot's salary and the salaries of all other Forest Service officials. If Roosevelt did not sign the bill by March 4, there would be no Forest Service, except on paper. Pinchot's biographer tells the first part of the ensuing story:

> No sooner had Congress passed the bill than Pinchot was at the White House, where Roosevelt and he, almost gleefully, concocted a scheme for avoiding some of the crippling effects of the amendment. During the ten days preceding the final date on which the President could sign the bill, members of the staff of the Forest Service worked day and night preparing plans and proclamations for new forest areas which Roosevelt could create before the deadline.[16]

Roosevelt himself described what happened next:

> I signed the last proclamation a couple of days before
> by my signature, the bill became law; and when the
> friends of the special interests in the Senate got their
> amendment through and woke up, they discovered
> that sixteen million acres of timberland had been
> saved for the people by putting them in the National
> Forests before the land grabbers could get at them.[17]

By this act, Roosevelt and Pinchot set aside most of what are
now the national forests of the Pacific Northwest.[18] That her-
itage endures—but so does a legacy of resentment to which
Roosevelt cheerfully alluded in wrapping up his version of the
story: "The opponents of the Forest Service turned handsprings
in their wrath; and dire were their threats against the Executive;
but the threats could not be carried out, and were really only a
tribute to the efficiency of our action."[19]

Efficiency is one way to describe it, but at the heart of that
burning (and still burning) western resentment of the Forest
Service lay a repeated exercise of centralized sovereignty, one
that has always made large numbers of westerners feel abused—
feel, in fact, colonized. There is more than sarcasm in the Jeffersonian words chosen by one Colorado representative to
describe Pinchot:

> I hesitate to think what might happen to the forest
> service if in the course of human events it should lose
> the services of the genius from whose imperial imagi-
> nation this stupendous federal structure has issued like
> Minerva from the brow of Jove.[20]

It is far from coincidence that the president who set aside
more national forests than any other would never have become
president had it not been for his imperially expansionist views

and actions. The governing structure of the public lands of the United States is embedded in the course of empire. The Roosevelt of the midnight reserves was every inch the Roosevelt of San Juan Hill and the Panama Canal. But his Rough Riders would become the fathers of Sagebrush Rebels. Everything that made them Rough Riders would make them rebel against the ruling hand of empire on their own landscape.

Although neither Pinchot nor Roosevelt would have called his conservation initiatives imperial, neither man would have denied that those initiatives were part of a concerted effort to expand the reach and role of the nation and the national government, an effort that has left a permanent mark on the West. By the time of Roosevelt's Bull Moose Party run for re-election in 1912, he was calling this effort the New Nationalism. The first item on that nationalist agenda was economic. Harvard University political theorist Michael Sandel summarized the situation at the turn of the century: "Since most big corporations operated in interstate or foreign commerce, beyond the reach of individual states, only the federal government was suited to the task of controlling them. The power of the national government had to grow to match the scale of corporate power."[21] This empowering of the national government to do a job that state and local governments could no longer handle lay at the heart of the New Nationalism.

But that New Nationalism was about more than balancing big business with the countervailing force of big government. It was also about redefining democracy in America, a redefinition that might well have given Jefferson one more headache and that is now at the heart of the conflict over the West. "More than a program of institutional reform," Sandel wrote, "the New Nationalism was a formative project that sought to cultivate a new sense of national citizenship."[22] In other words, the New Nationalism concerned not only the assignment of new duties to the national government. It was also designed to cultivate a deeper sense of national identity so that people would increasingly think of themselves not as Bostonians or Philadelphians, not as Virginians or Californians, but as Americans. Moreover, they should not only identify themselves as Americans but also formulate policy and purpose and a sense of direction together as Americans. In *The Promise of American Life*, published in 1909, Herbert Croly, the philosopher of the New Nationalism, argued that now the great American experiment in democracy could fulfill itself only by developing a widely shared sense of national purpose.

Even out of office, Roosevelt remained the most visible (and audible) spokesman for this perspective, which he summarized in a 1910 speech:

> We are all Americans. Our common interests are as broad as the continent. I speak to you here in Kansas exactly as I would speak in New York or Georgia, for the most vital problems are those which affect us all alike. . . . The New Nationalism puts the national need before sectional or personal advantage.[23]

The modern sense of nationhood, of having to do what needs to be done to solve problems or pursue agendas *as a nation*, only barely existed before the presidency of Theodore Roosevelt. The setting aside of public lands was one of the most visible ways in which Roosevelt injected into American public life this now pervasive strain of national democracy. With stops and starts but generally with forward movement, the nationalization of American public life accumulated force throughout most of the twentieth century. Woodrow Wilson soon created the Federal Reserve System, and Franklin D. Roosevelt's New Deal added immensely to the range of concerns Americans came to see as national in scope. From securities regulation to agricultural price supports, from social security to labor relations, the nationalization of public life proceeded apace during the reign of the second Roosevelt. The 1960s brought another surge of this momentum with the war on poverty and all its attendant national programs and with the reassertion of national policy in the field of race relations. The civil rights movement had no choice but to turn to the national government to enact its agenda, and within a few years the environmental movement did the same.

The National Environmental Policy Act of 1969 (NEPA) serves as the capstone to the entire national environmental statutory structure. The language of the act describes succinctly and matter-of-factly the nationalist perspective that permeates that structure. The purpose of the act is "to establish a national policy for the environment."[24] In setting forth that policy, the act declares that "it is the continuing responsibility of the Federal Government to use all practicable means . . . to the end that the Nation may . . . assure for all Americans safe, healthful, productive, and esthetically and culturally pleasing surroundings."[25]

In the absence of anyone else claiming stewardship for the environment, it is fortunate that the national government was willing to do it. The good that has been done by such environmental statutes as the Clean Air Act, the Clean Water Act, and the Endangered Species Act of 1973 has been of genuinely historic proportions. The need to invoke jurisdictional power at a level higher than that of the states to deal with environmental threats and depredations reaching across state boundaries can hardly be disputed. Indeed, in the effort to match scale of response to scale of problem, the Endangered Species Act even looked beyond national boundaries. Although it uses typical nationalist language in declaring that endangered species of animals and plants "are of esthetic, ecological, educational, historical, recreational, and scientific value to the Nation and its people," it also recognizes that "the United States has pledged itself as a sovereign state in the international community to conserve . . . the various species of fish or wildlife and plants facing extinction."[26] Apart from this one guarded acknowledgment of global interests, however, the environmental laws speak in straightforward nationalist terms. The purpose of the Wilderness Act is "to establish a National Wilderness Preservation System for the permanent good of the whole people,"[27] and the National Forest Management Act of 1976 is dedicated to "assuring that the Nation maintains a natural resource and conservation posture that will meet the requirements of our people in perpetuity."[28]

All of this nationalist language made perfectly good sense in the historical context within which these statutes evolved. Yet the fact remains that the choice of the national government (or, rather, the self-appointment of the national government) as "trustee of the environment" was a historically contingent phenomenon; it might not have happened that way, and it might not always be that way. The West in particular keeps asking whether in fact it should be that way. The reason is that the West feels the burden of this national agenda in a way no other region does. With the possible exception of civil rights, no other element of the national project has had as focused an effect on one particular region of the country as the convergence of national conservation and environmental movements has had on the West.

Because of the historical timing of the nationalist project of reserving lands from settlement, the last-settled interior West was the only place where that project could be carried out on a broad scale. Then, because of the concentration of public lands in the West, the subsequent national environmental framework became far more noticeable in this region than in any other. The "major Federal actions"[29] to which NEPA applies take place across the country, but they occur vastly more often in that region where the national landlord's every move is a "major Federal action." And the regional effect of national environmental laws is not confined to the operation of NEPA itself. The public lands bring with them a whole array of their own federal statutes, and the influence of these is also highly regionalized. The Federal Land Policy and Management Act of 1976 (FLPMA), for example, the operational framework for the Bureau of Land Management (BLM), has no effect anywhere but in the West because the BLM essentially manages no lands outside the West. The Forest Service does manage some non-western forests, but the fact that 85 percent of the national forests are located in the West means that the National Forest Management Act of 1976 is part of the Law of the West. So, by the same token, is the Wilderness Act.

The concentration of all this national democracy in the West has had a pervasive and complex effect on the region's politics. On one hand, the nationalist vision of what is best for western landscapes continues to be deeply, passionately, and genuinely held by a range of people both within the West and beyond it. Specifically, this nationalist vision is an article of faith within the environmental movement. The faith is genuine, the belief is real, and this is, among other things, a tribute to the power of the New Nationalism of Theodore Roosevelt. The injection of this form of nationalism into the conservation movement accounts for the fact that the public lands still carry with them precisely the sense of "belonging to all of us" that Roosevelt sought to instill into American public life in general. For many people—and especially for nonwestern environmentalists—the public lands are among the noblest achievements of national democracy. They stand for the farsighted wisdom and stewardship of which Americans are capable at their collective best. As such, they represent still, a century after their reservation, a stirring fulfillment of what Herbert Croly called "the promise of American life." These public lands exemplify democracy in two particularly important ways: by allowing equal access for all Americans and by including all Americans in the decision-making processes that determine how those lands are managed.

On the other hand, the concentration of national democracy in the West has had the effect of making the region feel pervasively tyrannized and colonized. If anyone in the country might have a visceral appreciation of the anti-colonial democratic arguments of Jefferson's Declaration of Independence, it is westerners, who have been subjected to more national democracy than they can well tolerate. Many westerners encounter the public lands system as anything but an empowering, democratic experience. Instead, their experience is too often one of a frustrating, alienating bureaucratic paternalism. The often-repeated reaction of westerners to what so many of them have experienced as an imperial presence is the subject of the next chapter.

Chapter 3

A
Century of
Rebellion

"Our Western states have long since passed from their swaddling clothes and are today more competent to manage much of these affairs than is the Federal Government. Moreover, we must seek every opportunity to retard the expansion of Federal bureaucracy and to place our communities in control of their own destinies. . . . The Federal Government is incapable of the adequate administration of matters which require so large a matter of local understanding."
—Herbert Hoover

Like many another people throughout history who have found themselves under the sway of a remote government seated in a distant, dissimilar region, westerners have long nursed a deep resentment toward Washington, D.C., in particular toward the Washington-based control of public lands. In fact, for as long as there have been public lands in the West, there has been western opposition to their national ownership and management. Arguments against national domination of the region have not changed fundamentally since the early twentieth century. This chapter reviews the story of this ongoing resistance, introducing some of its major actors and discussing in a preliminary way the recurrent themes of western discontent. We begin with Theodore Roosevelt and his chief forester, Gifford Pinchot.

By 1909, denunciation of Pinchotism had become a common theme of the western press. This focused resentment soon led to the formation of anti-conservation groups such as the Western Conservation League (WCL) in the state of Washington and the National Domain League (NDL) in Colorado. The purpose of the WCL was to "'destroy Federal tenantry' by . . . free[ing] the natural resources from the clutches of the Eastern socialists," while the NDL sought "to restore the rights of farmers, stock-men, and miners to the public domain."[1] Although such groups fairly readily secured the support of western representatives and governors, they were never well enough organized at the grass-roots level to have any lasting effect. During Roosevelt's admin-istration they were further restrained by the fact, noted in the previous chapter, that Roosevelt, who had himself ranched in Dakota Territory and whose Rough Riders had been drawn pri-marily from the West, enjoyed a great personal popularity among westerners. Pinchot, an easterner through and through, did not share in this popularity, but even the easy target of Pinchotism was eliminated by President William Howard Taft's removal of Pinchot from his position as chief of the Forest Service in 1909. Greater cooperation between individual western states and the Forest Service (including the establishment of state conservation commissions after 1908) led, at least briefly, to a better accept-ance of conservation policy among western state politicians.[2] This was the beginning of a long and still ongoing genesis of state and local advisory entities occurring parallel to, and sometimes as a result of, outright opposition to national ownership of public lands.[3] In any event, western resentment of and resistance to "federal tenantry" would raise its head many more times in the course of the century. Increasingly, the politics of resistance would center in the Republican Party, the party of Roosevelt and Pinchot, and the policy focus of western resistance would shift from forests to grasslands and remain there for several decades.

Following the two terms of Woodrow Wilson's presidency, the Republicans recaptured the White House in the 1920 election and held it for the next twelve years. The West almost brought that tenure to an early end when President Warren G. Harding became embroiled in a scandal involving leasing of nationally owned petroleum reserves in the Teapot Dome formation of Wyoming. Senator Thomas Walsh of Montana led the investigation, which might have ended Harding's presidency had his death not done so first. But when his vice president, Calvin Coolidge, assumed the presidency, the country settled into the false security of the Roaring Twenties, and the West faded once again from national awareness. The stock market crash of 1929 and the ensuing Great Depression eventually ended this era of Republican hegemony. Yet even before that crash, the West underwent years of its own agricultural depression. Those hard years may have played a role in launching the next chapter in the saga of the public lands.

In 1929, President Herbert Hoover, the last Republican president of the 1920s era, sent a message to the annual meeting of the Western Governors' Association proclaiming that when it came to rangeland management,

> our Western states have long since passed from their swaddling clothes and are today more competent to manage much of these affairs than is the Federal Government. Moreover, we must seek every opportunity to retard the expansion of Federal bureaucracy and to

place our communities in control of their own destinies. . . . The Federal Government is incapable of the adequate administration of matters which require so large a matter of local understanding.[4]

In the same message, Hoover framed his suggestions for change within an explicit conservation message:

The surface rights of the remaining unappropriated, unreserved public lands should . . . be transferred to the state governments for public school purposes and thus be placed under state administration. . . . It is my desire to work out more constructive policies for conservation in our grazing lands, our water storage, and our mineral resources, at the same time check the growth of Federal bureaucracy, reduce Federal interference in affairs of essentially local interest, and thereby increase the opportunity of the states to govern themselves, and in all obtain better government.[5]

Following this overture to the western governors, Hoover established a commission, under the chairmanship of James R. Garfield, to study "the whole question of the public domain, particularly the unreserved lands."[6] Despite the aggressive reservation of forested public-domain lands under Presidents Cleveland, McKinley, and Roosevelt, much of the arid lands of the public domain—especially grasslands and desert lands—still had been neither homesteaded nor officially reserved. In 1929, more than 200 million acres of public land remained unsettled, unreserved, and unappropriated. Although this land was technically open to settlement and privatization, much of it was used as open grazing land.[7] Now, at Hoover's recommendation, the President's Committee on the Conservation and Administration of the Public Domain (also called the Garfield Commission) was appointed, with the Hoover administration making sure the commission included several leading citizens of the public land states. Hoover's primary concern, as expressed in his instructions to the commission, was overgrazing. "The destruction of the natural cover of the land imperils the water supply," he observed; " . . . the problem in this sense is really one of water conservation."[8] In 1931, the commission brought its recommendations to Congress. The grazing lands were being ruined, the commission concluded, and they should be regulated by the people who knew how to do so—the residents of the western states themselves.[9] The recommended course of action was to set aside some additional federal reserves (including, according to Hoover, "all possible oil and coal lands") and then grant the remaining areas to the states.[10]

Despite its apparent generosity to the states, the commission's proposal was not popular with many state governments, which balked particularly at the decision to exclude mineral lands from the cessions. Without any of the income such lands could generate, the states were understandably dubious about their ability to manage the least productive lands effectively. On the other hand, a recommendation to allow selected national forest land to remain in the public domain but be placed under state administration satisfied western states while incensing conservationists. Attempts to enact the commission's recommendations became snarled in a battle among states, conservationists, stockmen, and critics within the U.S. Department of Agriculture.[11] But the Hoover administration was not ready to give up.

In his 1931 annual report to the president, Hoover's secretary of the interior, Ray Lyman Wilbur, described eloquently and passionately the high price the federal government was exacting from western landscapes by denying locals a greater hand in land management:

In eleven of our States a great part of the land is owned by a landlord from two to three thousand miles away who has done nothing to protect his neighbors from the floods, erosion, and other consequences of allowing overgrazing on his own lands. . . . In county after county the desert rains now rush down through the gullies, flooding the farms and carrying off the surface soil to ruin the reservoirs, whereas when the white man first came the sagebrush and the desert grasses retained the rains, held the soil, and protected the watersheds. . . . The time has come when we must allow these western citizens to protect their property if we will not protect our own.[12]

But the time had not come. Eventually, as Hoover noted mournfully in his memoirs, this effort to denationalize a substantial portion of the public domain "had to give way to depression legislation and never became a reality."[13]

In 1932, Hoover was succeeded by Franklin D. Roosevelt, who with solid Democratic support in both houses of Congress began battling the Great Depression by invoking national power over an unprecedented range of economic and social activities. It was this nationalist and activist administration and Congress that in 1934 took a big step toward securing the previously unreserved grazing lands to the federal public domain by declaring in the Taylor Grazing Act (named for Representative Edward T. Taylor of Colorado) that the "Secretary of the Interior is authorized to create grazing districts from any part of the vacant and unappropriated public domain."[14] President Roosevelt, on approval of the act, noted, "The passage of this act marks the culmination of years of effort to obtain from Congress express authority for Federal regulation of grazing on the public domain in the interests of national conservation and of the livestock industry."[15] With these dual, and for many people contradictory, objectives, the act organized about 80 million acres of public land into grazing districts. The act also established a system of local advisory boards. Users of the range elected board members to represent their interests as the boards drafted new rules and regulations. (A similar reform in the Forest Service at this time established local advisory boards for national forests.)

In spite of the establishment of local, user-dominated advisory boards, westerners were far from satisfied by these developments. In a House debate on the Taylor grazing bill, Representative Harry L. Englebright of California declared that the legislation would merely perpetuate national ownership of the lands and leave eleven states "half Federal and half state."[16] Representative Vincent Carter of Wyoming described the bill as "federalism in the extreme," charging that it would give the secretary of the interior "dictatorial power."[17] In response to such criticism, the new Division of Grazing (also called the Grazing Service), which the act had created, went out of its way to win the support of cattlemen. The Grazing Service was now thoroughly decentralized and staffed exclusively by residents of public land states. Advisory boards, elected by the users of the range, were to participate in drafting rules and regulations for the Grazing Service.[18] However, even this did not quell western dislike for the retention of these grazing lands in national ownership.

In 1940, Senator Pat McCarran of Nevada introduced a resolution in the Senate on behalf of the Livestock Association leveling criticism at the new Grazing Service, specifically for its recent increase in range fees, and calling for a "full and complete investigation of the purchase, withdrawal, and allocation of lands and the administration and use thereof" by any agency of the national government.[19] McCarran was named to head a subcommittee of the Committee on Public Lands and Surveys, which held an extensive and protracted series of public hearings on grazing throughout the West. At the conclusion of the four-and-a-half-year process, the subcommittee members were unanimous in concluding that state ownership and utilization of the public lands was preferable to national control and that private ownership should be the eventual objective for the rangelands.[20] In 1946, Republican senator Edward Robertson of Wyoming introduced a follow-up bill to convey to the states the unappropriated and unreserved lands within them.[21]

As Robertson's grazing lands bill began working its way through Congress, Representative Frank A. Barrett, also from Wyoming, introduced a bill to draw the Forest Service back into the action. Barrett's bill authorized a series of public hearings throughout the West on the grazing policies of the Forest Service. Although most nationally owned grazing land came under the jurisdiction of the U.S. Department of the Interior, the lines between grasslands and forestlands have never been clean. From its creation to the present, the Forest Service has not only managed forests but has also leased some grasslands to ranchers. By the late 1940s, the agency's administration of that program had rankled enough ranchers to move western congressional delegations to seek passage of Barrett's bill. During the hearings, stockmen, arguing for conversion of public rangelands to private ownership, vigorously attacked the credibility of the Forest Service, and opponents of grazing on public lands were virtually silenced.

One voice, however, pierced the silence so eloquently and insistently that the attempt to restructure the public lands system was once again brought to a halt. *Harper's Magazine* columnist Bernard De Voto—historian, critic, and native westerner—closely followed the hearings and brought into public view the efforts of the committee and the stockmen in several *Harper's* essays. Although he asserted that there was "no chance" this "landgrab" would win the support of Congress, De Voto worried that these hearings were part of a "many-sided effort to discredit all conservation bureaus of the government, to discredit conservation itself."[22] De Voto, with the assistance of other defenders of the public lands, succeeded in blunting the attack on the Forest Service and scuttling Roberston's bill to transfer lands to the states. The grazing lands in question remained in the National Forest System, and the Forest Service, along with the newly created Bureau of Land Management, continued to cut the number of livestock permitted on rangelands. "The reason why the landgrab did not succeed in 1947," wrote De Voto, "and the reason why the continuing attack on the public lands system since then has not succeeded, is that journalism has kept the public informed about what was going on."[23]

In building his case against the "landgrab," De Voto held an often unflattering mirror up to his native region's face. Many westerners still have not forgiven the Utah-born writer for pointing out some of the West's most glaring contradictions, if not outright hypocrisies. The same ranchers who supported huge federal subsidies for such things as western water development projects and farm price support programs, he noted, sought repeatedly to take the public domain away from the national government and turn it over to the western states. Among his most lacerating observations was his characterization of the West's attitude toward Washington in the sarcastic formula "Get out and give us more money."[24] Although most westerners still cannot admit it, De Voto identified a contradiction that pervades western politics to this day. With a seemingly inexhaustible supply of acid observations about his native region, De Voto played no small part in defeating the postwar effort to denationalize the public lands. In one last gasp in this round of anti-federal efforts, when the Republicans finally returned to the White House with Dwight D. Eisenhower's election to the presidency in 1952, Eisenhower's new secretary of the interior, Douglas McKay, enunciated and endorsed a "policy of liquidating the public lands, to states and private parties, as rapidly as feasible."[25] But with De Voto and company still bird-dogging the issue, the proposal made no progress.

As we will see, this story of western resistance to national ownership and management of public lands was to continue for at least another fifty years, right up through the turn of the century, with most of the themes of the first half of the century repeated in variations throughout the second half. It may be helpful in this review to pause at midcentury to summarize and reflect on some of those themes before they begin reappearing. What becomes clear is that the pattern is more complex than many defenders of the public land system (including De Voto) have generally been willing to acknowledge.

It is all too easy, for example, to attribute the repeated attempts to localize control over western landscapes to raw greed and to overlook the genuine and often well-founded perception that locals should, as a matter of sound public policy, have substantial authority over landscapes and ecosystems they understand better than anyone else. President Hoover clearly articulated that theme in his assertion that "the Federal Government is incapable of the adequate administration of matters which require so large a matter of local understanding." If the West, or indeed the rest of the country, is ever to break out of the unending cycle this chapter details, it will be because each side in the debate finally begins to hear something true and enduring in the arguments of the other. There is some reason why the theme enunciated by Hoover keeps recurring, and will keep recurring until its truth is recognized and reflected in the structure of public lands governance. It is easy to dismiss anything Hoover said simply because Herbert Hoover said it, or simply because it is all too demonstrable that his saying it served the interests of a portion of his political base that had never shown sufficient concern for the health of the rangeland in question. But those raw political facts, in whatever guise or whichever decade they replicate themselves, do not and cannot erase the equally raw truth of what Hoover insisted on, and what every successive opponent to the centralized system of public land management insists on—that the national government, from its East Coast base, simply cannot know enough about western landscapes and ecosystems to manage them appropriately. Hoover's invocation of "local understanding" is echoed in the modern phrase *local knowledge* and carries with it, even more forcefully now than it did then, an inescapable truth: that people who live on a landscape, who have struggled to sustain themselves and their families on its bounty and against its hardships, will have learned lessons about that place that nothing else can teach.

Or consider the way in which Bernard De Voto's acerbic pen burned into the minds of a small but highly influential segment of America's reading public an image of westerners—particularly western ranchers—that still is a major determinant in public land policy debates. Most nonwestern environmentalists remain comfortably convinced that they know everything they need to know about western ranchers—and indeed about westerners in general. Even though very few modern-day environmentalists may have ever read a word of De Voto's writing, their image of the West and its politics fits into a conceptual framework of which De Voto was the chief author. For all the undoubted good De Voto's work did for the cause of conservation in the late 1940s and the 1950s, it may be time to recognize that the hard truths he spoke about the West and about westerners were themselves only part of the truth, and sometimes less than half the truth. Today, as westerners of many callings—not least among them western ranchers—challenge themselves to find new ways to address public land issues, they continue to be haunted by the stinging characterizations of De Voto and those he influenced. Without denying the considerable extent to which westerners have contributed to that unflattering image, those who genuinely care about the fate of public lands may, for the sake of those lands themselves, need at last to give western-ers a chance to prove that they have begun to outgrow their lesser selves. There is now a danger—a very real danger—that the image De Voto created of the West and of westerners has itself become a western myth that is keeping both the West and the rest of the country from doing well by western landscapes, communities, and ecosystems.

But this gets us well ahead of our story. The uncontestable fact is that the defeat the western rebels suffered at De Voto's and others' hands at midcentury would only goad those rebels to more of the same kind of self-defeating behavior in the follow-ing decades. The effort to denationalize the public lands lay largely dormant between 1950 and 1975. It was stirred up again, however, to an even higher pitch, by the volume of environ-mental legislation passed in the 1970s. As noted in chapter 2, because of the prevalence of public lands in the West, that national environmental framework became much more notice-able in this region than in any other. In many cases, the legisla-tion felt to westerners like salt being rubbed into slowly healing wounds.

When the Federal Land Policy and Management Act of 1976 (FLPMA) was passed, it expressly reaffirmed the national gov-ernment's intention to keep BLM-administered lands in public ownership. In Utah, San Juan County commissioner Calvin Black called FLPMA "the worst piece of legislation ever passed against the people of the West." According to Black, the legisla-tion "established colonialism as a practice."[26] These were not isolated sentiments. In 1978, the Western Regional Conference of the Council of State Governments and the Western Interstate Region of the National Association of Counties agreed to join forces on the issue of ownership of public lands through creation of the Western Coalition on Public Lands. They sent a delegation to Washington, D.C., to publicize the coalition's official position and to present its case to Congress and the Department of the Interior.[27] Looking back at the passage of FLPMA, the *Washington Post* reported in 1979 that "this law may be the match that finally lit the Sagebrush Rebellion."[28]

In any event, it was in 1979 that the Nevada state legislature passed Assembly Bill 413 (later dubbed the Sagebrush Rebellion bill), drafted in part by Deputy Attorney General Harry Swainston, claiming all Nevada land administered by the BLM as state property. The legal argument behind the bill rested on the "equal footing" theory—the constitutional doctrine that a new state must enter the Union on an "equal footing" with other states. The core contention was that states dominated by federally owned land (more than 82 percent of Nevada's acreage is owned by the national government) cannot possibly operate economically or in any other way on an equal footing with other states. Swainston summed up the argument on Nevada's behalf by contending that "such an overwhelming [national] presence lessened the state's sovereignty."[29]

Following introduction of the Sagebrush Rebellion bill in the Nevada legislature, more than 300 delegates from western states attended the first regional meeting of the Western Coalition on Public Lands. On the heels of this meeting, Republican senator Orrin Hatch of Utah introduced Senate 1680, a bill to transfer ownership of public lands to the states. The bill would have established a Federal Land Transfer Board for each state wishing to participate in a land transfer. States would select any or all of the BLM lands, Forest Service lands, or wilderness areas within their boundaries. Emboldened by such support from their own senator, a few hundred Utahans attended a demonstration in Moab, where several Grand County commissioners, including chairman Harvey Merrell, delivered political speeches from the back of a bulldozer. After the speeches, the same bulldozer was used to plow a road into a BLM wilderness study area that blocked access to a parcel of state land believed to contain minerals.

In 1980, more than 500 people attended a conference in Salt Lake City sponsored by the League for the Advancement of States' Equal Rights (LASER). Representatives of the group stated that it was formed "to create a broad base of support in favor of divesting the federal government of the public domain."[30] Senator Hatch spoke at the conference, stating his opinion that "the vesting of ownership and management of the public domain with the respective western state governments means a rebirth of the prestige and power of state government."[31] Presidential candidate Ronald Reagan sent a telegram to the conference stating: "I renew my pledge to work toward a 'sagebrush solution.' My administration will work to insure that the states have an equitable share of public lands and their natural resources."[32] Later in the campaign, Reagan proclaimed, "Count me in as a rebel!"[33] By the end of 1980, Nevada, Utah, Wyoming, New Mexico, and Arizona had all enacted bills claiming federal public lands as state property. Washington State had passed similar legislation putting the issue before the public in the form of a referendum; Hawaii, Alaska, and Idaho had passed "supportive resolutions."[34]

In 1981, Reagan, now president, appointed self-professed Sagebrush Rebel James G. Watt of Wyoming as secretary of the interior. Watt's initial approach, though, was not to divest ownership of the public lands so much as to involve the West more in public lands decision making, believing that "a 'good neighbor policy' with the West was far more likely to allay western anger than a radical turnover of lands the states might not be able to administer."[35] This approach caused Nevada state senator Norman Glaser to worry that "Watt . . . might do too good a job and defuse the vitality of our movement."[36]

Environmentalists and other opponents of the Sagebrush Rebellion were by no means content to rely on Watt's inadvertent undermining of the movement, however. Instead, they went to court, where they persuaded U.S. District Court Judge Edward Reed to reject Nevada's Assembly Bill 413, the Sagebrush Rebellion bill. "No state legislation may interfere with Congress' power over the public domain," Reed declared.[37] This legal reversal was accompanied by a loss of political momentum within the rebellion. Accustomed as the rebels had become to opposing federal officials simply because they were federal officials, it appears that having one of their own in the White House took some steam out of their movement, exactly as Norman Glaser had feared. Reagan and Watt did put forward an administration plan to sell off "unneeded" federal property, but when even that effort failed, the rebels began turning their attention to the burgeoning property rights and "wise use" movements. They started mobilizing support at the level of local government rather than relying on an immediate solution from the center of power.

When the rebellion surfaced again a decade later, its locus had shifted from Capitol Hill and the western state capitals to county courthouses. In 1991, Catron County, New Mexico, published its Interim Land Use Policy Plan, in which the county asserted jurisdiction over all federal and state lands, waters, and wildlife within its borders. The plan purported to require county approval for all actions on state and federal land, allowed for no wilderness designation inside the county, and named the county as the designated planning agency for the future of the land. The plan's stated intent was to protect the county's "custom and culture."[38] The county also proposed an ordinance requiring all families to own guns in order to be prepared to protect the county's interests in opposing the federal government, but this was eventually modified to become a simple assertion of the right to bear arms.[39]

From Catron, what came to be called the county movement spread rapidly across the West. By 1993, the National Federal Lands Conference claimed to have 175–200 counties enlisted in the movement, with no lack of Washington-supplied fuel to feed the fire. In Nevada, for example, Nye County commissioner Richard Carver, angered by Secretary of the Interior Bruce Babbitt's announcement that the department would soon raise grazing fees, sent a letter to the governor of Nevada, the secretaries of the interior and agriculture, the director of the BLM, and the chief of the Forest Service stating that public lands were not reserved to the United States at the time of statehood and referring to a wide range of statutes that, Carver argued, revealed the constitutionality of the move to give control of federal lands to individual counties.[40]

In 1994, the Nevada Association of Counties voted unanimously to sign on to Carver's letter and asked that the letter's recipients meet with state and county officials to arrange for the transfer of public lands. On Independence Day of that year, in what would come to be known as the Jefferson Canyon incident, Carver earned himself an appearance on the cover of *Time* magazine when he bulldozed open a closed Forest Service road.[41] Nye County then promptly passed a resolution claiming county jurisdiction over all land within its borders.

Meanwhile, the Kelley Spring incident was unfolding in Elko County as the federal government took resident Don Duval to court for installing a pipe to carry water from a spring on national forest land to his private pasture. Republican state assemblyman John Carpenter organized a demonstration during which 500 people built a fence around the spring and declared it the property of Nevada. Duval eventually lost the case and dismantled the pipe, but 40 people replaced it the following day. The *Elko Daily Free Press* reported that Carpenter claimed, when questioned by the Forest Service about the incident, that if the government continued to push the issue, "there probably would be bloodshed."[42]

As the county movement spread across the region, it began to fire up a new round of the old western effort to denationalize the public lands. In 1994, the Western States Summit, a coalition of western state legislators, met in Phoenix, Arizona. A primary objective of the summit was to have BLM lands turned over to the states. The furor was fanned by Babbitt's further pursuit of his proposal to increase BLM grazing fees—the same proposal that had set Richard Carver in motion. (A Senate filibuster led by Republican senators Pete Domenici of New Mexico and Bob Bennett of Utah eventually defeated Babbitt's initiative.)

Emboldened by the spread of the county movement, by the defeat of the grazing fee increase, and by the "Gingrich revolution" in the 1994 elections, western conservatives moved their efforts to a new level of organization. Met Johnson, a Republican member of the Utah House of Representatives, convened a two-day Western Summit of conservative state legislators, county commissioners, and public land users in Salt Lake City. Five hundred people attended the 1995 summit, including Senator Orrin Hatch. Republican representative James Hansen of Utah, sounding the same theme Herbert Hoover had articulated more than sixty years earlier, told the crowd: "I believe with all my heart, that the legislative bodies of the West absolutely can take as good care of the ground as the federal government and do it cheaper and better."[43] Later that same year, Hansen and Republican senator Craig Thomas of Wyoming introduced companion bills in Congress requiring the BLM to give 270 million acres of land, including all its minerals, to the states. Their effort was buttressed by substantial local support; in 1995, the *Washington Post* reported that more than seventy western counties had passed or proposed laws to "take back" the public lands.[44] But the legislation, like all similar efforts, went nowhere.

During the last half of the 1990s, the county movement, like so many earlier phases of the western rebellion, began to fade. In 1995, the U.S. government filed suit against Nye County, Nevada, in response to the drafting of a county land-use plan (based on Catron County's land-use plan) that would have given the county control over national forests and other federal lands and ownership of the roads passing through them. (Federal land makes up 93 percent of Nye County, which is the third largest county in the United States, with a land area of 18,064 square miles.) The federal lawyers argued that the resolutions in the Nye County plan were unconstitutional. Assistant Attorney General Lois Schiffer called the lawsuit a "firm but restrained" approach to the county movement, saying, "It should send a message, loud and clear, that . . . the federal government has sovereignty over federal lands."[45] In 1996, U.S. District Court Judge Lloyd George ruled against Nye County in a decision stating that the federal government "owns and has the power and authority to manage and administer the unappropriated public lands and National Forest Service lands in Nye County, Nevada."[46] The following year brought a resolution of sorts, with adoption of a "settlement agreement" between the federal agencies and Nye County. The agreement, designed to create a "more cooperative working relationship," established a framework for discussing solutions to public land disputes.[47]

Here, we need to pause again in the chronological narrative to observe another persistent theme running through the story: the multifaceted effort to oppose or dismantle the federal public lands superstructure by claiming another form of jurisdiction or sovereignty over the lands in question. In the case of the Sagebrush Rebellion, the states were said to have sovereignty over the lands; the next episode, however, focused on claims of county jurisdiction. These arguments have never enjoyed any significant legal success, a fact that leads readily enough to the conclusion that there simply is no real issue of sovereignty at stake. Yet here again, just as with the recurring argument that local knowledge is finally a better base for public land management than a centralized national regime, there is more validity to the sovereignty concern than the legal arguments have managed to capture. In fact, the two themes go hand in hand. There is something about the current centralized structure of sovereignty over the public lands that the people who live surrounded by those lands seem to find fundamentally flawed. Although none of the alternative claims of sovereignty made so far has succeeded in court, the issue of sovereignty remains unresolved in the minds of many westerners. In later chapters, we will examine in more depth why the issue of sovereignty has been so persistent and consider some new, less ideologically brittle ways to address that enduring issue. For now, we return to the Sagebrush Rebellion.

By the turn of the century, the steam had largely evaporated from efforts to develop and sustain legal theories that could challenge national dominance over the West. But that is not to say that western resistance to the "imperial presence" had ended. Once again, the deeply embedded strain of western resistance simply shifted its ground, now relying more on symbolism and theatrics than on constitutional doctrines. As the old resource extraction economy of the West continued to be undermined by new economic forces, the focus of western resentment, though still held in place by anti-Washington dogma, began to play in a global arena. The story unfolded most dramatically in the unlikely nexus of two remote western towns: Elko, Nevada, and Libby, Montana.

Anti-government leaders in Elko County have repeatedly displayed a flair for the symbolic, media-friendly gesture, honing their skills during the 1994 uproar created by Don Duval's irrigation project and Assemblyman John Carpenter's bold, sound-bite threats of violence and bloodshed. Four years after the Kelley Spring incident, some of the same characters mobilized to push their agenda onto new territory. In 1998, Elko County commissioners joined with Carpenter and others to plan for the repair and reopening of the washed-out South Canyon Road, an access route to a popular campground and the Jarbidge Wilderness Area. In practical terms, this might have been a simple proposition, a matter of a bulldozer and a few loads of fill. However, the road traverses a national forest, and the river that had washed out the road was home to the Jarbidge bull trout, listed as a threatened species under the Endangered Species Act of 1973. In deference to the bull trout, the Forest Service had decided not to repair the road. In true western vigilante fashion, Carpenter and his followers took matters into their own hands.

A series of unsuccessful attempts to repair the road in violation of the Forest Service closure led to plans for an October 1999 "shovel brigade" work party. Richard Carver, the Nye County commissioner who in 1994 had driven his bulldozer into Jefferson Canyon, promised reinforcement from his county. Days before the scheduled event, U.S. District Court Judge David W. Hagen issued a temporary restraining order against the shovel brigade. Before issuing a permanent injunction, he ordered all the parties involved, including members of the Elko County Commission and Assemblyman John Carpenter, to enter into mediation with a representative of the U.S. Institute for Environmental Conflict Resolution.[48] But the matter did not end there.

The pervasive climate of anti-federal hostility surrounding the Jarbidge dispute was largely responsible for Gloria Flora's

November 1999 resignation from her position as forest supervisor for Humboldt-Toiyabe National Forest. Flora's resignation came five days before a special congressional hearing about South Canyon Road called by Republican representative Helen Chenoweth-Hage of Idaho. Flora called the planned Elko hearing a "public inquisition" of federal employees, one more example of the "fed bashing" and intimidation tactics that had plagued her term as forest supervisor.[49]

Meanwhile, a few small communities in northwestern Montana started to pay attention to the news coming out of Elko County, seeing a common western story in the articles. Eureka sawmill owner Jim Hurst began to collect shovels for a show of solidarity with Elko citizens. "We are the forgotten species," he declared. "We've got common issues here. We've got bull trout and endangered species. We've got people who have lost their access to the woods. It's the same thing all over the West."[50] Cary Hegreberg of the Montana Wood Products Association commented: "Public concern for forest management is what got us here. And public concern for our rural communities and lumber mills is what can turn us around. . . . Maybe sending a shovel will send a message that we count and our communities matter."[51] As the shovel solicitation picked up speed, Gloria Flora toured Montana, calling for citizens in the West to come together in a civil manner and avoid divisive rhetoric. An editorial in the *Elko Daily Free Press* criticized Flora's Montana speaking tour and analyzed the situation in terms now long familiar across the West:

> Criticism in a democracy against a federal agency— and there are many good reasons to find fault with the forest service—does not necessarily constitute harassment. . . . The real and critical issues swirling around the South Canyon Road debate are obscured . . . the great grassroots shovel crusade headed for Elko this

weekend reflects a nationwide concern over how a behemoth federal bureaucracy is trampling states' rights and personal freedoms. President Clinton's capricious and unconstitutional classification by executive order of more than 50 million acres of public lands as "roadless areas" epitomizes an administrative arrogance that redefines the notion of an imperial presidency. . . . In the state case, as well as the federal case, the Elko County Commission has remained adamant that no permits were needed during a county-declared emergency because the county has sovereignty over the road.[52]

On January 29, 2000, 1,000 protesters marched or drove through Elko's streets, carrying by hand or by truck 10,000 shovels sent from across the West. Carpenter's parade speech called for unity in the fight against federal land managers. "We have learned we must stand together, shoulder to shoulder," he declared, "to defeat those who would destroy our way of life and the West as we know it."[53]

Back in Libby, Montana—a town still reeling from recent disclosures of widespread asbestos contamination from a nearby vermiculite mine—Terry Andreessen, a former Forest Service employee, sat down with Republican state representative Scott Orr to plan a rally on April 15—the day most Americans like their government the least—to protest "the Clinton environmental regime's war on the West." Flyers advertising the event read, "No more negotiating, no more public meetings." Andreessen quoted Theodore Roosevelt to support his cause:

> Eastern people, and especially Eastern sportsmen, need to keep steadily in mind the fact that the Westerners who live in the neighborhood of the forest preserves are the men whom in the last resort will determine whether or not these preserves are to be

permanent. They cannot in the long run be kept as forest and game reservations unless the settlers round-about believe in them and heartily support them.[54]

Missoula's daily newspaper countered this quotation in an editorial with another Roosevelt statement dating from the establishment of grazing fees for federal land: "The rights of the public to natural resources outweigh private rights and must be given its first consideration."[55]

At least a few residents of northwestern Montana viewed the Libby protest with a cynical eye. One commented: "They want to rally together the snowmobilers and off-road vehicle users to combat the big federal government, but the people funding this Western uprising are the Japanese off-road vehicle manufacturers. There is no global government, but there is a global economy, and these guys are playing right into it."[56] Others pointed out the modern manifestation of De Voto's "Get out and give us more money" mantra as Libby residents decried the heavy hand of the federal government while simultaneously seeking millions of federal dollars to help address the asbestos contamination from the vermiculite mine. Passions ran high on both sides. Human rights activists entered the fray, charging the rally organizers with use of hate tactics. They invited Mark Potok, a speaker from the Southern Poverty Law Center, to come to Libby. Potok eventually canceled his Libby speech when organizers began expressing fear of a backlash from the organizers of the April 15 event. Potok criticized the organizers of the rally for buying into conspiracy theories regarding the United Nations' intentions to create a global government.[57] The organizers of that rally eventually canceled their event as well, but three dozen people showed up in spite of the cancellation and in spite of the spring rain. The little crowd expressed its concerns about globalism by burning a United Nations flag in the drizzle.

The linked dramas in Montana and Nevada came to a head in the weeks leading up to Independence Day 2000. On June 21 in Missoula, 2,000 timber workers and motorized recreation advocates gathered to vent their opposition to President Bill Clinton's Roadless Area Initiative, an attempt by his administration to preserve by executive action more than 40 million acres of wilderness, mostly in the West. It was a show of high theatrics that included a mock funeral procession crossing the Clark Fork River to deliver a coffin full of comments to the public hearing at which hundreds of people had gathered to speak out in support of the contentious proposal. Two weeks later, 500 people gathered in Jarbidge, Nevada, where they removed a boulder they had dubbed the Liberty Rock from the center of the Forest Service roadblock and then, for good measure, engaged in a symbolic cleaning of Forest Service outhouses at the now inaccessible trailhead. As the buckets were carried to a septic truck, Shovel Brigade president Demar Dahl told the gathering, "That's known as government waste."[58]

Increasingly, the long tradition of western resistance to the national presence in the region has moved away from an explicit assertion of state and county rights and toward a less legalistic and more symbolic attack on federal land management in general. There is something increasingly pathetic about these protests. Whether it is shovels or bulldozers, Elko or Libby, it all has the feel of a rearguard action that could at any moment turn into a rout. The forces against which the western rebels struggle are so massive that none of the actions seems any more effective than burning the United Nations flag in the rain in Libby. The momentum of the global economy will not be affected by such gestures, nor will that economy's effect on a small, resource-dependent community such as Libby be in any way modified. It becomes easier every moment simply to dismiss the rebels out of hand as an increasingly irrelevant anachronism.

Yet, as we will see in the next chapter, the centralized system against which westerners have struggled for a full century has itself become more than a little pathetic as it grasps at ever newer formulas to maintain its governing legitimacy. Like two punch-drunk fighters, the Empire and the Rebellion both sag on the ropes, and spectators can only hope that the fight is called before they have to endure another round.

Chapter 4

The Decline
of the
Empire

"The world's nations, having exhausted their natural bounty one by one, may still find a way to survive on the wings of artifice, but they will do so interdependently and together: globally or not at all. The nation-state's days are numbered."

—Benjamin Barber

"Fifty years ago, the Forest Service was one of the most highly regarded agencies in government. Today, the agency is besieged from without, demoralized within, and many wonder whether it will survive to see its centennial in 2005."

—Forest Options Group

The two deep historical strands traced in the previous two chapters now play themselves out rather incongruously against a twenty-first-century backdrop, with an entirely different set of forces bringing their weight to bear on the American West. This chapter describes one set of these new forces, with special attention to their implications for the West. The chapter begins by noting the steadily expanding number of observers who now argue that around the world, national governments are becoming less relevant and less capable of responding to the challenges of globalism. The United States is experiencing that phenomenon primarily in terms of devolution: the transfer of responsibility and authority over many functions previously performed by the national government to state or local governments. In the West, where the national government's presence is more evident because of the existence of a greater proportion of public lands, the prospect of devolution is especially contentious. But the worldwide forces weakening national governments everywhere are also at work in the West, manifesting themselves in declining vitality, effectiveness, and legitimacy of the land management agencies.

Libby's soggy flag-burning ceremony will endure, if at all, as a minor footnote in the history of the American West. The contradictory forces that inspired the event, however, offer a study in confusion that might help westerners understand where they are headed in the next millennium, provided they can sort out the tangle of intertwined forces and ideas. Start with the fact that the people who burned the United Nations flag in Libby are generally the same people who would support an amendment to the United States Constitution either to outlaw burning of the American flag or to require recitation of the Pledge of Allegiance in the country's schools. Yet they burn the flag of the United Nations, concocting conspiracy theories about black helicopters financed and flown by that organization, which they believe may itself be only a stalking-horse for a much more sinister "one-world government." Since the heyday of the John Birch Society, regionalism has been seen as an integral and menacing component of that purported conspiracy. This gives us a glimpse at the strands of confusion that tend only to conceal where the West fits into the real world: the new and indeed confusing world of globalism, continentalism, regionalism, and declining nationalism.

There are, in fact, forces at work at the global and continental scales that are rightly troublesome to old-economy communities such as Libby and Elko. With that said, however, the United Nations is nothing like the threat the conservatives make it out to be, simply because it is a fairly harmless holdover from a passing era: the age of the nation-state. The operative world order is no longer fundamentally an inter*nation*al order, in which an organization such as the United Nations might play a prominent role. Rather, the new order is becoming genuinely global. Kenichi Ohmae, in a book titled *The End of the Nation State*, summed up a steadily expanding body of thought when he concluded that "the nation state is increasingly a nostalgic fiction."[1] Benjamin Barber, in *Jihad vs. McWorld*, sounded the same note in a different key: "The world's nations, having exhausted their natural bounty one by one, may still find a way to survive on the wings of artifice, but they will do so interdependently and together: globally or not at all. The nation-state's days are numbered."[2]

It is becoming more and more clear that postindustrial capitalism has little use—or, indeed, patience—for nations as they have come to be known over the past two centuries. In the fiercely competitive global order, artificial jurisdictional boundaries, whether national, state, or county boundaries, end up interfering with commerce in a way that cannot long be tolerated or indulged. More organic entities such as continents, city-regions, and coherent subcontinental regions are rapidly emerging as considerably more relevant economic entities than states, provinces, and nations.

Nor is the economy the only arena in which old, arbitrary

jurisdictional boundaries are being slowly but steadily rendered irrelevant. Global ecology moves in exactly the same direction as does the globalized economy, sorting itself into layers of organic places, none of them corresponding to the old linear, mechanical order. Some issues, such as global warming and the thinning of the ozone layer, must be dealt with at the utterly organic level of the earth itself. Some, such as desertification and rain-forest issues, are essentially continental. Yet others, such as species loss and degradation of water quality, are best dealt with at the level of bioregion and river basin. No ecological issue has anything to do with national, state, or provincial boundaries, and people only make things more difficult for themselves by trying to deal with such issues through arbitrarily shaped political jurisdictions. Andrew Hurrell, a fellow in international relations at Oxford University, offers this analysis of the nation-state's incapacity to address ecological concerns:

> The . . . fragmented system of sovereign states [is] less and less able to guarantee the effective and equitable management of an interdependent world in general, and of the global environment in particular. . . . The [nation] is too big to develop effective strategies of sustainable development, which must come from the bottom up, and too small to effectively manage global problems such as climate change or biodiversity protection.[3]

Although they often seem at odds with each other, then, global economy and global ecology speak with one voice in proclaiming the growing irrelevance of existing structures of sovereignty and the inevitable emergence of much more organic global, continental, regional, and local forms of governance.

It has been easier for Americans to recognize the decline in relevance of the nation-state abroad than at home, but the

declining potency of national structures is a global and historical phenomenon from which they cannot remain (and have not
remained) immune. Devolution is the form in which Americans
have become most familiar with the nation's diminishing role.
The most far-reaching example of American devolution to date
has been the dismantling of the national welfare system. This
decommissioning of a major national program was motivated in
part by the substantial contribution that move could make to
balancing the national budget, but the savings could be achieved
only because of the deeply rooted and steadily widening conviction that here was a function the national government was no
longer capable of performing in a satisfactory way.

In the United States, the diminishing role of the national
government is rooted particularly in the cold war and its after-
math. The cold war, like any other war, was a battle of both wills
and arms. In this case, the arms did not have to be (indeed, could
not be) used in order to be effective. In fact, their effectiveness
ultimately lay less in their throw weight or the accuracy of their
delivery systems than in their astronomical costliness. In the
end, the United States simply spent the Soviet system into a
state of collapse.

But the collapse of the Soviet empire was purchased at a huge
price at home, both in straightforward monetary terms and in
the more subtle but perhaps more lasting terms of loss of governing legitimacy. If the United States fought and won the cold
war fiscally, if it essentially spent the Soviet Union into the
ground, it also in the process spent itself into overwhelming
indebtedness. During the Ronald Reagan–George Bush years
alone, between 1980 and 1992, the national debt quadrupled,
rising from $845 billion to $3.6 trillion. This massive borrowing
in turn contributed significantly to an already well advanced
weakening of the national government's legitimacy—a weakening that the cold war had at first obscured. The Vietnam War

and the Watergate scandal had seriously undermined the national government's credibility in the 1960s and early 1970s, but the cold war—the righteous battle against what President Reagan called the Evil Empire—had continued to invest the national government with a big and important task to which most Americans could give their consent. With the end of that war, that key legitimizing task was suddenly completed.

But to the surprise of many, the result was not to make people say, "What a great government—it did just what we wanted it to do!" Instead, the result was to strip away the one piece of work that had given the government broad legitimacy. Because nothing had occurred in the meantime to remove the cynicism bred by Watergate and Vietnam, people were left asking, "What exactly is this government now good for, anyway?" Although answers certainly could have been (and were) offered, the question was given a particularly sharp historical bite by the overwhelming debt the cold war had occasioned. Citizens giving permission to borrow money in their name is one good measure of the popular legitimacy a government carries. Through the Great Depression, World War II, and the cold war, Americans had been fairly liberal in granting that permission. With the overwhelmingly costly completion of its last great mission, though, the national government found that it had exhausted its permission to borrow money.

In fact, the need to keep expanding and extending the government's borrowing authority became a key point of contention in the 1990s, leading at one point to a government shutdown of several days' duration—a constitutional crisis that was itself a symptom of a growing crisis of legitimacy on the government's part. Although the government survived that immediate crisis, it found it had permanently lost its mandate to perform a variety of functions for which it had previously been granted both popular support and borrowing authority.

The welfare system was the first major casualty of this loss of legitimacy, but if devolution is in fact a manifestation of a broader, deeper historical phenomenon having to do with the collapse of continental empires and the declining significance of nationhood in general, welfare reform is likely to be only one in a series of major shifts in governing responsibility. Of particular relevance to the West is the likelihood that sooner or later, something analogous to welfare reform will occur in the arena of public lands and resource management. For those who sincerely believe that the current land management system needs to be defended or strengthened, not dismantled, this is bound to be an unwelcome suggestion. In fact, it is guaranteed to evoke defenses of the current system reminiscent of the last-ditch defenses of the welfare system. In the case of the public lands, the pressure for devolution will also inevitably invoke among the heirs of Bernard De Voto visions of one more round in the glorious battle against the forces of greed and exploitation. But the eminently well intentioned defenders of the current structure of public land governance now run a serious risk of losing their ability to influence events in a constructive way by defending too uncritically a system that history itself may be bypassing.

What the West already sees, far more clearly than the rest of the country can be expected to perceive, is the deepening inability of the national government to fulfill all the responsibilities it has undertaken in this region. The land management agencies in particular often seem to westerners to be in a state of paralysis, unable to move decisively in any direction, even as continuing migration of newcomers into the region over which these agencies have such vast jurisdiction puts unprecedented pressure on the public lands. Each agency manifests this paralysis in its own way, but the variety of manifestations should not be allowed to obscure the underlying historical phenomenon of a loss of governing legitimacy.

Start with the Bureau of Land Management (BLM), which owns and manages 264 million acres of land, all but tiny jots and slivers of it in the West. This small agency has total management responsibility for an area roughly equivalent in size to the combined acreage of the (very large) states that make up the region known as the Four Corners: Utah, Arizona, New Mexico, and Colorado. So how is the agency doing? Consider this: the BLM went through five different directors and acting directors in the first six years of President Bill Clinton's administration. Although personalities and other momentary factors no doubt played a part in the revolving door phenomenon in the director's office, the more fundamental problem may simply be that the national government no longer has the capacity or the legitimacy to govern from the banks of the Potomac River those vast stretches of western landscape assigned to the BLM's jurisdiction.

Bruce Babbitt, who served as secretary of the interior throughout Clinton's administration, ultimately decided to fill the leadership void within the BLM by proposing an entirely new identity and mission for the agency. Babbitt's tool of choice in this quest for a meaningful mission for the beleaguered BLM was the Antiquities Act of 1906, which authorizes the president to designate as national monuments sites of historical or scientific interest that are situated on federal land, and authorizes the secretary of the interior to accept these tracts of land on behalf of the government.

At an agencywide staff meeting in March 2000, Babbitt outlined his ambitious plan to salvage the agency's self-respect:

> In the 21st century, the BLM faces a choice. It can become the greatest modern American land management agency, the one that sets the standard for protecting landscapes, applying evolving knowledge and social standards, and bringing people together to live in harmony with the land . . . or it can become a relic,

a historical artifact, its most desirable lands carved up and parceled out to other land management agencies, with the remainder destined for the auction block of divestiture. . . . For a half century, from 1946 to 1996, every single large new national monument established under the Antiquities Act was taken away from the Bureau of Land Management. . . . The new BLM must have at its core a system of specially protected and managed conservation units, including landscape monuments and National Conservation Areas.[4]

Including the famous (or infamous) 1996 designation of the Grand Staircase–Escalante National Monument in Utah, Babbitt and Clinton had by the summer of 2000 designated no fewer than eight new BLM-managed monuments in six western states. Aside from Grand Staircase–Escalante, newly designated national monuments included Canyons of the Ancients in Colorado, Hanford Reach in Washington State, Cascade-Siskiyou in Oregon, California Coastal, and three in Arizona: Agua Fria, Ironwood Forest, and Grand Canyon–Parashant. Babbitt's desire to give the BLM something worthy of its management skills was a little reminiscent of Gifford Pinchot's ambition on behalf of the Forest Service a century earlier. By 1900, Pinchot had become America's chief forester, but he held his title within the Department of Agriculture, whereas all the nationally owned forests were under the jurisdiction of the Department of the Interior. Pinchot worked tirelessly to change that situation, finally succeeding in 1905 with the creation of the Forest Service as an agency of the Department of Agriculture and the assignment to it of the already reserved national forests. Then, with Theodore Roosevelt's help, Pinchot proceeded to add millions of acres to his domain through the use of the presidential prerogative to create forest reserves. Babbitt's president never enjoyed that reservation power, which Congress had taken out of the hands of the presidency in 1907, but Clinton did openly invite comparison of his use of the Antiquities Act to Roosevelt's bold strokes in the cause of conservation.

However Roosevelt might have felt about the comparison, we can be certain Pinchot would have bridled at Babbitt's suggestion that the BLM was poised to become "the greatest modern American land management agency." That was what Pinchot had created the Forest Service to be, and his heirs within the agency today would scoff at Babbitt's in-house claim. But the real question is whether either the Forest Service or the BLM can any longer claim anything even remotely like the distinction Pinchot established for his agency.

Even as Babbitt worked relentlessly throughout the last months of the Clinton administration to create more and more national monuments and national conservation areas and to ensure that they would remain under BLM jurisdiction, many old-timers within the agency expressed concern about whether the BLM actually had the wherewithal to manage several (or indeed to manage any) new tourist destinations. In fact, they knew it did not have that capacity, and they doubted whether Congress would ever consider increasing the agency's base budget enough to build such capacity. In the new age of balanced budgets, they had become hardened to steady reductions in force, and they remained appropriately skeptical about any looming reversal of that trend. Furthermore, they knew that the politics of the situation were driven not only by the sharpened knives of the "budget hawks" but also by the spreading perception that the old model of centralized national jurisdiction over western landscapes was ripe to be replaced by a far more decentralized model. That perception was clearly articulated by one group of county commissioners whose counties either bordered or overlapped the freshly minted Hanford Reach National Monument. These local officials spoke for hundreds of their colleagues across the West when they offered an alternative management structure to Babbitt's monolithic "greatest modern American land management agency" approach:

> The federal government will make all the decisions regarding the Hanford Reach and surrounding lands, and although it may seek local input, it won't be obligated or required to consider our perspective. And that's where the problem begins. We think it is unfair and irresponsible to exclude local people from the decision making and management of an area that has proven to greatly impact our quality of life. Management of these lands should be placed in the hands of a partnership that allots all government agencies—federal, state, local and tribal—a seat at the decision-making table.[5]

Whether or not anything like this proposed partnership will be created at Hanford Reach, the concerns expressed about "the federal government [making] all the decisions" are part of a larger pattern that no amount of cheerleading by secretaries of the interior can now overcome. The George W. Bush administration may actually succeed in getting a BLM director confirmed; it may even keep one in office for a few years running; but in no event will the BLM be to the twenty-first century what the Forest Service was to the twentieth.

Nor will the Forest Service itself, an agency in which the loss of governing capacity—the loss of legitimacy—is even more evident than it is in the BLM. Since its creation in 1905, the Forest Service has become responsible for 192 million acres of land, 86 percent of this area located in Alaska and the eight contiguous western states. Through much of the twentieth century, the Forest Service enjoyed a sterling reputation for its management of those lands. But those days are gone, and they are almost certainly gone for good. In 1998, former chief of the Forest Service

Jack Ward Thomas described in typically blunt fashion both the agency's former glory and its fall from grace: "From the 1950s until the early 1960s, the Forest Service was held up by many as a paragon of virtue. The scholars proclaimed that IBM and the Forest Service were the two most effective, efficient bureaucracies in the world." Now, he admitted, the agency "faces its greatest challenge since its birth."[6] The challenge had been building for some time. As forest supervisors, who had gathered at a conference in 1989, described the situation in a memo to Thomas' predecessor as chief, Dale Robertson, "We have become an agency out of control."[7] A decade later, *High Country News*, a Colorado-based weekly covering the interior West, described the Forest Service as "an agency deep in decline, plagued by spiraling morale, paralyzing lawsuits from environmental activists and property-rights advocates, suppression of scientific research and the collapse of public confidence."[8] The Forest Options Group, a diverse collection of environmentalists, industry representatives, academics, and agency officials committed to devising alternatives for the national forests, noted, "Fifty years ago, the Forest Service was one of the most highly regarded agencies in government. Today, the agency is besieged from without, demoralized within, and many wonder whether it will survive to see its centennial in 2005."[9]

How could the Forest Service have undergone such a monumental change of fortune in such a short time? The answers to this question are many and complex, and they depend, to a certain extent, on who is supplying the answer. Whereas the rhetoric of some western politicians and political activists places the blame on Forest Service employees themselves, neither they nor their counterparts in the BLM or other federal agencies deserve that blame. Although those agencies no doubt have some inefficient or ineffective employees, the vast majority are deeply dedicated public servants who bring a high level of professionalism and commitment to their jobs. If there are severe problems of morale and effectiveness within the land management agencies (and there are), the fault does not lie with the employees; rather, it is to be sought at another level altogether.

Paul Hirt, in his 1994 book *A Conspiracy of Optimism*, went to that deeper level when he diagnosed within the Forest Service a chronic pattern of agency avoidance of unavoidable problems, with a resulting pattern of deferred, but finally inevitable, consequences. Above all, the post–World War II level of timber production from national forests contained within itself all the elements of this "conspiracy of optimism." Hirt claimed that "the Forest Service too often substituted theory for wisdom and expediency for courage," and "politicians in charge of the agency's resources called for responsible management but then failed to enable the agency to act responsibly; Americans demanded illusions of abundance in order to avoid setting limits to production and consumption."[10] According to Hirt, the Forest Service was able to respond to the postwar demand for timber resources only by inflating harvest levels well beyond sustainable limits.

Meanwhile, the problems this shortsightedness would eventually create for the agency were being quietly compounded by administrative changes. In 1998, the Pinchot Institute's V. Alaric (Al) Sample observed: "Strategic planning requirements under the Resources Planning Act of 1974 (RPA) reinforced in the Forest Service a government-wide trend toward centralized planning. . . . In theory, land management planning under the National Forest Management Act of 1976 (NFMA) should have provided a [decentralizing] counterbalance, but the politics of the day imposed centralized constraints on local planning assumptions and then strongly influenced the alternatives."[11]

Hirt explained the centralizing "politics of the day" in this way:

The Reagan Administration represented an aggressive and somewhat successful—if temporary—backlash to the environmental trends of the 1960s and 1970s. During Reagan's tenure, Assistant Secretary of Agriculture John Crowell ordered the Forest Service to plan for a doubling of its harvests over the next few decades. . . . Senior members of Congress . . . began attaching amendments to Forest Service appropriations bills in the 1980s containing specific timber harvest quotas to keep production high.[12]

This quickly became a self-perpetuating cycle in which various interest groups learned that the way to influence Forest Service behavior was not to work directly with the bureaucracy but to go over its head, pulling either congressional or administrative strings. Pat Williams, who served for nearly two decades as a congressman from Montana, described the situation at the end of the century:

> As the second decade of this struggle ends, the Forest Service has been in a near free fall, with lands virtually unmanageable and the politics worsening. . . . A recent Congress passed the Salvage Sale Logging Act with massive support from Republicans and lesser— but still important—timely support from at least one well-placed Western Democrat on the House Appropriations Committee. That act, an end run around traditional environmental standards, was then countered by Secretary of Agriculture Dan Glickman. He ordered the setting aside—beyond the reach of the new law—of more than one million acres of federal land in Montana.[13]

Al Sample described what this consistent use of political pressure has done to the agency's relationships with local communities: "Intensified political centralization of decision-making has made it impossible for local managers to keep the promises they make to local communities. Once it becomes evident that local managers can be second-guessed on everything, it is of little value to local community leaders to work out plans and agreements with them."[14] The Forest Options Group saw much the same picture, concluding that

> current governing and budgeting systems are the source of many of the core problems with the Forest Service. Top-down governance structures promote polarization and discourage people from working with the agency at the local level because of the risk that a higher level would overturn their decisions. The budgetary process encourages people to view both the national forests and federal funds as a commons, available mainly to those who stake their claims.[15]

During the Reagan–Bush years, timber interests were usually the ones best positioned to "stake their claims." Hirt described their efforts to force harvest quotas upward as follows: "All these political efforts to focus the Forest Service on logging resulted in a temporary jump in timber production . . . [but] it was an artificial boost to production, like deficit spending, that could not be sustained and that entailed significant environmental and economic costs."[16] Although those costs could be obscured for some time, the complex system of statutes, regulations, and appropriations within which the Forest Service by then operated guaranteed that sooner or later the costs would come home to roost and Forest Service operations would feel their effect.

The first bird to alight was the environmental one. As layer after layer of national environmental statutes, from the National Environmental Policy Act of 1969 (NEPA) and the National Forest Management Act of 1976 to the Endangered Species Act of 1973, were overlaid on the Multiple-Use Sustained-Yield Act of 1960, the timber harvest quotas that Congress had often forced on the agency began to crack and crumble. Jack Ward Thomas had it right when he said that as far as the Forest Service's timber policies went, the environmentalists had already won out over big timber, but the two interests were "still fighting the last battle of a war that's been over for years, still arguing about allocations decisions that have already been made."[17] Thomas' observations merely underscore the revolutionary changes Forest Service timber policies had undergone during the last decades of the twentieth century. Nationally, annual timber sales on Forest Service land had fallen by no less than 68 percent, from 12 billion board feet in the early 1980s to 3.8 billion in 1997. California's national forests gave up 400 million board feet of timber in 1997, compared with the 2 billion board feet harvested in 1965, an 80 percent decline in the cut. Most dramatically, in the forests of Region 1, which includes Montana and northern Idaho, the cut dropped by 89 percent, from 2.8 billion board feet in 1970 to barely 300 million in 1997.[18]

If the problem with the Forest Service had been its one-dimensional commitment to sawlog production, by now the agency should be well on its way to recovery. But that is anything but the case. Part of the reason, of course, is that the timber interests are deeply distressed with the sharp decline in production from national forests. That distress now links up with the finally inescapable recognition that U.S. taxpayers had long been subsidizing national forest operations, including timber production itself. Below-cost timber sales have long been the target of criticism from environmental groups. These critics have often relied on reports of the General Accounting Office (GAO) to support their push for timber sale reform. A 1984 GAO report, for example, found that in 1981 and 1982, 96 percent of timber sales in the Forest Service's Rocky Mountain Region had lost money.[19] Western conservatives long resisted these findings and might still wish they were not true, but the combination of falling harvest levels and red ink finally led them to threaten a whole new approach to Forest Service funding.

In 1998, the chairs of all four Senate and House public land and natural resources committees (all four of them from the West) suggested in a memo to Forest Service Chief Michael Dombeck that his agency be scaled back to what they called a "custodial maintenance" mission. Republican senators Frank Murkowski of Alaska and Larry Craig of Idaho and representatives Don Young of Alaska and Helen Chenoweth-Hage of Idaho proposed a policy that would have effectively relieved the Forest Service of many of its managerial duties, as well as the budget to perform those duties. "Since you seem bent on producing fewer and fewer results [i.e., sawlogs] from the National Forests at rapidly increasing costs," they wrote, "many will press Congress to seriously consider the option to move to custodial management . . . in order to stem the flow of unjustifiable investments."[20] The committee chairs proposed downsizing the agency and contracting out most management functions. Their message, some of it explicit and some clearly enough visible between the lines of the letter, was roughly, Since you continue to ask for subsidies but no longer produce anywhere near the timber that once justified the subsidies, why don't we just pay you enough to do minimal maintenance on the forests and let it go at that?

The letter was, of course, the height of cynicism, given that these resource industry–backed western conservatives wanted anything but the solution they proposed. Yet in terms of leverage, the letter carried a certain credibility because the western Republicans could, if they chose, readily join their nonwestern "budget hawk" colleagues who cared little about cutting timber from western forests but cared deeply about cutting needless subsidies from federal budgets. Here, once again, the post–cold war era of balanced budgets had created an utterly different operating environment for the Forest Service than the construction-driven post–World War II operating environment. The turn-of-the-century balancing of budgets caught the Forest Service in a double bind. The cold war years had subjected the agency to a steadily mounting set of requirements for environmental analyses and other varieties of paperwork, which could easily lead to the conclusion that the Forest Service was consuming more paper than its forests were producing and that its people were spending more time "doing NEPA" and in general "doing bureaucracy" than in managing actual forests with actual trees. The natural resource committee leaders, for many of whose constituents the production of commercially harvestable timber had been and still should be the guiding mission of the Forest Service, now described the situation as a lack of "agreement on a discrete mission for the National Forest System." They went on to observe that "neither Congress, the Administration, nor the Forest Service have been able to consider together, let alone find, cost efficient and effective ways to streamline the legislative, regulatory, and legal morass in which the Agency currently finds itself."[21] It was not that the agency lacked prodding to address the morass. The GAO had conducted more than 100 investigations into the Forest Service's finances, many of them lacerating in their findings. But nothing stops what former congressman Pat Williams called the agency's "free fall."[22]

One manifestation of the Forest Service's apparent paralysis was the Interior Columbia Basin Ecosystem Management Project (ICBEMP, popularly pronounced "Icy Bump"). Several federal agencies (the Forest Service, the BLM, and the U.S. Fish and Wildlife Service) collaborated with various state agencies on this project in hopes of developing a comprehensive management and restoration strategy for a substantial segment of the

Pacific Northwest's landscape and natural resources. The area covered by this ambitious and profoundly well-intentioned plan includes 72 million acres in parts of seven states and involves twenty-three national forests, nine BLM districts, and twenty-two tribal governments. The impulse behind the plan, in addition to returning some control to local branches of the Forest Service and the BLM, was regional cooperation, but after six years and $47 million, the enterprise had generated little beyond dissent and dissatisfaction. Presented to the public and Congress as a draft (and then a revised draft) environmental impact statement (EIS), ICBEMP drew criticism from conservatives and liberals alike. Environmentalists attacked its scientific credibility, expressing doubts about the state and local government agencies' ability to care for the ecosystems in question; industry representatives said ICBEMP was too generic and failed to take into account the vast diversity among different areas. Republican office holders repeatedly voiced their opposition to the entire project, producing at least two unsuccessful but demoralizing attempts to kill it in Congress.

Forest Service officials met in Coeur d'Alene, Idaho, in April 2000 to pitch the latest development on the belabored ICBEMP—release of the supplemental draft EIS. According to project manager Susan Giannettino, the government's preferred alternative centered on three components: "people, restoration of resources and protection."[23] Giannettino emphasized the expanded role of local decision makers under the preferred alternative, although she promised continued oversight by agency managers at the national level. "We will set the direction, but how the local [forest] supervisors get there will be up to them," Giannettino said.[24] Some outside groups found the plan an improvement on the earlier version released in 1997, which was sharply and variously criticized as either too broad in scope, overly restrictive on land users, or lacking environmental protections. Environmentalists, however, said the preferred alternative still fell short in terms of ensuring that Columbia River basin ecosystems would be adequately protected; in fact, they charged, it weakened protections for old-growth forests in Oregon and Washington. Industry groups said the document offered them too little access to federal land, even with a 22 percent increase over 2000 timber harvest levels. Republican senator Slade Gorton of Washington said, "It's another attempt by Bill Clinton—and to a certain extent Al Gore—to lock up land in Eastern Washington without an awful lot of input" from people in the region.[25] The agencies, for their part, were more than ready to close the book on the long-drawn-out, contentious process. "It's time to get done," Giannettino said. "Nobody knows that more than me and my staff."[26]

At the close of the Clinton administration, it was impossible to predict what further challenges ICBEMP would face before it ever affected a single fish or tree in the Pacific Northwest ecosystems it was intended to manage. What is already clear, however, is that in attempting to broaden the scope of its planning to an entire drainage, the Forest Service seems to have alienated almost all the parties involved and may well see its entire effort vitiated by old-fashioned western politics. At least in the Columbia basin, in trying to please everyone, the agency is pleasing no one. This is what a loss of governing legitimacy looks like.

Former Forest Service Chief Jack Ward Thomas may well have been right when he reflected, "My experience has convinced me that the period in conservation history between 1995 and 2005 is going to be just as critical as the period between 1895 and 1905 when the national forests were first established."[27] This period may indeed be as crucial to the Forest Service and to the public lands system in general as was the turn of the past century. But the conditions under which that system now operates are not the same—indeed, they are nearly the reverse—of what they were a century ago. And those changed circumstances do not bode well for the future of the agency. As Al Sample said, "the combined effect of these two factors—the loss of broad-based local community support and the breakdown of decentralized decision making within the organization—leave the Forest Service today more vulnerable to collapse than ever before in its history."[28]

It is simply impossible to understand this radical reversal in the reputation and effectiveness of the Forest Service except by taking account of the larger historical forces at work around it. The centralization of power, authority, and governing functions that Theodore Roosevelt's New Nationalism inaugurated at exactly the time the Forest Service was being created has given way a century later to the worldwide phenomenon of decline in the relevance, effectiveness, and legitimacy of the nation-state. It is within this historical context that the loss of legitimacy of American land management agencies should be understood, and it is against this broad historical backdrop that devolution of responsibility for the West's public lands is now very likely to occur in one form or another. But that devolution cannot be approached in a constructive way unless another side effect of these historical trends is better understood and more effectively incorporated into western thought and politics.

As the stories of Libby and Elko so clearly demonstrate, the relentless, implacable forces of globalization are having a paralyzing effect not only on the land management agencies but also on traditional industrial-era economies and communities. As *New York Times* correspondent Thomas Friedman put it in *The Lexus and the Olive Tree*, "globalization involves the inexorable integration of markets, nation-states, and technologies to a degree never witnessed before—in a way that is enabling individuals, corporations and nation-states to reach around the world farther, faster, deeper and cheaper than ever before, and in a way that is also producing a powerful backlash from those brutalized or left behind by this new system."[29]

The danger is that the West as a region may become paralyzed by these historical forces. If both the land management agencies and the region itself seize up in the face of change, western landscapes and communities will both lose. There are few promising signs of adaptive viability within the agencies. But, as described in the next chapter, history may have positioned the West to rise to this challenge.

Chapter 5

A
Maturing
Region

Reinhabitation means learning to live-in-place in an
area that has been disrupted and injured through past
exploitation. It involves becoming native to a place
through becoming aware of the particular ecological
relationships that operate within and around it. It
means understanding activities and evolving social
behavior that will enrich the life of that place, restore
its life-supporting systems, and establish an ecologically and socially sustainable pattern of existence
within it.

—Peter Berg and Raymond Dasmann

While the previous chapter focused on the decline of national
governments, with emphasis on the loss of governing capacity
on the part of American land management agencies, the coming
decades need not be primarily an era of decay and decline, for
either the country at large or the West in particular. Vital new

forms of political and economic organization are beginning to emerge in the midst of what often seems to be nothing but a chaos of alienation and gridlock. These new, still barely discernible ways of organizing human affairs are most often landscape driven, and because the American West is the part of the continent where landscape is still most potent and present in human affairs, this region is poised to play a major role in the creation of those new forms of governance uniquely appropriate to twenty-first-century circumstances. This chapter will explore the convergence of two historical trends. On one hand, the forces of globalism seem to be producing renewed interest and experimentation in the phenomenon of regionalism in general. This coincides with a period in the history of the American West that may come to be seen as its passage into political maturity, or at least into a heightened awareness of its regional identity. The coincidence of these two historical forces may present the West with an unusual opportunity at least to survive and perhaps to thrive upon the changes sweeping across the region.

But to be prepared to assume such a role, the West will need to free itself from old, narrowing, and blinding ideologies and myths. The region needs to be developing modes of thinking and tools of analysis radically different from its often antiquated ways of viewing the world. Above all, a region positioning itself to operate effectively in the twenty-first century needs to be able to perceive possibilities within the deeper structures of global forces and trends that more traditional ways of viewing the world tend only to obscure. Consider just one aspect of globalization as an example. There is a widespread fear, an understandable fear, that the forces of globalization will make the West just like every other place in the world, obliterating any distinctiveness that might buttress a sense of regional pride and identity. Undeniably, there is and will continue to be a homogenizing thesis running through the evolving course of globalism.

But just as undeniably, although less noticeably, runs a compelling antithesis of diversity and differentiation. If we apply even the most rudimentary form of systems analysis to capitalism, we become immediately aware of how fundamentally dependent the system is on competition. The essence of competition is diversity, not homogeneity; particularity, not universality. We know how dependent capitalism is on competition among firms, but as a system, capitalism thrives on a richly textured fabric of competition, including competition among places. During the industrial era, nation-states played this "competitive unit" role admirably, but as capital has achieved a new plateau of global integration, it no longer finds the national form of geographic differentiation congenial. Yet even though capital is now more fully integrated globally than ever before— to the point at which it has largely escaped national control—it is by no means the case that capital, or capitalism as a system, is ready to dispense with geographic differentiation or the ways in which that differentiation lends itself to competition. It is simply choosing new, more appropriate units of competition. Increasingly, it is not nations but continents and, within continents, regions that are emerging to fulfill this role.

But to gain an accurate appreciation of how irresistible this global reorganization is and what it might mean for a region such as the West, we need more powerful and more historically up-to-date analytical tools. The prevailing understanding of the dynamics of economic diversity and competition is based on what is now fairly ancient scientific theory, namely Darwin's nineteenth-century study of species dynamics. There is nothing new about such borrowing of scientific theory to explain economic reality. In an essay on the "geopolitics of complexity," James Gardner, president of the Conference of World Regions, explains that "powerful new scientific ideas tend to reverberate, in rough relation to their power, far beyond the confines of the scientific academy." We see evidence of what Gardner calls "intellectual resonance" having shaped political institutions throughout American history.[1] The political thought of America's founders, for example, was closely entwined with the science of their day. Newtonian physics, with its emphasis on the mechanics of the natural world and the laws governing motion, was the science not only of the Industrial Revolution but also of the nation-state. The drafters of the United States Constitution were fascinated with the strict action-and-reaction, cause-and-effect relationships Newton had revealed in the world all around them. As children of the Enlightenment, they sought to build those physical principles into what they often referred to as the "machinery" of the government they were creating. Because of its high degree of predictability, which lent itself to an equally high degree of control, Newtonian physics was destined to be the science of the machine age and of those machine-like governments that characterized that age. But those are the very governments that are now, around the world, losing their relevance and their effectiveness. Does science offer any insight into this phenomenon or any help in our thinking about new institutions and forms of human organization?

What we know is that by the twentieth century, the radical predictability of Newtonian physics had begun to be assaulted by the equally radical unpredictability of what would finally emerge as quantum physics. Werner Heisenberg's uncertainty principle turned the Newtonian world on its head by asserting that some physical phenomena or relationships were not only unpredictable at that time but fundamentally and forever unpredictable regardless of any conceivable advances in technology. Although there remained, of course, a vast range of highly predictable natural phenomena, much of the universe now had to be understood as inherently impossible to forecast and therefore impossible to control. As this startling reality began to settle in, it produced a new way of thinking about the relationship between chaos and order. Out of this learning grew chaos theory and then complexity theory.

Complexity theory tells us, in a nutshell, that from situations that appear to be utterly chaotic, order is constantly emerging. It emerges not on the terms humans might impose, based on our powers of analysis and prediction, but in patterns embedded within and determined by the emerging order itself. Life itself and the evolution of life are now understood as emerging in just this sense, which means that complexity theory is adding new dimensions of understanding to the old Darwinian concepts of biology. The most adaptive life-forms, at either the individual level or the group level, are now seen to be those that learn how to operate at what complexity theorists call "the edge of chaos." These life-forms walk the line between a system so thoroughly ordered that it can no longer claim the vital advantages of chaos and one so chaotic that it forgoes the competitive advantages of order.

Complexity theorists teach us to see these unfolding patterns in the animal kingdom in the tendency of birds to flock, fish to school, sheep and bison to herd. There is definitely order in these phenomena, and order with high adaptive value, but part of the adaptive value derives from the fact that a healthy dose of chaos is left in the system. Often, these chaotically ordered patterns organize themselves into fractal formations. Fractals are patterns within patterns within patterns that complexity theory has called to our attention and that, when we become attuned to them, we see everywhere in the universe. Look on the surface of a sand dune and you will see small sand dunes making up that surface, and even tinier dunes on the surface of the small dunes. Notice how often spirals appear in nature, from spiral nebulae to hurricanes to water draining from your bathtub. Complexity theory says that these forms play back and forth on one another:

what happens at a large scale is related to what happens at a much smaller scale, but not in a Newtonian, billiard-ball way. Rather, they influence one another through a process the complexity theorists call emergence, in which new forms suddenly begin to emerge simultaneously, often at several different scales at once, in the same way crystals emerge within crystals in a supersaturated solution.

What we are now beginning to perceive is that exactly this kind of simultaneous emergence of organic forms at many different scales may be the determining characteristic of the postindustrial, postnational order. Complexity theory sees these structures as a logical extension of biological evolution. In *At Home in the Universe*, Stuart Kauffman writes:

> For what can the teeming molecules that hustled themselves into self-reproducing metabolisms, the cells coordinating their behaviors to form multi-celled organisms, the ecosystems, and even economic and political systems have in common? The wonderful possibility . . . is that on many fronts, life evolves toward a regime that is poised between order and chaos.[2]

Kauffman's description of emergent life-forms leads to a question that brings complexity theory to the edge of the new regionalism. "I wonder," he mused, "if the political structures we have created will continue to serve us?"[3] That question is one that life in all its forms has always addressed: the question of optimum adaptability. What this adaptability seems now to require in the political realm is a radical reorganization of governing forms, in which political power is moved both upward and downward from the level of the nation-state, where it became concentrated during the industrial era. Political theorist Michael Sandel has argued that both economic reality and the human desire to stay in control of our own destiny move us toward this dual dispersal of national sovereignty. "Only a politics that disperses sovereignty both upward and downward," Sandel writes, "can combine the power required to rival global market forces with the differentiation required of a public life that hopes to inspire the allegiance of its citizens."[4] Strobe Talbot, a journalist who became deputy secretary of state in the administration of President Bill Clinton, similarly predicted a transfer of power "upward toward supranational bodies and . . . common markets" and downward "toward freer, more autonomous units of administration that permit distinct societies to preserve their cultural identities and govern themselves as much as possible."[5]

The Rocky Mountain West is home to one of those "distinct societies" that Talbot describes as wanting to "preserve their cultural identities" but needing, in order to do that, to "govern themselves as much as possible." One objection that is immediately and understandably raised against such a suggestion is that the forces of global capitalism are so powerful that a place such as the American West cannot in the age of globalism either preserve its identity or in any important way govern itself—that both its identity and its destiny will be determined by forces larger than itself. What those observations always lead to is the conclusion that the West (or any other region—but perhaps especially the West) needs the protection of the national government against those economic forces. What this ignores, though, is that global capitalism has essentially overleaped the bounds of nations and escaped their jurisdiction. This is precisely why both Talbot and Sandel insist that even as power is devolved downward from the nation to smaller, more culturally and socially meaningful units, political power must also be organized at scales larger than the nation-state, "to rival global market forces," as Sandel puts it.

We will take a closer look in chapter 8 at how those supranational, continental, and global forms of government might be expected to organize themselves to serve as effective counterweights to the power of supranational corporations. Here, what we want to keep in mind is the way global and continental forms of human organization and governance are emerging from the same historical forces that are creating a new regionalism. These historical forces do not lend themselves to any neat and orderly analysis or classification. They are in many ways a chaotic and in all ways a complex set of forces, but they are creating their own kind of order, and the forms that are emerging are exactly the kinds of inner-directed, organically evolving forms that complexity theory teaches us to watch for.

Continents, subcontinental regions, bioregions, watersheds, and city-states are slowly beginning to emerge, to gain coherence and vitality as the nested and sometimes overlapping units of the new order. As the forces of global integration mature, economics and politics seem increasingly to operate as symbiotic forces moving us closer to this transformation. It is often difficult to tease out cause and effect, but more often than not, persistent economic realities seem to be forcing new forms of political responsiveness and adaptation, rather than politics and policies shaping economic realities. One reason for a region such as the American West to try to understand more clearly its place in this larger picture is to enable it to mobilize the political power to direct, rather than be directed by, economic forces. To gain that leverage, the West, or any other region, needs to understand how regionalism, continentalism, and globalism relate to one another in this emerging picture. Complexity theory urges us to view the picture fractally—to see similar forms emerging at many different scales simultaneously. Consider one increasingly relevant western example of such fractal layering. Imagine a small creek as a building block within a fractal formation. One step up from the creek is the subwatershed, a river valley such as the Swan River valley in western Montana. The Swan River is one tributary to the Flathead River drainage, which in turn is one component of the Clark Fork River watershed, which itself is a subwatershed of the vast Columbia River basin. Structurally, the small creek we started with and the Columbia basin itself are very similar. One is much smaller than the other and fits within the other, but a picture of one would closely resemble a picture of the other. This is how fractals work. We know they work that way physically, and now we are starting to see that they might also work that way socially and politically. Later chapters will examine how at each level in this fractal watershed formation, individuals, especially in the West, are in the process of testing out new forms of governance and economic self-determination to match their geographic context. Meanwhile, we can use this nesting of watersheds in a fractal pattern to help us understand how globalism, continentalism, regionalism, and localism are emerging as similarly layered or nested organizing structures in the political economy of the twenty-first century.

Although our focus here is on the emergence of regionalism as one layer in this fractal order, it is easier to understand regionalism against the backdrop of continentalism, from which it naturally emerges. Within the new global order, Europe was the first continent to recognize the need to move beyond the nation-state as the primary political jurisdiction and to create a new, globally competitive continental economic and political entity. The emergence of a strong form of continental integration in Europe has lent impetus to the incubation of a still fairly immature form of North American continentalism. The most sweeping manifestation of this to date is the North American Free Trade Agreement (NAFTA), which has smudged—although not yet erased—the economic and jurisdictional borders along the forty-ninth parallel and the Rio Grande.

The first decades of the twenty-first century will almost certainly see further moves toward continental governance in North America. What may seem paradoxical is that this continental integration may well go hand in hand with a certain kind of national disintegration. The likeliest starting point for this dynamic is the ever threatening dissolution of the Canadian federation. Whether or not Quebec ever actually secedes, Canada seems increasingly unworkable as a unit, with globalism and continentalism only furthering the already substantial strain within the structure. If the Canadian union does break apart or restructure itself, there will probably be repercussions throughout the continent. *Atlantic Monthly* correspondent Robert Kaplan played out this scenario in *An Empire Wilderness*:

> Canada's demise might accelerate not only the melding of like-minded northern European farming and ranching economies in western Canada with those in the northern United States, but also that of the Hispanic-influenced Southwest with Mexico, bilingual South Florida with the Caribbean and Latin America, Quebec with New England, and so on, because it would destroy the myth of the permanent nation-state in North America . . . and thus unleash cross-border energies everywhere on the continent.[6]

Kaplan's reference to the "myth of the permanent nation-state in North America" recalls our attention to the forces that have shaped the American West and that still create tensions of historic proportions within it. Remember that the manifest destiny that powered forward the settling of the West was merely one way of expressing a very potent and long-standing continental imperative. America's very founding had occurred under the aegis of continentalism. Most Americans have a vague recollection that it was a Continental Congress, meeting in Philadelphia, that declared the nation's independence from Great Britain. Because Americans focus on the creation of what became the United States, they almost universally overlook the name the colonists chose to give their assembly. In fact, this was the second time the colonists assembled as a Continental Congress—the first having been convened a few years earlier to fashion a response to the five "intolerable acts" enacted by the British Parliament in 1774: the Boston Port Act, the Massachusetts Government Act, the Administration of Justice Act, the Quartering Act, and the Quebec Act. When resistance to these acts only brought further repression, the Second Continental Congress finally declared American independence. Both continental congresses brought together what were until then totally distinct colonies, attempting to aggregate enough power to resist what they had come to see as British tyranny. Their intention was to coalesce continentally—to mount a continental resistance movement. The fact that British Canada had been a French dominion until just a few years earlier, and that the British Parliament had in the Quebec Act given Canada what the other colonies saw as unwarranted privileges, meant that the congresses would not include representatives from that part of the continent. But when the Second Continental Congress began raising and provisioning the Continental Army, one of its first strategic objectives was Quebec. They meant it, in other words, when they called themselves a "continental congress," and it was not until late in the peace negotiations with Britain that the congress relinquished the hope of prying Canada free of British dominion.

For the next few decades, then, America's continental tendencies looked westward more than northward—but the distinction was never absolutely clear-cut. From Jefferson's Louisiana Purchase and his commissioning of the Corps of Discovery onward, America had determined that its nationhood must assume coast-to-coast continental proportions. From that moment on, American nationhood became indistinguishable from American empire, and the West above all other regions was affected by and continues to suffer from this blending of nation and empire. Because Americans tend to think that the way things are is the way they had to be and must remain, they forget that the boundaries eventually drawn on the continent might easily have been drawn elsewhere. How much of the continent America's "destiny" required it to rule remained unclear for some time. "Fifty-four forty or fight" was a serious battle cry of American empire that could readily have made most of what is now British Columbia "American Columbia" instead. Americans decided not to fight the British over that border but to pick a fight with Mexico over the border of Texas instead. Then the question became whether America should not only conquer but also absorb Mexico. Soon, Americans were asking whether they should annex Cuba, or Nicaragua. These questions remained alive up to and into the Civil War period, when even Canada came back into the imperial picture, with Secretary of State William H. Seward urging Abraham Lincoln even before he was inaugurated to use the southern rebellion as a fulcrum to consolidate America's continental empire both southward and northward.

Looking back on these events from the twenty-first-century vantage of a new postnational era of continentalism, it is possible to imagine that even during the period of manifest destiny something was at work that had more to do with the continent's "trying to become a continent" than with American (or Canadian or Mexican) nationhood. As we watch continentalism assert itself now like a great bear emerging from hibernation, we can imagine that the continent had stirred repeatedly during its overwintering but could not yet rouse itself in its organic, continental form. As it prepares to do so at last, it is not surprising that the largely arbitrary, nonorganic structures of the nations that have been imposed on the continent are found wanting. Above all, it is not surprising that Canada, always the least geopolitically coherent and indeed the least nationalistic of these nations, should show the most unmistakable signs of disintegration, and should in the process send tremors throughout the continent.

The redefinition of the North American continent into meaningful subregions has been working its way to the surface conceptually for the past few decades. In his 1981 book *The Nine Nations of North America*, Joel Garreau identified nine subcontinental regions as functional divisions for the North American continent.[7] Since then, certain subregions have begun to emerge as real actors with skeletal frameworks for economic and political integration. Spurred by the distinct economic advantage offered by their regional positioning within the global economy, the separate metropolitan regions of Portland, Seattle, and Vancouver, British Columbia, are rapidly developing the infrastructure for a subcontinental region dubbed Cascadia or the Pacific Northwest.[8] Southern California, Arizona, New Mexico, and Texas have growing ties, through language, culture, and economics, with northern Mexican states. These ties may be harbingers of what could someday emerge as a unified region: what Charles Truxillo, a professor of Chicano studies at the University of New Mexico, has dubbed Republic del Norte.[9] Such cross-border regional realignments still seem quite literally outlandish to most people, who cannot imagine North America's internal borders ever changing. A little historical perspective, however, reminds us both how recent "in the course of human events" and how fundamentally arbitrary those borders are. Although the synergies inherent in natural or organic subcontinental regions could be ignored and overlooked during the ascendance of the nation-state, in the fierce new competitiveness of the global order such natural connections must be acknowledged and cultivated simply because of the competitive advantages attached to them.

A cross-border, continental reconfiguration of the kind Garreau and Kaplan have suggested probably lies some distance in the future. But some trends and determinants are already clear. One is the fact that the creation of meaningful regions cannot be dictated from above; indeed, it cannot be dictated at all. As complexity theory helps us to perceive, regionalism is an utterly organic phenomenon: either a place is a region inherently, by its own internal logic, or it is not a region at all. As a result, regionalism stands in stark contrast and challenge to the Newtonian, industrial, command-and-control structures we have placed on the landscape, structures such as state and county boundaries by which we attempt to tell places what they are and are not part of. At every level, but perhaps most unexpectedly at the regional level, we are witnessing the emergence of organic forms of human relatedness driven by life's own imperative to adapt in order to thrive.

What becomes clear when we pay attention to the North American continent in these terms is that almost all of its natural regions run north to south, cutting straight across the east-to-west axes on which American and Canadian nationhood have so fundamentally depended. With a few exceptions, the physical superstructure of the continent—from its coasts to its interior plains and great interior river—all run north and south. So do its mountain chains, including most commandingly the great spine of the continent, the Western Cordillera. The Rockies are nothing if not continental in their significance. These mountains are the eruptive result of continent-creating plate tectonics and can be understood only in continental terms. Just as Thomas Jefferson's search for the "height of land" brought geologic and geopolitical time into a momentarily significant relationship, so may the Rockies, the geologically most alive part of the continent, now have a special role to play in the reconfiguration of the continent's internal jurisdictions. As the continent emerges into greater self-awareness (and into some globally competitive form of self-governance), the region that centers on the mountain spine can be expected to play a leading role in redefining the meaningful subcontinental places within the continent. Stephen Maly, a long-time observer and analyst of Montana–Alberta relations, captures the tectonic-like vibrancy of the Rockies when he refers to this cross-border region as a "remote but promisingly fertile transnational mixing zone."[10] Joel Garreau put the same transformative power in terms reminiscent of the major themes of this book: "Between the U.S. federal control of such huge quantities of the land and resources . . . and the Canadian West's political impotence, this high, arid, resource-rich, beautiful, often still pristine Empty Quarter is the last colony of the rest of North America."[11] Such language recalls our attention to the colonial roots of the Second Continental Congress and to those colonies' willingness to create something new and previously unimagined in the world. Whether the Rockies will ever transcend their colonial status and emerge as a politically and economically coherent cross-border region is impossible to predict and beyond the scope of this book. If this does happen, it will almost certainly follow a period of region building on each side of the border. Certainly on the American side, the colonial or imperial themes identified by Garreau will be a major determinant in the emergence of any historically important form of Rocky Mountain regionalism.

With or without a connection to the Canadian Rockies, the American Rocky Mountain West is almost certain to play a leading role in rethinking the relationship of regions to nationhood. There are at least two overlapping reasons for this. First is the link between the West's history and the history of American nationhood. The defining presence of federal land in the West, the chief legacy of this historical link, has fostered anti-nationalist tensions throughout the West that do not go away and cannot be ignored. Because so much western acreage is controlled by Washington, D.C., and because so much of the West so deeply resents that national domination, the public lands are the likeliest fulcrum against which the West as a region might eventually leverage its way to genuine regional self-government.

The second, related, reason why the West can be expected to take a leadership role in the redefinition of governance structures is the fact that the global sorting out into more organic, less arbitrary places is so powerfully driven by landscapes and landforms, such as continents themselves. The West's identity is fundamentally bound up with land, and regionalism is about nothing if not about land. A later chapter will argue that the West's global competitive advantage now depends centrally on its establishing a sustainable relationship of people to landscape, and that it must do this as a self-determining region. Yet here, where self-determination with regard to landscape is of ultimate importance, that self-determination has often seemed precluded by the absentee (national) ownership and control of most of that very landscape. What this all adds up to, in the context of a world in which regionalism is one of the forces challenging nationhood, is that the American region most likely to mount such a challenge is the West. But that will be only a theoretical possibility if the West is not prepared to see itself as a distinct region and to act accordingly. That sense of regional distinctiveness and capacity has been a long time coming, and it has often been stalled or diverted. But there is reason to believe that the West is maturing just as regionalism itself is gaining a new significance.

John Wesley Powell, an acute observer of the West and later director of the U.S. Geological Survey, argued more than a century ago that the West was different and that because of its uniqueness it would be especially important to organize human activity there—including political jurisdictions—according to the lay of the land and the particularities of the place, not according to an artificial, straight-line, square-cornered grid or by means of top-down management from the East Coast. Americans ignored Powell with a vengeance—basically trying for a century to fit the West into an undifferentiated pattern of national policies and programs, as if it were no different from anyplace else. Yet despite this imposition of artificial boundaries and misfit policies, westerners persisted in forming a meaningful regional identity based primarily on a strong relationship with their home landscape. The emergence of this sense of regional identity is a story of its own—a story that began roughly in the middle of the twentieth century and now feeds into the larger regional, continental, and global stories unfolding at the beginning of the twenty-first. We might look for the beginnings of this story not in the West but far off, in New England.

Wallace Stegner described the annual Bread Loaf Writers' Conference, a writers' workshop convened at Middlebury College in Vermont, as "something special in [Bernard] De Voto's life—a focus, a trying ground for ideas, a vacation, a reunion, an annual renewal of acquaintance and energy."[12] There, in a comfortable, camplike setting in the woods, among a circle of writers assembled every summer around Bread Loaf old-timer and guru Robert Frost, De Voto did what Bread Loaf still invites its guests to do: he sharpened his skills as a writer, improved his eye, toned his voice. De Voto had begun attending Bread Loaf conferences in 1932, hardly missed a summer throughout the 1930s, and after a wartime hiatus attended all the conferences during the late 1940s. By then, the Utah native had been joined at Bread Loaf by several other western writers, including A. B. Guthrie Jr., Joseph Kinsey Howard, and, later, Stegner himself.

By the late 1940s, as we saw in chapter 3, De Voto had become deeply engaged in resisting western efforts to dismantle the public lands system. He was spending more time in the West than he had for several decades, drawn there, among other things, by the work of finishing *The Course of Empire*, his long-awaited book on the Lewis and Clark Expedition. In the summer of 1951, De Voto accepted an invitation from his old Bread Loaf buddy, Montana journalist Joseph Kinsey Howard, to participate in a writing conference at what was then Montana State University in Missoula. There, they were joined by another Bread Loaf alumnus, A. B. Guthrie Jr. "They turned Missoula into a 'Bread Loaf, Montana,'" Stegner wrote in his biography of De Voto, "and, like Syracusans writing back to Corinth or Athens, sent long messages of report and humorous adjuration to their mother institution in Vermont."[13] The colonial metaphor from classical Greece certainly captured an important dimension of the scenario, but there is also a sense in which that summer conference in Montana, and the summers and conferences that followed, marked the beginning of the end of the West's colonial status—the beginning, indeed, of a West capable of thinking its own thoughts and speaking them in its own voice.

The American West had always been seen as a unique region of the country and had played a central role in America's national imagination and self-conception. From Henry David Thoreau's "westward I go free" through Frederick Jackson Turner's frontier thesis to the decades-long reign of the western movie, Americans had used the West as a stage for national self-reflection. But this national fascination with and mythologizing of the West is not by any means the same thing as the development of regional identity or regional consciousness—and indeed it has often stood in the way of the emergence of a genuine regional identity. Western historian David Wrobel describes the difference:

In examining the process by which regional consciousness formed, it is worth distinguishing between
the sense of place that develops among those people
living in various parts of the West and the construction of regional characteristics for the whole of the
West by outside observers. We might call the former
"internal regionalism" . . . and the latter "exterior
regionalism."[14]

For a century or more, the West had been subjected to far
more than its share of "exterior regionalism." But in spite of
such obstacles, the West finally began and then continued slowly
and steadily to develop its own sense of regional self. "Bread
Loaf, Montana" both symbolized and advanced that cause.

For some reason, the time was ripe. In September 1946, *The
Nation* had published an article by political economist Morris E.
Garnsey titled "The Rise of Regionalism in the Mountain
States."[15] Garnsey wrote, "There are many signs today of the
rise of a new and significant regional spirit in the Mountain
West."[16] He went on to identify the 1943 publication by Yale
University Press of Joseph Kinsey Howard's *Montana: High,
Wide, and Handsome* as "the first significant landmark in the rise
of the new spirit."[17] Within a year of publication of Garnsey's
article, A. B. Guthrie published *The Big Sky*, which many have
seen as a similar regional landmark in the field of fiction.
Regardless of which writer or which book we focus on, something new was clearly emerging in the late 1940s—some new
way of writing about the West that made a regional phenomenon such as "Bread Loaf, Montana" nearly inevitable.

It was Stegner who noticed the phenomenon and named it.
"No place is a place," he wrote in one of his last books of essays,
"until it has had a poet."[18] The essay was titled "A Sense of
Place," and the place in question was, of course, the American

West. If the West had been needing a poet—needing someone who had learned to speak in an authentic western voice—many of us might settle on Stegner himself as the single best candidate. But in fact we do not have to name one, and no one writer could have accomplished alone what was accomplished on behalf of the region during that postwar period. Whether we look at Guthrie's *The Big Sky* or Howard's *Montana: High, Wide, and Handsome* or a growing number of books from other "Bread Loaf, Montana" writers, we encounter a voice that the West had not heard before but that the region seemed instantly to recognize as its own. From roughly that point on, westerners began to have a new kind of confidence about the West as a real place both deserving and capable of a real and distinctive voice.

How does such a thing happen? Why does it happen at one time and not another? Bioregionalists would see this phenomenon as a crucial element of what they call reinhabitation. Here is one definition of that term, which fairly well describes what was happening in the West at midcentury:

> Reinhabitation means learning to live-in-place in an area that has been disrupted and injured through past exploitation. It involves becoming native to a place through becoming aware of the particular ecological relationships that operate within and around it. It means understanding activities and evolving social behavior that will enrich the life of that place, restore its life-supporting systems, and establish an ecologically and socially sustainable pattern of existence within it.[19]

"Becoming native" had happened before on those western landscapes, of course, and the best of the western writers had made a careful study of the deep knowing of the place that generations of tribal inhabitation had produced. In fact, the passing of place-lore from one generation to another seems an inescapable seedbed for any genuine reinhabitation. Stegner put it this way: "A place is not a place until people have been born in it, have grown up in it, lived in it, known it, died in it—have both experienced and shaped it, as individuals, families, neighborhoods and communities over more than one generation."[20]

Perhaps, then, we can understand the years around 1950 as a time when the white settlers in the West had finally been there long enough to begin actually to know the place. In one sense, the writers of that time may have been working out their own western version of what their mentor Robert Frost meant when he wrote that "the land was ours before we were the land's."[21] By the late 1940s, Stegner, Guthrie, and De Voto had all come to understand that Anglo westerners had claimed the land before they knew how to allow it to claim them; that they had laid title to it long before they had learned how to let it speak through them. But these writers also understood that after a few generations of living on the land and paying attention to it, westerners might actually be ready to let the power of the land speak through them. That is what westerners seemed to hear above all else in the writings of Guthrie and Howard and then Stegner— that hard, straight, honest voice of the place speaking up through its people. It takes time for something like that to happen, generations of hard country beating its lessons into its people, but when it does happen, it is real; it is decisive; it dwells among the people of that place. It becomes part of their lives together; it reaches them as a great gift to accompany them on the next stage of inhabiting their place. Westerners have received that gift wholeheartedly. They have not let go of that voice, and they have tried their best to use it to work out the challenges of life on this land.

It was this West, which had become accustomed to hearing itself loyally but unflinchingly described by its own writers, that could hear with relative equanimity later voices such as those of historians Patricia Nelson Limerick and Richard White. Most westerners would not at first (and many still do not) accept Limerick's concept that conquest is what the West has been most about, or either White's or Limerick's contention that what the West now needs to do is come to terms with some way in which its many ethnic groups and cultures can inhabit the place together. There can be, and there is, disagreement about these themes, but it is disagreement within a region that now has a strong enough sense of identity to carry on a serious and constructive conversation about what in fact most characterizes (or challenges) it. The West now has more and more clear, strong voices with which to carry on that conversation. William Kittredge, Terry Tempest Williams, Charles Wilkinson, Mary Clearman Blew, James Welch, William deBuys, Donald Snow, Alvin Josephy, Teresa Jordan, and Ed Marston are only a few of the excellent writers who day after day and year after year hold the West critically and constructively before itself.

This maturing sense of western identity is also evident in the rapid proliferation of regional and subregional magazines, newspapers, and reference works throughout the West. *The New Encyclopedia of the American West*, published in 1998 by Yale University Press, and the *Atlas of the New West*, a project of the Center of the American West at the University of Colorado (Norton, 1997), offer portraits of the West as it is emerging today, a far cry from the West of a century or even a half century ago. *Northern Lights* magazine, *Chronicle of Community*, *High Country News*, and the latter's syndicated column *Writers on the Range* all comment on people and current events throughout the American Rockies, and the Center for the Rocky Mountain West's *Headwaters News* provides an on-line source of up-to-the-minute regional information along the entire spine of the continent, from Alberta to Arizona. Regional organizations such as the

University of Colorado's Center of the American West and Natural Resources Law Center; the Sonoran Institute and the University of Arizona's Udall Center for Studies in Public Policy, both based in Tucson; and the Wallace Stegner Center for Land, Resources and the Environment at the University of Utah are only a few institutional manifestations of the interest in regionalism that is steadily gathering momentum throughout the West.

The variety of historical forces now at work both within the West and at the national, continental, and global scales now seem set to bring the region's distinctiveness into much clearer focus than ever before—indeed, to bring it into action in genuinely historical terms. The West is beginning to understand itself in a new way, as a region with its own cultural identity, an identity strongly shaped by the landforms that define the territory and give shape to its communities. The love of the land that brought so many people to the West and keeps them there is common ground on which westerners can articulate and enact a commitment to a shared agenda of living well in a well-loved place.

But will they? The question might be paraphrased in Stegner's terms as whether, in the end, a place can be a place without its own politics. Listen first to how Stegner himself described the politics of the West: "I have pretty consistently despised its most powerful politicians," he wrote, "and the general trend of their politics."[22] One can certainly understand what would have led Stegner to say that. There are multitudes who have generally despised the politics of the West. But westerners must ask themselves whether it is possible to be a mature people, or indeed to inhabit a place in Stegner's terms, while continuing to loathe the politics of that place. In the literary realm, it is easy enough to recognize the impossibility of inhabitants of a place taking pride in it if they "pretty consistently despise" the work of their own writers. America itself did, in effect, despise the work of its writers for many decades before a recognizable and credible American voice began to emerge, and it was not until then that America could truly outgrow its colonial legacy. In its turn, the West went through a similar self-effacing phase, and it was the great gift of writers such as those who assembled in Missoula in the summer of 1951 that they began to show the region the way beyond its own particular form of colonialism. But if westerners still despise their politics as thoroughly as ever, we must ask whether the region has yet become "a place" in the sense it needs to be if it is to thrive and prosper in the new global order.

When we compare the most recent attacks of western conservatives on the federal land management agencies with the same attacks against which De Voto fought half a century earlier, we might well conclude that nothing has changed, that western politics are as hopeless as ever. But on the ground in dozens of communities, watersheds, and ecosystems throughout the West, something has indeed begun to change. As the region has steadily built a stronger sense of its own identity, it has also at last begun to outgrow its political infancy by developing a genuinely western way of dealing with western issues. That story is the subject of the next chapter.

A Homegrown Western Democracy

"Angry as one may be at what heedless men have done and still do to a noble habitat, one cannot be pessimistic about the West. This is the native home of hope. When it fully learns that cooperation, not rugged individualism, is the quality that most characterizes and preserves it, then it will have achieved itself and outlived its origins. Then it has a chance to create a society to match its scenery."
—Wallace Stegner

For several decades after Wallace Stegner wrote those lines,[1] it would have been almost impossible to find any but the most scattered bits of evidence of westerners having learned lessons of cooperation. If anything, the region became increasingly polarized after the adoption of the national environmental laws that overlaid their confrontational tone so pervasively across an already fractured region. But then, against all odds, something new started emerging in the West, and it soon began to gather force in a way that would eventually make Stegner appear prophetic indeed.

There is a story almost totally unknown outside the West but urgently discussed every day now in the western press: the story of a steadily growing number of local agreements among western environmentalists, ranchers, loggers, miners, and recreationists about how the public lands and natural resources should be managed in a particular river drainage or ecosystem. It is almost uncanny to see how important a part of the West's emerging identity is now occupied by this phenomenon, and to remember Stegner's insistence that the West would never realize its potential until something exactly like this happened. The list of such local collaborative efforts is growing too fast now to be cataloged, but names such as the Henry's Fork Watershed Council, the Quincy Library Group, the Willapa Alliance, the Malpai Borderlands Group, and the Applegate Partnership are beginning to add up to a matter of genuinely historical proportions. A steadily expanding number of westerners on both sides of the political fence are coming to believe that they can do better by their communities, their economies, and their ecosystems by working together outside the established, centralized governing framework (which had taught them only how to be enemies) than by continuing to rely on the cumbersome, uncertain, underfunded, and increasingly irrelevant mechanisms of that old structure.

The Western Governors' Association has articulated both the frustration and the promise in its Enlibra principles, or what the governors call the Shared Doctrine for Environmental Management:

The regulatory tools we have been relying on over the last quarter of a century are reaching the point of diminishing returns. In addition, environmental issues tend to be highly polarizing, leading to destructive battles that do not necessarily achieve environmental goals. Successful environmental policy implementation is best accomplished through balanced, open and inclusive approaches at the ground level, where interested stakeholders work together to formulate critical issue statements and develop locally based solutions to those issues. Collaborative approaches often result in greater satisfaction with outcomes and broader public support, and can increase the chances of involved parties staying committed over time to the solution and its implementation.[2]

While the governors sometimes sound as if they had invented collaboration, what they have actually done is recognize how important this upwelling of collaboration and cooperation has become to the shared western awareness of the region's distinctiveness. After a half century of steadily deepening and strengthening their sense of regional identity in other ways, westerners have now begun giving that identity teeth by turning cooperation into a watchword in dozens of western watersheds as old enemies learn to solve hard problems together. In the process, the old dynamic of national control versus western rebellion has begun to give ground to something much more like Stegner's vision. One or two stories will illustrate this phenomenon.

In 1978, as the Sagebrush Rebellion began brewing across the West, Tony Tipton rented a bus, filled it with neighboring Nevada ranchers as fed up as he was with trying to make a living off their combination of private land and BLM grazing leases, and drove to Carson City to join the nascent rebellion. Tipton might well have stayed on that path and followed it into the symbolic politics of shovels and bulldozers, but within a few years of the bus trip, he had begun to suspect that simply fighting the feds was not going to produce any real on-the-ground solutions to his or his neighbors' problems.[3] For one thing, the "other side" was also fighting federal land policies—with such slogans as "Cattle Free by Ninety-Three!"—and by the late 1980s those efforts seemed at least as likely to succeed as did the ebbing Sagebrush Rebellion. Determined to explore all viable options for saving his ranch, Tipton set out on another journey, this time heading for Lincoln, Nebraska, to attend a course in holistic resource management. Holistic management, as it would come to be called, teaches landowners to investigate and minutely inventory their land—its features and ecology, every creature or plant that lives on or near it—and then bring together all the people who have an interest in the property and its management in order to set goals for the land and strategies for achieving those goals.[4]

Back in Nevada again, armed with these ideas, Tipton and his wife, Jerrie, sent out invitations to neighboring ranchers, public land agencies, and even environmentalists, inviting them to come and discuss management of the ranch and its publicly and privately owned environs. Those who responded to the invitation eventually created the Toiyabe Wetlands and Watershed Management Team. The first task (and the first test) of the team was to reclaim an old dam site on leased Forest Service land, a "steep, barren pile of clay" that had functioned as a dam retaining an old mining pond.[5] The team spread hay on the slopes, encouraging cattle to come and graze there, where the animals' movements would plant the seeds that were in the hay and till and fertilize the soil. Then the animals were removed from the site and the land was allowed to regenerate, which it did, growing thigh-high grass in its first season. With these sorts of experiments, the Tiptons attempted to prove that cattle can be not only benign but also beneficial to the land on which they graze, whether the land is privately or publicly owned.

The Toiyabe experiment is one small example of what proved to be a steadily growing number of instances of an entirely new way of dealing with issues on the public lands. In the early 1990s, to take another example, the BLM found itself unable to respond effectively to an alarming increase in off-road recreational activities at the Sand Flats Recreation Area in Grand County near Moab, Utah. The number of mountain bikers on the Slickrock Trail in Sand Flats had exploded from 140 in 1989 to more than 100,000 just five years later. The resulting damage to the fragile desert environment had become a major concern of both agency officials and environmentalists. The BLM adopted stronger restrictions on camping and recreation, but these proved impossible to enforce in the face of the tremendous influx of tourists. Grand County officials were upset that their community and its unique surroundings were being destroyed by "industrial-strength tourism."[6] They persuaded BLM planner Mike O'Donnell to try something entirely new. Together, they organized a symposium in which they proposed the idea of "cross-jurisdictional land management." Out of this symposium the Canyon Country Partnership emerged.

The participants in this partnership realized that the crisis at Sand Flats demanded their immediate attention.[7] More staff needed to be assigned there to enforce restrictions and to teach tourists how to behave on this delicate landscape. But the BLM was constrained by federal hiring restrictions, which in turn were driven by the need to balance the federal budget. Someone suggested charging user fees, but federal procedures required that such fees travel through a complicated appropriations process before a portion of them could return to where they were collected, and even then only a small percentage could be returned. Intent now on overcoming all such obstacles, the group decided to have the county collect and allocate visitor fees, thereby making the county a managing partner with the BLM. This suggestion, along with a grant from AmeriCorps, broke the logjam, allowing the partnership to hire nine new members for the Community Sand Flats Team, which did the day-to-day work of fixing traffic barriers, cleaning up trash, and replanting damaged areas. Within a few years, the group had become financially self-sufficient and had availed itself of the ongoing advice of a citizens' stewardship committee. Before long, the group's formal relationship with the BLM (via a cooperative management agreement) was running smoothly, according to its director, Michael Smith, because the group dealt directly with only two BLM staffers, both of whom were enthusiastic about the partnership. Of the BLM's institutional opinion of the partnership, Smith was less sure.[8]

Another notable collaborative effort, arising in another part of the West during the 1990s, was the Malpai Borderlands Project. This project focused on an area of public and private grazing land along the Mexican border at the corner of southeastern Arizona and southwestern New Mexico. In the early 1990s, a group of ranchers and other parties started to share their concerns about loss of native grasslands and increased fragmentation of the countryside as a result of development pressures. The Malpai Borderlands Group eventually emerged from those discussions, and it went on to develop strategies to promote prescribed burning across public and private ownerships and to implement a voluntary grass-banking program. One result was that partners from the private sector began cooperating with local, state, and federal land management agencies in a community-based ecosystem management effort. The group's stated goal was to "preserve and maintain the natural processes that create and protect a healthy, unfragmented landscape to support a diverse, flourishing community of human, plant, and animal life in the borderlands region."[9] As with many other successful collaborative efforts, the Malpai group has attempted to meet this goal through a diversity of approaches, including public education and collaboration with government agencies, universities, and environmental organizations.

These stories about specific people and places can only begin to suggest the complexity and synergy of the emerging and steadily growing collaboration movement in the West. The movement has been so powerful and persistent that it has generated a growing literature replete with analyses and critiques of the collaborative phenomenon, as well as a recounting of its historical roots. The *Chronicle of Community*, an important component of that literature, defines collaboration in technical terms as a process based in alternative dispute resolution (ADR), a movement that came out of mid-1970s environmentalism seeking to "resolve difficult environmental issues through mediation, negotiation, and the building of formal agreements among disputing parties."[10] Most commonly, collaborative efforts emerge as interest groups with a stake in a particular local issue come together to try to solve problems that no one party could resolve by itself. Donald Snow of the Northern Lights Institute coined a now widely used phrase when he referred to collaborative groups as "coalitions of the unalike."[11] Agreements reached by these groups run a gamut between formal written documents and highly informal forms of consensus. Generally, coalitions emphasize stakeholder inclusiveness (so that even groups or individuals with whom any given party would rather not talk are nevertheless invited if they have a stake in the outcome); volunteerism (as opposed to required or mandated participation); flexibility (meaning a kind of shared, committed openness to new, untested ideas and solutions); and direct communication among the parties (as opposed to use of lawyers or other paid "mouth-pieces"). Although not all groups work to achieve formal consensus on issues, most groups do work hard to craft viable solutions that are at least minimally acceptable to everyone at the table.

This way of solving problems involving public lands or natural resources is a far cry from, and a direct response to the inadequacies of, the approach that has been emerging and evolving since the early 1900s. The Progressive movement at the beginning of the twentieth century had succeeded in persuading policy makers that a technical elite, working primarily within federal bureaucracies, should be responsible for the majority of natural resource management decisions. Lawmakers of the era institutionalized this philosophy when they established the Forest Service, the Bureau of Reclamation, and the National Park Service. In many ways, the culture of these agencies retains to this day the Progressives' faith in technical decision making.

By the middle of the twentieth century, the institutionalization of what Cornell government professor Theodore Lowi called the Second Republic had fundamentally changed the face of American democracy.[12] What Lowi encapsulated in the term *Second Republic* was an approach to public policy making that combined the use of professional elites with "pluralism," a system in which government serves as a kind of ringmaster in a field of competing interest groups. It was this pluralist strain of American public life that was reflected, for example, in the Forest Service's inclusion in its 1990s jargon of a repeated reference to the agency's "publics." This pluralization of the word *public*, which many would argue is inherently singular, hints at some of the deepest problems of pluralism—problems that finally contributed to the emergence of collaboration as an alternative way of making natural resource decisions. Michael Sandel summed up these problems in the early 1990s in an essay titled "The Procedural Republic and the Unencumbered Self."[13] The "proce-dural republic" is the form of decision making so familiar to participants in environmental impact statement reviews and, especially, public hearings. As government became more and more focused on maintaining fair and balanced procedures that gave everyone equal access to the decision makers, the "publics" seeking that access became increasingly "unencumbered" from any responsibility to help solve the problems that self-government finally exists to resolve. These "unencumbered selves," in Sandel's terms, or the "publics" of the Forest Service, came to stand increasingly outside the decision-making processes, seeing their role only as making sure the agencies heard their point of view, and, more important, put it in the record, where it could support litigation.

Paul Hirt, in his book *A Conspiracy of Optimism*, took a somewhat different slant on these developments and made them specific to the Forest Service when he argued that after World War II, instead of bringing together the different communities interested in the public lands to resolve how the forests could and should be used, the Forest Service promised all parties that they could get what they wanted—wilderness, recreation, timber, minerals, habitat—from the same land.[14] In fact, meeting everyone's demand proved to be impossible (hence the phrase *conspiracy of optimism*) and helped create the deep fissures that now exist among the different groups of users. Since World War II, competing groups have increasingly sought support for their claims not from the agencies, which seemed increasingly unable to move in any direction, but from the courts or from the United States Congress. The result has been an even more divisive and hostile political environment.[15]

The contemporary environmental movement was launched against this political and social backdrop. Environmentalism focused on the failure of technocratic and pluralistic governance as it had evolved across the country, especially throughout the West, to adequately address environmental values and social equity. Other social movements such as civil rights and feminism presented similar critiques of the established governing system. But these movements, in the process of addressing serious substantive issues, tended to exacerbate the proceduralism of the Second Republic. In 1970, for example, the National Environmental Policy Act (NEPA) became the law of the land, largely as a result of concerns over the prevailing decision-making structures. But for all the environmental advantages that have accrued because of NEPA and other environmental legislation of that era, the new approach to decision making also brought a new and substantial set of problems in its wake. Over the ensuing decades, NEPA litigation stalled many decisions or sidetracked them in long-drawn-out, confrontational, narrowly defined debates. Among both resource users and environmental interests, the entire procedural, bureaucratic framework of decision making created steadily deepening anger and frustration. People blamed the polarization and impasse on a range of causes: fragmented agency thinking; the high costs of those formal decision-making processes; the subordination of local communities to national interest groups; limitations in the public involvement processes; and the subordination of science to special interests and politics. In particular, the West, as the region with the majority of the country's public lands, became increasingly polarized as a more or less direct result of 1970s environmental legislation.

By the 1980s and 1990s, some of the veterans of these frustrating procedures had begun experimenting on their own with an entirely different way of dealing with public land and natural resource issues. A growing number of people began to see a new form of public participation—collaboration—as one possible solution to the perceived flaws in the system. As the first issue of the *Chronicle of Community* put it, those who have come to be most enthusiastic about collaboration as a problem-solving tool believe that "solutions to today's difficult natural resources challenges do not lie exclusively in the emergence of new technologies or management prescriptions [but] in the creative energies of individuals and groups organized around particular places they care about."[16]

The first generation of western collaborative groups coalesced primarily around watershed protection and water management issues. Western watershed "councils" proliferated and then began to move beyond water-related themes. In the late 1990s, the scope of these efforts broadened considerably, taking on issues such as species reintroduction, timber and rangeland management, and habitat protection. Increasingly, collaborative groups began stepping into advisory, if not comanagement, roles with government agencies across a full range of local and regional issues.

Working in this environment, on these issues, is not easy. In fact, it is very hard work, which would not surprise anyone who pays attention to the structure of the word *collaboration*. Its Latin derivation is a combination of *com*, meaning "with," and *laborare*, meaning "to labor." To collaborate, then, is "to work with" others. The work is always hard and often exhausting. The amount of work involved and perseverance required is graphically captured in the title of a recent book on the subject—*Beyond the Hundredth Meeting*.[17] However, while collaborative work is always laborious, often frustrating, and sometimes downright unproductive, the reason more and more groups and individuals have turned to it is not because of any of the feel-good motivations with which critics of collaboration so often mock the phenomenon but because collaborative work so frequently succeeds in fashioning solutions to hard problems that are more adaptive, more creative, and more sustainable than the old, highly adversarial system could produce.

The emergence of this indigenous form of western problem solving is almost precisely what Wallace Stegner predicted and urged when he spoke of the West outliving its origins by learning lessons of cooperation. The collaboration movement, then, is one crucial dimension of the maturing of the West, and the real historical promise of this movement will become apparent only as the West prepares to assert the degree of sovereignty over its own landscape that a mature region must exercise. But even as the West takes this collaborative step on the path toward genuine self-determination in the face of changes that deeply threaten the region, the centralized system of public land management also looks to this new approach to save it from the historical forces that now so seriously undermine its legitimacy.

The steadily expanding recourse to local, place-based collaborative problem solving in western land and natural resource issues is now seen by the federal land management agencies as a way out of the crisis of legitimacy described in chapter 4. This is a natural and healthy response on the part of the agencies, and one to which both the Forest Service and the BLM seem genuinely committed. A case in point is Michael Dombeck's proclamation of "collaborative stewardship" as the hallmark of his reign as chief of the Forest Service. In a message to all Forest Service employees on his first day as chief, in January 1997, Dombeck offered this assessment of the agency's purpose:

> Our task is to help bring people together on the land. That's what collaborative stewardship is all about. Whether we are engineers, support staff, or line officers, we are the educators and communicators, the teachers and technical experts who can bring communities of interests together to help define the policies and practices needed for healthy sustainable forests. In doing so we must streamline our regulations and simplify the way we implement the laws toward the goal

of a "government that works better and costs less."[18]

Later that year, Dombeck introduced an ambitious revision of the agency's forest-planning regulations with a "vision for the 21st century" in which "the Forest Service becomes a convener, facilitator, and information provider in helping the stakeholders define the desired goals, outcomes, and issues; collecting and analyzing relevant information; and finding the solutions."[19] At Dombeck's urging, a Committee of Scientists proposed significant changes in Forest Service operations, making collaborative management a standard feature of those operations.

It is, of course, a good thing for the Forest Service to try to transform its operations in this way. But such efforts always run the risk of getting bogged down in the embedded culture of the agency, which is deeply imbued with the forester-as-expert ethos. In the case of collaborative stewardship, this all too easily results in any approach to collaboration initiated by the Forest Service coming at communities from the agency, not at the agency from communities. Even worse, the agency makes it clear that it wants collaborative help only up to a point, but that the ultimate decisions must still be made by the "experts." And that is fatal to genuine collaboration. People will not do the hard work of collaboration over extended periods of time if their work is going to be merely advisory to the "experts." The kind of people with the skill and perseverance to make collaboration work will not long be satisfied with a governance structure that leaves either the most important decisions over the issues they have labored so hard to resolve, or the crucial follow-through oversight of management, in hands other than theirs.

At the bottom of this difficulty lies the fact that the collaboration movement represents a form and philosophy of decision making fundamentally different from the decision structure in which the land management agencies are embedded. One is an inherently decentralized, democratic form of governing; the other is inherently centralized and hierarchical. The effort to make something like collaborative stewardship an integral part of Forest Service operations, for example, cannot really succeed unless the agency is willing to turn some actual decision-making and management authority over to the people who are doing the collaborating. But that is exactly what the agency seems incapable of doing. This, once again, is not the agency's fault. The structure of sovereignty within which it operates requires the federal agency to be the decision maker. If the agency does not make decisions, it is guilty of what George Coggins, a leading authority on public land law, identifies as an abdication of its responsibility.[20] So the agencies are caught between, on one side, a legal responsibility to be the decision makers within the existing framework and, on the other, a new, collaborative decision-making process that finally depends on much more broadly shared responsibility. On their own, the agencies cannot get out of this trap.

One example of the agencies' legal bind is provided by the Applegate Partnership, which arose out of disagreement over forest management issues in the Rogue River basin in southern Oregon. A series of smaller cooperative efforts preceded the bold decision of local environmentalist Jack Shipley to draft a proposal for a "comprehensive ecosystem management plan" for the entire Applegate watershed (some 500,000 acres) and then to distribute it to various interest groups for comment.[21] Environmentalists, representatives of the timber industry and of government agencies, and farmers and ranchers agreed to come together to rework and refine the plan. At the first meeting, attendees were asked not to reveal the interest they represented but to speak about their broader concern for the watershed in which they lived. Out of this assemblage a board of eighteen members was selected, each individual chosen because he or she represented a key stakeholder group and had demonstrated an ability and willingness to "build bridges" among participants.[22] After several months, the group developed four basic objectives: to formulate a "comprehensive ecological assessment" of the watershed and a "comprehensive community assessment" of its human inhabitants; to initiate efforts leading to responsible harvesting of forest products (these negotiations were under way in 1992, after the listing of the northern spotted owl as an endangered species had led to a moratorium on logging on public lands); and to "create a research and monitoring strategy capable of evaluating and improving activities in the watershed."[23]

The Applegate Partnership attracted the attention of President Bill Clinton, whose administration's Northwest Forest Plan included the establishment of ten Adaptive Management Areas, which would act as the Applegate Partnership did to "facilitate creative solutions."[24] But then, in an effort to stop Clinton's forest plan, the timber industry challenged this process under the Federal Advisory Committee Act. When the court issued a judgment in favor of the industry, the federal agencies concluded that their staff members could no longer attend partnership meetings. While the Applegate Partnership continued to enlist volunteers and secure funding to restore watersheds, improve irrigation, and initiate local economic development, its promise had been permanently impaired because of a fundamental misfit between the "procedural republic" and the homegrown form of problem solving the partnership represented.

Local collaborative efforts run into this kind of conflict with the prevailing system of rules, regulations, and procedures so often that both the agencies and local collaborators have become increasingly innovative about creating "running room," both by looking for something akin to loopholes in the existing framework and by creating pilot projects. Although the agencies have sometimes been effective partners in these efforts, the most innovative and promising collaborative management experiments on federal lands have been driven not by top-down agency directives but by western communities themselves, experimenting with new solutions to seemingly intractable problems. The Ponderosa Pine Forest Partnership and the Grand Canyon Forests Partnership exemplify these citizen-initiated forest management experiments, and they also demonstrate the agencies' tendency to borrow, if not co-opt, the innovations of localities.

In the early 1990s, "confrontation, polarization, and gridlock" characterized the debate over public lands in Montezuma County, Colorado, in the southwestern corner of the state.[25] The community exhibited familiar symptoms of disintegration and dysfunction: antagonism toward public land management agencies; formation of "wise use" and county supremacy groups; conflicts in values between newly arriving urban refugees and longtime rural inhabitants; degraded forest health; and increased wildfire risk. In 1992, the Montezuma County Commission decided more or less in desperation to test a new approach to resolving issues regarding federal lands. Rancher and commission member Tom Colbert persuaded his fellow commissioners to convene a group of local stakeholders, including the president of the Colorado Timber Industry Association, the director of the newly established Community–Public Land Partnership Program at the local community college, and a district ranger for the San Juan National Forest. After a field trip to a notoriously unhealthy forest stand, the group recognized that the problems plaguing their forests and their community were "shared problems" and that they might have "shared solutions."[26] The Ponderosa Pine Forest Partnership, as the group began calling itself, decided to try tackling the problems at hand through a deliberate effort centered on ecological research, economic analysis, community education, and coalition building.

The partnership emerged from a long series of talks and meetings with a community-based prescription for restoring the
region's badly degraded ponderosa pine forests on both public
and private lands. The partnership agreed on a long-term vision,
stating that "forests in southwestern Colorado will be managed
across jurisdictional boundaries in balance with ecosystem and
human needs."[27]

As a first step, the partnership began implementing this
vision through a series of pilot timber sales. The Forest Service
took advantage of an obscure clause in the agency rule book
that allowed it to contract directly with counties; Montezuma
County, in turn, subcontracted the logging work to local timber companies. This was an instance, then, of local collaboration providing a constructive suggestion to the Forest Service
and the agency responding with a willingness to move beyond
its standard way of doing business. As the *Chronicle of Community* told the story, "The business relationship [that emerged]
between local and federal levels of government provides a
direct, unencumbered way to pursue ecological and economic
interests—very much unlike the highly inflamed relationships
that exist between counties and federal agencies elsewhere."[28]
Trying out such new working relationships may, in at least some
instances, prove to be an effective way to overcome the effects
of decades of mistrust between the land management agencies
and many western communities. "Pilot projects provide a
forum for interaction around something tangible," according to
the partnership's self-analysis; "seeing a concept on-the-ground
helps people crystallize their desired future condition."[29] In
other words, the work of actually maintaining a forest gives
local people and agency personnel a chance to relate differently
from the way they ever could within the old management
framework.

In 1999, the Ponderosa Pine Forest Partnership reflected

on its restoration pilot projects as one piece in a much larger puzzle:

> The story of the Ponderosa Pine Forest Partnership is part of a larger story that is being written throughout the rural West. It is a story of western communities and western landscapes trying to absorb the influx of new people, changing economies, and diverse values. Public lands, which make up more than half of the western landscape, are places where the natural still dominates the man-made, and where public policy can engage the market forces of the global economy. The public lands are also a focal point in the interface between national and local values and interests. It is little wonder that the public lands have become a battleground and, in some places, a healing ground in the transformation that is sweeping the rural West. . . . We believe that protecting and restoring these rural landscapes provides a focal point for restoring the sense of community, civility, and empowerment essential for communities to adequately address the challenges of the 21st century.[30]

The partnership rightly takes pride in the success it has achieved in these terms. But it sees its continued success as being dependent on the flexibility and adaptability of the Forest Service. "A great deal of the capacity needed to make things work comes from the U.S. Forest Service," the partnership observed. "It is up to this agency to stabilize supply, offer timber at affordable prices, keep administrative costs down, and maintain working relationships with the community."[31] Whether the agency can actually deliver such flexibility over the long term is a key question that a period of deliberate experimentation should seek to answer.

As the Ponderosa Pine Forest Partnership was taking shape,

another partnership coalesced in northern Arizona around a very similar set of needs and objectives. Around the fringes of Flagstaff, Arizona, 120 years of grazing, logging, and fire suppression—combined with the effects of a four-year moratorium on timber sales in national forests—had generated high wildfire risk and a degraded forest ecosystem.[32] In 1996, the Grand Canyon Trust, a regional nonprofit environmental organization, came forward with a proposal to create the Grand Canyon Forests Partnership. This partnership sought broad-based participation from local, state, and national organizations with an interest in advising the Forest Service on community-based forest restoration. It aimed, in its own words, to "research, develop, and demonstrate new approaches to improve and restore ecosystem structure, function, and resilience in endangered Southwest forest ecosystems."[33] The partnership spun off an independent organization called the Grand Canyon Forests Foundation, which then entered into a cooperative agreement with the Forest Service. The agency, in a pass-through situation similar to that of the Ponderosa Pine Forest Partnership, conveyed timber rights to the foundation, enabling it to subcontract with local logging operators. This allowed the revenues from timber cutting to be kept in the community and used for forest restoration.[34] Although the Forest Service retained final authority and responsibility for all decisions, the cooperative agreement established a framework for collaborative research, development, testing, and demonstration of restoration management approaches.

In June 1998, Forest Service Chief Michael Dombeck and Vice President Al Gore designated the Grand Canyon Forests Partnership a National Reinvention Laboratory. This designation, a product of Gore's National Performance Review (later renamed the National Partnership for Reinventing Government), was intended to improve government effectiveness and efficiency by offering innovative projects an added measure of support, flexibility, and freedom from restrictive regulation. While this sounds promising, it is not clear that there was ever much substance behind the National Reinvention Laboratory title. As one of the coordinators of the partnership observed:

> We had high hopes for the Reinvention Lab status at the beginning, but as time went on those hopes faded entirely. It became abundantly clear that no one at the Office of Reinventing Government had done the hard work of determining exactly what legal authority the lab designation conferred for real change. Because of the resulting ambiguity regarding its legal authority to act, the Forest Service was unwilling to risk changing any procedures of real importance. In the end, the benefit of lab status was relegated to having a plaque on the wall signed by the Vice President and the Chief of the Forest Service.[35]

These observations describe a fundamental problem with this kind of agency-sponsored experiment. For all the good intentions behind the efforts of federal agencies to support and extend local collaboration, there is reason to doubt that this level of experimentation will ever result in real change. In almost every instance, the agencies are simply responding to local collaborative initiatives, with the agencies themselves remaining all too closely bound to the embedded framework of rules and procedures. In relation both to particular local situations and to the collaboration movement in general, the agencies seem to be perpetually running to catch up with a train that by its nature has more momentum than the bureaucracy can generate. Not infrequently, an agency's inability to respond to local ingenuity leads to severe frustration among the people who have worked so hard to create a sustainable solution to a local challenge.

A classic case of conflict between the existing machinery of public land management and the new, vibrant force of collaboration is the story of the Quincy Library Group. Quincy, as it is now called throughout the West, had a fairly textbook beginning. Made up of the by now standard recipe of loggers, environmentalists, citizens, and local government officials, it was founded in 1993 in Quincy, California, as a result of a conversation between Plumas County supervisor Bill Coates and timber lobbyist Tom Nelson. Both men had figured out that a selective logging plan backed by environmentalists a decade before would actually produce four times more timber than the Forest Service's contentious (and certain to be appealed) clear-cutting proposal. The pair contacted local environmentalist Michael Jackson, who had long lobbied for such a proposal, to offer their support for an alternative forest plan combining environmental protection and selective logging. After a number of meetings at the Quincy town library, the group came up with an alternative five-year management plan for 2.5 million acres of forest surrounding Quincy (constituting sections of Plumas, Lassen, and Tahoe National Forests) that would preserve old-growth forest, endangered species habitat, and roadless areas and still keep the town's sawmills in business.

At first, the group enjoyed an enthusiastic response from the Forest Service and the federal government. In February 1994, forty-three members of the group traveled to Washington, D.C., to promote their Community Stability Proposal to congressional delegates, Forest Service officials (including Forest Service Chief Jack Ward Thomas), and Assistant Secretary of Agriculture Jim Lyons. Quincy Library Group member Michael Kossow, who attended the meeting, reported that Thomas "told all three forest supervisors 'to go back and start forest plan amendments' to examine and possibly adopt the [group's] suggestions."[36] The group met with Lyons in July of that year to discuss development of a strategy for implementing the proposal, and Secretary of Agriculture Dan Glickman offered the Forest Service $4.7 million for projects suggested by the group. President Clinton even selected the White House Christmas tree from the Plumas National Forest in recognition of the group's work.

For the next two years, however, nothing happened. Twice, the Forest Service offered a timber sale in an area that in the group's plan was off limits to logging. In an interview conducted after his retirement, Thomas stated that he had been uncomfortable with the fact that the Quincy Library Group was "not properly chartered" to draft a forest plan and, especially, that industry representatives were included in the group. Of one participant, Thomas was quoted as saying, "'I don't like [Sierra Pacific Industries owner Red] Emmerson; who the hell turned over my national forests to him?'"[37] Lyons later attributed Thomas' resistance in part to the fact that the Forest Service was "steeped in a professional tradition and in science" and did not appreciate external, lay opinion.[38] But as strong as Thomas' feelings might have been, the Quincy Library Group was not made aware of them, and the agency's unexplained lethargy prompted the group to turn to other options. In April 1996, the group wrote a first draft of a bill to force agency officials to implement its proposal.

The Quincy Library Group Forest Recovery and Economic Stability Act of 1997 was passed by the U.S. House of Representatives by a vote of 429–1 on July 1 of that year. The bill was introduced into the Senate on July 17 with the support of California senators Dianne Feinstein and Barbara Boxer. In response to opposition from national environmental groups, Boxer later withdrew her support, expressing doubts about whether the proposal adequately protected old-growth timber stands. Boxer eventually put a hold on the bill, ending its chance for passage in 1997. But Quincy Library Group legislation was finally passed by both houses in October 1998, attached as a rider to the omnibus appropriations bill.

Having met with bureaucratic obstructions to its natural flow, the collaboration movement had naturally begun to explore alternative watercourses. The legislative route had offered the best hope of salvaging the Quincy Library Group's work when that collaborative effort could not engage the decision-making structure of the Forest Service. Even though this legislative approach succeeded in Quincy's case, its success was due in part to its uniqueness. Congressional representatives and staffers had a certain enthusiasm for the Quincy legislation, but this would quickly have grown stale had they thought they would have to approve an endless series of collaborative results after the fact. But given the not infrequent hesitancy or outright unwillingness of the land management agencies to adopt collaborative results, what are the alternatives to such after-the-fact congressional intervention? One alternative would be to have Congress give some form of approval to collaboration before the fact. A small step in that direction is a program called stewardship contracting.

Early in the 1990s, Congress authorized a small stewardship demonstration program that never came to completion, but in 1998 an amendment to the Omnibus Appropriations Act gave the Forest Service the green light to engage in forest stewardship contracting on an experimental basis. The idea was to streamline land management in national forests and render it more effective by focusing on end results and desired future conditions instead of the traditional target-based timber outputs. Essentially, instead of hiring different contractors for each type of work needed on each tract of land, stewardship contracting arrangements encourage the Forest Service to hire one contractor to do all types of work—including restoration—on a specified tract. The contract itself is drafted by a committee consisting of local, regional, and national participants. A typical stewardship contract outlines a set of goals these stakeholders have set for a certain area and describes how they want the place to look at a given future date. When a consensus is reached on those issues, the Forest Service hires a contractor to do whatever work is required to accomplish these multifaceted goals. Rather than being awarded to the highest bidder, as in the traditional timber sale framework, stewardship contracts are awarded on a "best value to the government" basis. This best-value provision means that quality of work, as well as long-term treatment of the land, can be taken into consideration in the contract-awarding process.

Traditionally, various goals for a given tract of land have been approached more or less separately, with the timber cut being handled by one contractor (most likely a logging company) while each type of conservation, restoration, or remediation work is executed by a different agent. This piecemeal approach has generally proven ineffective for achieving sustainable land management goals and unsatisfactory for almost everyone involved in the process. Several perceived benefits motivated the departure of stewardship contracting from this traditional approach to federal land management. First, the contracting process is intended to bring local communities more effectively into the planning and decision-making processes. In addition, stewardship contracting allows timber companies to compensate the Forest Service with services instead of cash for timber removed from demonstration project forests. The agency may, for example, enter into a contract with a logging company for as long as a ten-year period to achieve comprehensive land management goals, which may involve not only timber removal but also watershed and wildlife habitat maintenance and restoration, prescribed burning, noxious and exotic weed control, and road and trail maintenance or obliteration. Under such a contract, it is in the company's interest to do ecologically conscientious work while removing timber.

According to supporters of stewardship contracting, this process represents a new way for the federal government to support local economies by continuing to provide economic activity, in the form of both wages and profits, from Forest Service land, slowing the drastic reductions in logging activities that so devastated many western communities in the 1990s. While existing environmental laws and regulations must still be implemented, stewardship contracting is intended to allow for greater flexibility and creativity in land management, with the aim of reducing the animosity, dissatisfaction, and frustration that currently accompany so many decisions regarding use of public land.

The Forest Service solicited proposals and selected the first round of twenty-eight projects in the spring of 1999. In the agency's Northern Region alone, contracts went to nine projects out of a pool of eighteen proposals. Despite the stewardship contracting program's apparent popularity on the ground, opposition came from familiar corners. Two specific provisions in the pilot projects—the ability to trade goods for services and the role of community advisory groups—drew fire from environmentalists and agency officials alike. National environmental groups that have a goal of ending all commercial timber production on federal lands saw stewardship contracting as a foot wedged in a door they fully intended to close. Predictably, several stewardship contracting projects were facing appeals as they moved into their second year of existence.[39]

Within the Forest Service, however, there is a kind of desperate optimism that stewardship contracting may be an effective tool to redirect and revitalize the agency's operations. At a meeting in Missoula, Montana, in May 2000, Regional Forester Dale Bosworth commented, "Land stewardship contracting may be the best hope for us to take care of the land and to meet the expectations of the American people."[40] Bob Shrenk, regional director of forest and range, went a step beyond Bosworth's "best hope" language. In his closing remarks, Shrenk stated bluntly, "Without this tool we have no hope."[41] Although Shrenk may have overstated the case, both his comments and Bosworth's convey a sense of the importance the land management agencies are beginning to attribute to experiments such as stewardship contracting. Given the increasingly difficult conditions under which those agencies operate, it is important to give the agencies the greatest possible leeway to try such new approaches.

It is also important, however, to begin hedging policy bets against the chance that the old framework is just too brittle, that there is "no hope" of salvaging that structure, and that it is time to begin experimenting not only with new ways of doing business within that framework but also with some far-reaching alternatives to it. In fact, voices from several distinct constituencies had by the end of the twentieth century begun calling on Congress to approve the creation of pilot projects or laboratories in which local collaborative processes could be given legitimacy not after the fact, as in the case of the Quincy Library Group, but in advance, with clear congressional directives to the agencies to incorporate the processes of place-based collaborations in their own decision processes and—most important of all—to implement the results.

One such proposal for pilot projects emerged from a March 1999 workshop on the National Environmental Policy Act (NEPA). The University of Montana's Center for the Rocky Mountain West and the University of Wyoming's Institute for Environment and Natural Resources cosponsored the workshop to test the hypothesis that collaborative processes could and should be more fully and effectively integrated into the NEPA decision-making framework. Participants, who included environmental advocates, industry representatives, academics, collaborative process consultants, and staff members of land management agencies, identified barriers that would need to be addressed to fit collaborative approaches into the NEPA framework and to secure agency adoption of those methods. Many of the group's recommendations would not seriously depart from the existing statutory and regulatory framework, and none of the recommendations would alter NEPA itself. But having made a series of "inside the box" reform recommendations, the workshop report went on to recognize that "while some of the tension between the old statutory framework and the new methods of collaboration can be addressed in the ways recommended . . . some of that tension is simply not yet ripe for resolution without further debate and the gathering of more information."[42] In the foreword to the report, William Ruckelshaus and James Scott, the board chairmen of the two sponsoring organizations, made the following case for ongoing discussion and experimentation:

> Agencies have statutory responsibilities for making public land decisions, yet many people are concerned that expending time and energy to participate in collaborative groups is not worth it unless the group is actually making the decision, or at least having a direct influence on the decision. Otherwise, people often feel their input is meaningless.[43]

In this spirit, the pilot project proposal contained in the workshop report "emphasizes the selection of innovative pilot projects that test the possibilities and limits of collaboration. Workshop participants suggested that one possible use of the pilot projects would be to explore to what extent decision-making authority can be vested in collaborative groups."[44]

Where to vest actual decision-making authority is an open question that others have also suggested should be examined in pilot project settings. One of the most rigorous suggestions for such experimentation came from a consortium of environmentalists and timber industry representatives that called themselves the Forest Options Group. This group convened in the late 1990s to discuss and address the growing concern about the soundness and viability of Forest Service operations. The Forest Options Group found that the current budgetary and administrative framework of the Forest Service encouraged "polarization, not cooperation," and the group suggested alternative "governance structures" to restore public trust in the agency and alternative budgeting styles to reduce both subsidies and inefficiencies. Realizing that identification of the best combination of management and budget structures was an "empirical question," the group developed five different pilot models and recommended that they be tested on two forests each. While some of the models would focus on incorporating a revised budget plan with no changes in management, another presented a "collaborative governance" option whereby the forest plan would be written and the forest supervisor hired by a local board. The managers of the forests would adhere to all environmental laws but would be allowed to depart from internal agency directives. All the pilot projects would be evaluated for effectiveness after five years. According to Randal O'Toole, a convener and member of the Forest Options Group, "the proposals received a positive reception from Congress but a negative one from the [Clinton] administration, whose only concern appears to be to maintain or increase the Forest Service budget. Since some of the proposals would reduce forest budgets, [the administration was not] interested."[45] But whether or not the specific proposals of the Forest Options Group are adopted, pressure continues to build to try some experimentation that would test the viability of decentralized control over selected public lands.

Another group somewhat similar to the Forest Options Group began meeting at the University of Montana's Lubrecht Experimental Forest in 1998. This group recommended the creation of a new Region Seven within the organizational structure of the Forest Service. The original Region Seven, which included within its boundary Kentucky, West Virginia, Virginia, and Pennsylvania, had been absorbed into Regions Eight and Nine in 1966. Because the regions were not renumbered, there has not been a Region Seven for several decades. The Lubrecht Group proposed to reconstitute Region Seven not as a traditional, geographically contiguous tract but as a kind of "virtual region" consisting of pilot or experimental forests from the various existing regions. Some, if not all, of these forests would be managed by local collaboration. Within each participating forest, management plans would be written and their implementation overseen by a local collaborative group. One participant described the Region Seven idea as follows:

> Forests would compete to be one of four or five that would be carved out congressionally to operate under guidelines that give a great deal of freedom from present rules and regulations. The chief of the Forest Service should be the one to choose which forests should come into Region 7 when they've proven their ability to govern themselves on a local collaborative basis. I'd like to see a local governing group in a national forest with boundaries that more or less correspond to a watershed. Rather than have to come up with a budget and go to Congress like the Quincy Library Group, I'd like to tell them how much they have to work with but allow them the maximum amount of governing authority to use that money.[46]

Another participant summed up the discussion in this way:

> So we're talking about a region without geography,
> where individual national forests could voluntarily
> seek more latitude to make decisions outside of budg-
> ets, targets, and the other constraints on current deci-
> sion making. Part of that creativity would include
> evaluation, which might lead to a new vision for the
> Forest Service.[47]

These experiments, like some of the ones proposed by the
Forest Options Group and at the NEPA workshop, would actually turn planning and management responsibility over to local
collaborative groups. Just as "inside the box" experiments give
the agencies a chance to prove their capacity to incorporate collaborative methods within the established procedures, these
local control experiments would give westerners a chance to
prove they are capable of ecologically sustainable stewardship of
their own landscapes, including the public lands.

If such pilot projects are approved and allowed to operate,
what will be the possible outcomes? The community conservation or collaboration movement is an emergent phenomenon; it
is still too early to quantify results and present conclusive evidence about its effectiveness. Anecdotal evidence tells us that
these approaches often are effective, as does observation of
watershed and ecosystem conservation over the last couple of
decades of the twentieth century. The relative lack of documen-
tation, though, is one compelling argument for well-designed
pilot projects that call on the problem-solving abilities of local
people and draw on local knowledge and love of place.

As the collaboration movement has matured, it has had the
benefit of a number of thoughtful, well-meaning critiques, most
notably on the part of the *Chronicle of Community* and the Uni-

versity of Colorado's Natural Resources Law Center. In a sense, the focusing of such careful analysis on the movement is a tribute to the mark it has already made, and certainly any movement of genuinely historical significance must welcome and be prepared to answer critiques of this kind. Douglas Kenney of the Natural Resources Law Center has summed up the major criticisms under various headings. He points out that skeptics of collaboration often assert that

> existing processes of decision-making and problem solving, while admittedly far from perfect, are not fundamentally flawed, and will work now and in the future. Also, without this regulatory framework, it would be impossible to attempt collaborative processes. Third, skeptics argue that most collaborative groups have not been effective in solving on-the-ground problems, and this is not likely to change. In addition, there is the "low-hanging fruit" argument: that collaboration only solves the simpler problems, and cannot be counted on for more complex, larger-scale situations. Skeptics also criticize that requiring unanimity as a decision-rule can be problematic. Finally, they point out that as most natural resources are public resources, they should be managed in accordance with the values of society at large, not just a local constituency, and that conflict-oriented processes are part of the decision-making process of our form of government.[48]

These are substantial, serious, and well-framed concerns, many of which can best be addressed by continuing to observe and analyze collaborative work. The "low-hanging fruit" argument is clearly of that variety, as is the question of whether collaborative groups can consistently solve "on-the-ground" problems. Whether the existing framework "will work . . . in the future" is probably another "time will tell" question. Kenney goes on to suggest that these empirically open questions should not simply be left to the passage of time; rather, they should be more rigorously examined. "Tentative conclusions suggest that experimentation with collaborative processes continue, guided by a policy of 'guarded optimism' and scholarly techniques."[49]

Kenney's suggestion about how to proceed is consistent with the deliberate period of experimentation this chapter recommends. It is conceivable that pilot projects and other forms of experimentation will be one arena of consensus among the forces that otherwise would continue to battle one another over control of the West. Underlying nearly all the suggestions for pilot projects is a deep dissatisfaction (so familiar to western conservatives) with existing structures of public land management, combined with a perception (so crucial to liberals) that the only way forward at this stage is to give the existing structure a full and fair chance to prove its adaptability to new forms of decision making. If those warring ideologies can agree to disagree about most things but agree on a period of experimentation at selected western sites, the national system of public land management may respond with a resiliency beyond what it now appears to have, or westerners may prove more capable of sustainable stewardship than many would now predict. In any event, both the land management agencies and westerners should be given that chance, and pilot projects seem to be the best available means of doing that.

Results, of course, will have everything to do with the way people behave and the choices they make locally. They might be much worse than the federal managers, or about the same, or better. If they are worse, the current view of westerners as being incapable of genuine stewardship of their own landscapes will be confirmed, and any further devolution will be very hard to achieve. If they are better or even about the same, the myth of westerners as irresponsible exploiters of their homeland will begin to erode, both within the West and outside it.

C h a p t e r   7

An
Irrepressible
Conflict

"These antagonistic systems are continually coming into closer contact, and collision results. . . . It is an irrepressible conflict between opposing and enduring forces. . . . It is the failure to apprehend this great truth that induces so many unsuccessful attempts at final compromise . . . and it is the existence of this great fact that renders all such pretended compromises, when made, vain and ephemeral."
—William H. Seward, 1858

The rise of collaborative land management efforts in the West, while very recent, is also very compelling in terms of their rapid spread across the region and into a growing number of issues. Although it is conceivable that the collaboration movement is a passing phenomenon, it seems much more likely that it has become, as Wallace Stegner predicted, a fundamental feature of western political culture. The question, then, is how it will align itself as a historical force in relation to the deep strands of western history described in chapters 2 and 3—the strands of imperial or national control over the West on the one hand and of Sagebrush Rebellion–type resistance to that control on the other. The preceding chapter described various efforts by the national government to incorporate this new way of doing business into its operations. Those efforts will continue, and they should be encouraged. But what if there is something about collaboration as it has arisen so insistently in the West that makes it fundamentally incompatible with the existing public lands system? If there is any reason to think that such a basic incompatibility exists, Americans would do better to begin thinking their way into that eventuality while still giving the old decision-making system every opportunity to accommodate the new current of collaboration.

This chapter will explore the possibility that national sovereignty over the public lands will be unable to accommodate itself to the basic dynamics of collaboration. This exploration will move back and forth between political theory and history, but the unifying thread will be that of sovereignty. If there is now an irreconcilable conflict between the existing structure of public land governance and the expansion of collaborative efforts, that conflict is fundamentally about sovereignty. This chapter will trace out a pattern of such conflict over sovereignty throughout American history, noting how frequently the West has been at the heart of the matter. Sovereignty has always been at the center of the public lands debate, but it has also remained a live issue in the West in a very different context: that of Indian tribal sovereignty. Unresolved issues of tribal sovereignty are beginning to link up with the challenge to national sovereignty that lies embedded within the collaboration movement in the West.

If there is a fundamental and irresolvable conflict between collaborative efforts and the existing framework of public land governance, it is because both national sovereignty and collaboration contain within themselves a kind of quantum principle—a level below which it is not possible to break them down with out destroying their essence. In the case of collaboration, people are willing to do the tremendous amount of work these processes require because they have seen in dozens of cases that such work bears fruit—it solves problems that cannot otherwise be solved, and it produces solutions more lasting and satisfying than the "procedural republic" can produce. What has not yet been clearly grasped is how fundamentally democratic this phenomenon of grassroots cooperation actually is. Solving shared problems together on behalf of a shared place is the essence of democracy. This kind of democracy has its own irreducible requisites. As in pregnancy, it is impossible to be "a little bit" democratic. Either people are making decisions or they are not, and democracy means nothing if it does not mean making decisions. Americans, especially westerners, now need to keep their eyes open to the possibility that the more collaborative experiments they create, the clearer it will become that collaborators must be decision makers. There may continue to be instances in which they are willing to serve merely as advisors, but those instances seem likely to be increasingly outnumbered by cases in which people say, "If we are going to do all this work, we are going to make the decision." That is the most strongly democratic statement a group of people can make. Whether the collaborators intend it or not, when they make that statement—when they claim their democratic authority—they fundamentally challenge national sovereignty over whatever issue they are addressing. What this may well add up to is that this vibrant democratic movement in the West cannot finally allow the ultimate decision-making power over so much of the region's territory and its future to continue to reside in Washington.

But national sovereignty also has its own quantum principle, which says that it is not possible to be a little bit national. Public land legal authority George Coggins criticizes the resort to place-based collaboration in exactly these terms, calling it "abdication of legal management responsibilities by federal land managers."[1] Those legal responsibilities derive from the history of the public lands, which Coggins traces candidly to its imperialist roots while freely maligning westerners who resist that imperial legacy:

> First, the United States, not the individual western states, bought, conquered, or stole the present federal lands. Second, they are owned by the United States in trust for all of the people in the country (and, increasingly, in the world), not just for the souvenir sellers in Cody, Wyoming, or the mining claimant marijuana farmers in California, or the county commissioners in Garfield County, Utah. Third, Congress has determined, somewhere along the historical line, that all of these federal lands should remain federal because they serve some important national purposes.[2]

Where this leaves the West, in Coggins' view, is quite clear:

> The federal government is the only federal government we have. It owns the federal lands and resources and it must be responsible for allocating them in the fashion that a national majority—not a local group or partnership—deems appropriate.[3]

Or, as he put it in another context:

> The public lands are public. They are the property of all of the people, not just those who live in their immediate vicinity. They are national assets, not local storehouses to be looted in the deregulation riots.[4]

Coggins' perspective gains on-the-ground significance if we consider a story such as that of grizzly bear reintroduction in the northern Rocky Mountains, introduced in chapter 1. The U.S. Fish and Wildlife Service in the 1980s identified the Selway-Bitterroot region of Idaho and Montana as one of the few remaining areas in the lower forty-eight states capable of sustaining a viable population of grizzlies. What eventually emerged as the agency's preferred way of getting grizzlies into those mountains was the Citizen Management Alternative. Proposed by a coalition of local conservationists, timber producers, and labor unions, this plan, which *High Country News* called "a groundbreaking compromise,"[5] would require the governors of Idaho and Montana to appoint a team of citizens to monitor and manage an initially small but growing population of grizzlies in the Selway-Bitterroot.

At one juncture in the debate over this proposal, a group of environmental leaders reminded the chief of the Forest Service that in making decisions about grizzlies, "the Forest Service is managing National—capital 'N'—not local, forests."[6] The insistent capitalization of the word *national* is merely a colorful way of expressing that exclusive or irreducible claim of national sovereignty that makes any more localized form of decision making seem deeply threatening. It is important to recognize that this is inescapably a question of sovereignty—of who is in charge—but it is also a question of democracy, specifically of whether, in a case like this, by democracy we mean local, regional, or national self-determination. In this case, the issue of democracy was brought into play in another letter to the editor attacking the Citizen Management Alternative. This writer warned that such locally devised solutions, which seemed to be springing up everywhere around the West, would "drive a stake in the heart of democracy."[7] What he meant by democracy was, clearly and exclusively, national democracy. The passion of his defense of national democracy against any grassroots alternative comes close to the heart of the conflict between two forms of public land governance now locked in what may well prove to be mortal combat across the West. A mortal combat is by definition one in which one of the contestants does not survive. There is good reason to believe that this conflict is of that kind. And no one has understood this more clearly than national environmentalists.

More acutely than anyone else, national environmental organizations have recognized (and resisted) the revolutionary democratic implications of the collaboration movement. Almost without fail, these national groups have condemned consensus efforts, not out of ill will or mean-spiritedness but because they have clearly seen that the old, centralized system and the new, decentralized system of decision making are fundamentally incompatible. Because environmentalists were so instrumental in constructing the existing decision-making framework, because they understand how it works and still see it as the best available bulwark against the forces of greed and exploitation, they react with understandable anxiety to a movement that by its nature challenges the basic premises of that framework. One result has been a deepening ideological rift within the environmental movement itself, with some factions in staunch resistance to the new approaches to land management and others throwing themselves wholeheartedly into advancing and participating in those new approaches.

Increasingly, as the debate plays itself out across the West, those national environmental organizations that most strongly defend the existing system are referred to in shorthand as "the nationals." While on the surface this may simply be a reference to the fact that these groups are organized at a national scale, the name actually and accurately portrays the fact that their approach to environmental protection is, not incidentally but fundamentally, a national approach. These are indeed "the nationals," and they now, for very good reason, devote almost as much attention to defending national sovereignty over western landscapes as they pay to defending those landscapes themselves.

One of the strongest and clearest statements of the deep-seated conflict between collaboration and national sovereignty was provided in the mid-1990s by the longtime executive director and later chairman of the Sierra Club, Michael McCloskey. "A new dogma is emerging as a challenge to us," McCloskey wrote in a November 1995 memorandum to the club's board of directors. "It embodies the proposition that the best way for the public to determine how to manage its interest in the environment is through collaboration among stakeholders, not through normal governmental processes. Further, it proposes to do this at the community level through a consensus process. Advocates of this notion believe collaboration must be place-based, preferably at the scale of natural units such as watersheds."[8]

At the core of McCloskey's objection to the collaboration movement lay the departure of the movement from the nationalist foundations of conservation and environmental protection outlined in chapter 2 of this book. "Local interests do not necessarily constitute the national interest," McCloskey reminded his club's membership, "and instead of hammering out national rules to reflect majority rule in the nation, transferring power to a local venue implies decision-making by a very different majority—in a much smaller population."[9]

Here, we encounter the one key dilemma of the collaboration movement that no amount of testing or experimentation will be able to resolve. Collaboration as it has grown up out of western soil poses a fundamental threat to national sovereignty, and the most committed of nationalists know it. Coggins' or McCloskey's nationalist language, or the "stake in the heart of democracy" statement quoted earlier, are clear and perceptive articulations of this threat. They are also, in every case, extremely passionate, and the passion must be understood down to its roots if Americans are to understand why they may be facing a crisis of public land management and governance in the West.

Where, then, does this impassioned rhetoric of distrust toward local self-determination come from? Clearly, a large part of it comes as a response to the well-established record of greed and heedlessness of so many western leaders, from William "Big Bill" Stewart, Nevada's first U.S. senator and renowned 1860s mining champion, to Secretary of the Interior James G. Watt in the 1980s and Idaho representative Helen Chenoweth-Hage in the 1990s. Most national environmentalists are convinced that resistance to western greed is all that motivates their fierce defense of full-fledged national control of western landscapes and that it is a conclusive motivation. This "protect the West from westerners" argument is as powerful now as it was when Bernard De Voto made it half a century ago, and the West will not escape its sting until it finally begins consistently to elect more enlightened leadership. But regardless of what happens to electoral politics in the West, the collaboration movement will continue to gain strength, and the stronger it becomes, the more vehement will be the nationalist response. Something more is driving that vehemence than western greed. What is it? When national sovereignty is asserted over any arena, why do those who support the national approach become so fierce, so exclusive, so unyielding in defending that sovereignty?

The answers are manifold, but in the end they concern nothing less than a fundamental question of democracy and of sovereignty that has been debated for most of the history of the United States. The traumatic roots of this antagonism toward local control reach back beyond the Civil War. They can be traced straight through the twentieth century and they are at the core of today's battles over western landscapes. To begin to understand the emotional intensity that often accompanies environmental politics in the West, then, we must once again look back in U.S. history to the 1850s, when the issue of slavery thinly veiled an even larger issue: a deep-seated conflict over the meaning of American democracy and American nationhood.

Chapter 2 presented the argument that it was not slavery alone that brought those issues to the surface but slavery in the context of America's imperialist acquisition of the West. In fact, although we now think of the Civil War as a battle between the North and the South, it was really the West that was most fundamentally at issue. The question that finally became irresolvable was not that of slavery itself but of slavery extending into the western territories; the combination of slavery and empire was what finally brought on the Civil War. But the war came only after a decade of heroic efforts to find some solution to the crisis that westward expansion had precipitated. Those efforts are worth remembering because they resemble in so many ways the great variety of efforts to reconcile the two systems of public land governance now competing with each other in the West. While no civil war will explode out of the present conflict, the chances of reconciling the two systems may be as remote as they were in 1850—and their irreconcilability may in fact have the same roots.

Remember that the 1848 signing of the Treaty of Guadalupe Hidalgo, which ended the war with Mexico, started a decade of steadily escalating tension over the extension of slavery into the western territories acquired in the war. Throughout the 1850s, leaders in both parties and all regions tried every conceivable means of resolving the conflict that westward expansion had brought so obtrusively to the surface. No one worked harder at this than Illinois senator Stephen A. Douglas. Douglas, who would eventually emerge as the leader of the Democratic Party,

was convinced that local self-determination in the western territories was the only form of governance that would enable the
union of states to survive. On many occasions, Douglas declared
his belief in "that great principle of self-government," which he
described to a Chicago audience on July 9, 1859, as "the exclusive right of a free people to adopt their own fundamental law,
and to manage and regulate their own internal affairs and
domestic institutions."[10] Unfortunately for his historical legacy,
Douglas' "great principle," otherwise known as "popular sovereignty," would have allowed slavery wherever a majority favored
it. Douglas was convinced, and probably correctly, that over
time the arid West, inhospitable to cotton, would prove equally
inhospitable to slavery. In any event, Douglas' career in the U.S.
Senate represented a deep strain of American faith in local self-
determination, which in his case extended itself valiantly to a
faith that Americans as a people could find a way to be locally
self-determining and still stay together under one Constitution.

The first significant tear in the fabric of that faith occurred
when Douglas was challenged for re-election to the Senate in
1858. In Springfield, Illinois, on June 16, in the opening speech
of his eventually unsuccessful campaign to unseat Douglas,
Abraham Lincoln used a biblical passage to formulate a radically
new way of understanding the situation. "A house divided
against itself cannot stand," he quoted, and then continued: "I
believe this government cannot endure, permanently half *slave*
and half *free*. I do not expect the Union to be *dissolved*—I do not
expect the house to *fall*—but I *do* expect it will cease to be
divided. It will become *all* one thing or *all* the other."[11]

Four months later, on October 25, 1858, in Rochester, New
York, William H. Seward, who like Douglas was running for re-
election to the U.S. Senate, and who was at that time far more
famous and visible than Lincoln, borrowed heavily from the
prairie lawyer's speech and then went a step further. "Hitherto,

the two systems have existed in different states but side by side within the American Union," Seward explained. "This has happened because the Union is a confederation of states. But in another aspect the United States constitute only one nation."[12]

It is difficult for us now to appreciate the new constitutional territory Seward was entering, but there is a clue in what appears to us initially as a mistake in verb form. Today, we would never say "the United States constitute" because we now consider "the United States" to be a singular, not plural, noun. But Seward began his sentence in the old framework, in which "the United States" were in fact separate states, united only insofar as they chose to be united. However, that old Jeffersonian legacy—the concept of the nation as a weblike structure of independent, individually sovereign states—was now meeting its greatest challenge yet. Seward ended his sentence by turning this plurality of states into what the Civil War would force it to be: "one nation." And if it were to be one nation, both he and Lincoln were saying, it could not be of two minds about something as fundamental as slavery.

What is all too easily overlooked in these arguments and events is that the imperative of being one nation came in no small part from the fact that the nation had become an empire. Only a united nation could govern and defend that vast empire. It has become difficult for Americans to see clearly this connection between American empire and nationhood, in part because they shy away from the language of empire in describing their national experience. William Seward suffered from no such compunction.

As early as 1850, as Congress debated the free-state admission of California to the Union as part of Henry Clay's Compromise of 1850, Seward had proclaimed on the Senate floor that "the unity of our Empire hangs on the decision of this day." Seward never ceased being an unabashed imperialist. Seventeen years after California's admission, his undaunted imperialism produced a pair of phrases by which most Americans now remember the name of Seward, if they remember it at all. As secretary of state, it was Seward who negotiated the 1867 purchase of Alaska from Russia, provoking one skeptic to tag this farthest extension of American empire Seward's Icebox while others settled on calling it Seward's Folly. But midway between California's admission and Alaska's acquisition, Seward's philosophy of the empire-nation had led him to formulate one of the most prophetic phrases in American history. The setting, again, was his 1858 speech in Rochester.

Those senators who, like Douglas, thought America's leaders needed only to search harder for a compromise between the two systems of governance, "mistake the case altogether," Seward declared that day, and he finished with a formulation that political observers at the time considered even more radical than Lincoln's "house divided." "It is an *irrepressible conflict* between opposing and enduring forces," Seward thundered, concluding that "it is the failure to apprehend this great truth that induces so many unsuccessful attempts at final compromise between the slave and the free states, and it is the existence of this great fact that renders all such pretended compromises, when made, vain and ephemeral."[13]

By 1858, both Lincoln and Seward had become convinced that democracy and imperial nationhood must stand or fall together. They were both proclaiming that this kind of nationhood implied an exclusive claim: either we are a democracy together, as a single nation, or we are not a democracy at all. National democracy cannot brook an alternative system. It must either absorb it (to become all one thing) or be replaced by it (to become all the other). This fundamental choice can often be deferred but cannot finally be avoided whenever issues of sovereignty or self-determination are at stake. Efforts to accommodate one system to another sometimes simply fail, and then a choice has to be made. Whether this is now true of efforts to accommodate local collaboration to the national system of public land management is still an open question, but history suggests that Americans should be alert to that possibility. In fact, the history of this kind of choice is as old as the nation itself.

In the 1770s, American colonists tried in every way they could think of to remain within the British imperial system while not relinquishing that irreducible degree of self-determination that had turned them into a democratic people. Finally, with great reluctance, they decided that the two systems were in fact fundamentally incompatible. Thomas Jefferson had most clearly identified the roots of that incompatibility, and it was to Jefferson that his colleagues turned in 1776 to explain to the world why a new structure of sovereignty had to be created, why it had become "necessary for one people to dissolve the political bonds which have connected them with another."

The American Revolution and the Civil War may seem utterly remote from contemporary issues of land management in the West. Still, these historical clashes over sovereignty might give us enough perspective to see in today's West a possibility that almost no one wants to acknowledge: the possibility that the deeply democratic phenomenon of collaboration cannot be made compatible with centralized sovereignty over the public lands; that the conflict between them may be "irrepressible," and that public land management will have to become "all one thing" or "all the other." Whether or not current efforts to reconcile the two systems and accommodate them to each other turn out to be as fatally afflicted as the reconciliation efforts of the early 1770s or the compromises of the 1850s, it is time for all those concerned with the public lands, particularly westerners, to begin considering that possibility.

If this vibrantly emergent form of western democracy does

turn out to be irreconcilable with the system of national sovereignty that has been overlaid so pervasively across the West, it will be only another chapter in a long, never finally told story of the relationship between Washington, and the West. It is now, as it always has been, a story of empire, of sovereignty, and of regional autonomy. Consider two sharply contrasting historical views about regions.

At the end of 1862, as Lincoln labored to keep the skittish Congress behind the war effort, he set forth a less biblical, more geopolitical version of his "house divided" speech. Americans had to stay under one single system of government, he said, because the continent as a landform was fundamentally indivisible. He had already alluded to this in his first inaugural address:

> Physically speaking we cannot separate. We cannot remove our respective sections from each other nor build an impassable wall between them. A husband and wife may be divorced and go out of the presence and beyond the reach of each other, but the different parts of our country cannot do this.[14]

Now, two years into the war, he expanded on this theme:

> There is no line straight or crooked, suitable for a national boundary upon which to divide. Trace through from east to west, upon the line between free and slave country, and we shall find that a little more than one-third of its length are rivers, easy to be crossed and populated or soon to be populated thickly on both sides; while nearly all its remaining length are merely surveyors' lines, over which people may walk back and forth without any consciousness of their presence. No part of this line can be made any more difficult to pass by writing it down on paper as a national boundary. . . . And this is true *wherever* a

dividing or boundary line may be fixed. . . . *There is no possible severing of this but would multiply and not mitigate evils among us. In all its adaptations and aptitudes it demands union and abhors separation.*[15]

To reach this conclusion about the indivisibility of the continent, Lincoln had to close a question about regional autonomy that Jefferson had preferred to leave open. Lincoln's closing of this geopolitical question coincided with his closing of the question of slavery, which Jefferson had, of course, also left open. Lincoln had no choice but to address the questions of regional autonomy and slavery together because they were presented together. But in fact, they were very different questions. The issue of regional self-determination was not and could not be finally laid to rest by the Civil War, even though the issue of slavery was. Today, it is the West that seems destined to bring a regional challenge to national sovereignty as more and more westerners engage in the strongly democratic processes of local collaboration on issues that fall officially under national jurisdiction. But this is not the first time the West has brought questions of region and nation to the surface. An earlier West had confronted Thomas Jefferson with those same issues.

Jefferson, whose earliest pro-independence political base had been rooted in western Virginia when that was the West, was always looking farther west, always trying to discern what lay out there and what might become of it. That westward gaze became quite literal in his decision to build his home, Monticello, facing west into the misty depths of the Blue Ridge. His most famous westward-looking acts were the Louisiana Purchase and the Lewis and Clark Expedition, but even before that, he had thought about the West in terms Lincoln would later make nearly unthinkable.

As the Trans-Appalachian West began to fill with Anglo settlers in the 1790s and to express a broad and now eerily familiar range of discontents with domination from the eastern seaboard, Jefferson cast his democratic gaze on those developments:

> We think we see [westerners'] happiness in their union [with us] & we wish it. Events may prove it otherwise; and if they see their interest in separation, why should we take side with our Atlantic rather than our Mississippi descendants? It is the elder and the younger son differing.[16]

Or again:

> Whether we remain in one confederacy or form into Atlantic and Mississippi confederacies, I believe not very important to the happiness of either part . . . and did I now foresee a separation at some future day, yet I should feel the duty & the desire to promote the western interests as zealously as the eastern.[17]

It was precisely this Jeffersonian openness toward the possibility of regional autonomy that Lincoln felt compelled to foreclose in the process of closing the other great question Jefferson had left open: the question of whether or not Americans could be Americans and still hold slaves. It is easy today to conclude that, of course, Lincoln was as right about the geography as he was about the slavery—that both questions needed to be closed and were correctly closed. But there is danger in treating two temporarily overlapping issues as if they were the same issue. In the process, we run the risk of making a temporary linkage permanent, thereby freezing history in its tracks, or at least freezing institutions in their tracks so that they are no longer responsive to what Jefferson so responsively described as "the course of human events."

As this never-ending course of events begins to move beyond

the age of national predominance, the existing public lands system is brought more and more sharply into question. Under those circumstances, the assumption that a national system is the only possible or viable system threatens to freeze institutions in the path of history's course. Although Lincoln's defense of national sovereignty may well be invoked by "the nationals" in this struggle, the more useful historical memory may be the fact that Lincoln was no less responsive than Jefferson to the course of human events. "As our case is new, so we must think anew and act anew,"[18] Lincoln proclaimed when he had become convinced that the old arrangements of sovereignty had outlived their usefulness.

Perhaps it is time to notice with fresh eyes how often the debate over governance of public lands in the West has returned to issues of sovereignty. From the states' rights arguments of the Sagebrush Rebellion to the county movement that succeeded it, westerners seem to have had recourse to a bottomless reservoir of novel theories about sovereignty—about jurisdiction over western landscapes. None of these theories has fared well in the judicial system; in fact, none has ever reached first base. Because of this, it is easy to dismiss the entire issue of sovereignty as it applies to the public lands as a fringe phenomenon, something that need not be taken seriously. But behind the unorthodox, if not bizarre, theories about sovereignty raised by the Sagebrush Rebellion and the county movement lies a deeper truth: that there is an inherent tension about sovereignty over the public lands, indeed over the West in general, that no amount of zaniness can obscure and no amount of mockery can obliterate. No viable, democratic, ecologically sustainable institution for governing western landscapes can be successfully devised without in some fundamental and innovative way addressing the question of sovereignty. In the end, this is the question of who rules—of who will be in charge of the West.

The issue of sovereignty is kept terminally open in the West by two complementary vectors, both with great historical force. The first is the fact that people who live and work, raise their families and build their communities, on a particular landscape cannot be and will never be persuaded by any amount of purely legal reasoning that people who have no such dependence on or knowledge of those landscapes should have an equal say in their governance. In the end, sovereignty cannot be a matter of raw legal jurisdiction. Unless the way people actually live in a given place—their living relationship with land and landscape—is made a part of the pattern of sovereignty, that pattern cannot be sustained over time. It is this simple fact of life, more than greed or mere cussedness, that has kept westerners coming back time and again to the issue of sovereignty.

But the issue has also stayed alive because national sovereignty over western landscapes has itself always been problematic—and it is now more problematic than ever. It was problematic originally because it rested on conquest; it is now increasingly dubious because of the decline of national governing legitimacy discussed in chapter 4. These two historical strands actually overlap in current discussions of tribal sovereignty in the West.

Almost always, in any debate about the role of local collaboration in the governance of public lands, someone will say, "But these are federal lands," as if that legally incontestable claim were the end of the argument. But it is worth bearing in mind that "these are federal lands" not because of some natural law or divine decree but because the United States government took the lands away from the people who had for centuries lived and worked, raised *their* families and maintained *their* communities, on those landscapes, and then reserved the conquered land in national ownership. Even George Coggins, in making the legally conclusive claim of national sovereignty, recognizes the brute fact of conquest on which that claim rests when he declares that "the United States . . . bought, conquered, or stole the present federal lands."[19]

The point here is not to claim that national sovereignty over the public lands in the West is invalid because of the conquest, but rather to remind us how historically contingent the current structure of sovereignty actually is. The sense that things might have been otherwise, that the existing structure of sovereignty is not rock-solid, is reflected in the ongoing western rebelliousness against the public lands system, but it is reflected much more crucially in the ongoing assertion of tribal sovereignty. During the same decades when western rebels of various types have seen their claims of states' rights and county sovereignty go down in legal flames, western landscapes have been the locus of another set of sovereignty arguments that the courts have taken very seriously indeed. In the long run, the West may learn more of what it needs to discover about self-determination from its native tribes than from any other source. Those sovereign western tribes may prove to be key players in working out the previously intractable issue of sovereignty over western landscapes in general.

The fact is that the Indian tribes actually possess a form of sovereignty that carries the kind of potency western rebels have tried repeatedly (and repeatedly failed) to claim on behalf of states or counties. What is more, tribal sovereignty has steadily gained strength, credibility, and vitality at the same time western rebelliousness against national sovereignty has become increasingly symbolic and ineffectual. It may finally be time for nontribal westerners to find some way to avail themselves of the energy and robustness of the tribal sovereignty movement. It is not and probably cannot be clear at the outset what form such an alliance might take, specifically what the rest of the West could offer the tribes in exchange for their assistance in rethinking and reshaping the framework of sovereignty. Dennis Gibb of the Puyallup Tribe in Washington State sums the situation up succinctly: "Don't bring us your poor, your tired, your huddled masses yearning to breathe free," Gibb says. "Bring us a good deal."[20] What a good deal might look like to western tribes or to other westerners negotiating with them over issues of sovereignty would have to emerge from the negotiations themselves. But such negotiations are now a settled part of the western scene, and they are fundamentally concerned with issues of sovereignty.

Tribal sovereignty is already reshaping policy in the West through the negotiation of steadily increasing numbers of compacts between states and tribes. As a 1999 article in the *Harvard Law Review* summarized the situation, "compacts—working agreements between tribes and states that resolve jurisdictional or substantive disputes and recognize each entity's sovereignty—have become a 'device of necessity' for tribes and regional governments."[21] Many factors have led to the expanded use of compacts with tribes at the turn of the twenty-first century, but one of the most important is a factor that is encountered repeatedly throughout this book: the historical momentum of devolution. As the same law review article explained, "in an era of federal budget cuts and devolution of federal power to the states—in which Congress has been increasingly willing to delegate to tribes regulatory and implementation functions previously accorded only to states—the need for tribal–state cooperation in allocating scarce financial resources has increased."[22]

If we concentrate too sharply on the subject matter covered by compacts—whether gaming or child welfare or water rights—we can miss the actual historical significance of this phenomenon. In fact, it is part of the larger pattern described throughout this book: the pattern of a steady loss of governing capacity and legitimacy on the part of the national government accompanied by an equally steady strengthening of competence and confidence on the part of westerners. In this case, the westerners in question are Indian tribes. Just as other westerners, working together through local collaborative processes, have become aware both of their own capacity to solve public land issues and of the federal agencies' growing inability to deal effectively with many of those issues, so have Indian tribes gained confidence in their own self-governing capacity across a range of issues while becoming more and more dubious about the ability of the national government to protect or advance tribal interests.

In the case of tribes, the national government seems in fact to be standing on the brink of a dramatic collapse in its legitimacy. In a lawsuit filed in the 1990s against the United States government, concerning the Individual Indian Money trust accounts, Elouise Cobell of the Blackfeet Tribe provided leadership in bringing to light some particularly egregious examples of federal abuse in the management of Indian funds. "It would be difficult to find a more historically mismanaged federal program than the Individual Indian Money Trust," U.S. District Court Judge Royce Lamberth declared in an interim ruling in December 1999. "The court knows of no other program in American government in which federal officials are allowed to write checks—some of which are known to be written in erroneous amounts from unreconciled accounts—some of which are known to have incorrect balances. Such behavior certainly would not be tolerated from private sector trustees. It is fiscal and governmental irresponsibility in its purest form."[23] With that finding in hand, Cobell sought restitution for $10 billion that she claimed the federal government owed to more than 500,000 Indians.

Regardless of the outcome of this particular lawsuit, the national government is no more likely to succeed in reversing its loss of legitimacy over tribal matters than in reversing its loss of legitimacy over public land issues. In both cases, devolution—a shift in responsibility and authority from Washington, D.C., to those whose lives are most directly affected by the decisions that need to be made—is likely to continue to gain momentum. In chapter 8, we will return to the role tribal sovereignty might play in reshaping western institutions and governing structures. Any such reshaping seems almost certain to emerge from a growing awareness of fundamental incompatibility between two systems of sovereignty. Western tribes have kept that awareness alive for decades; now a similar awareness is dawning on a newer contingent of westerners.

The steadily expanding collaboration movement is an indigenous, democratic phenomenon through which westerners have begun to translate their land-rootedness into direct and effective control over their home ground. This movement is bringing together in a most unexpected way the western love of powerful landscapes with the old western strain of independence and rugged self-determination. Almost in spite of themselves, westerners have been learning that they can take good care of their land and be self-governing and that, indeed, the two seem to depend on each other. As more and more westerners learn from experience how capable they are of managing their own landscapes when they succeed in transcending their entrenched ideological differences, their impatience with what many of them have come to see as a worn-out centralized bureaucracy is leading to the emergence of a new western way of doing business. Throughout the West, watershed councils and other local, collaborative units of governance are transcending, ignoring, or wearing down outmoded procedures. These loose affiliations of citizens are getting on with the work of solving real, on-the-ground problems in a new world where the old forms of sovereignty and governance have simply proven too clumsy and unresponsive to get the job done.

As watershed democracy has gained momentum and legitimacy in the West through the spread of the collaboration movement, the existing national system's loss of legitimacy has inevitably been accelerated. Above all, this deepening experience of western democracy calls into question a basic assumption of the national system. The assumption is that for a broad range of issues affecting the public lands, a comprehensive national approach is the best way to formulate policy. This assumption is questionable at best, and the time may be at hand to recognize that it is simply false.

Fire policy provides an excellent example. From Gifford Pinchot's time to the present, the Forest Service has tried now one, now another national fire policy in its forests. The results have been, quite simply, disastrous. They have been far more disastrous than they might have been because of their very comprehensiveness—because they have been national policies, applied universally across the entire National Forest System. How different things might have been if John Wesley Powell had been heeded more and Pinchot less—if those living in various western watersheds had been given responsibility for managing the public lands within those specific watersheds, bringing to bear their local knowledge of the ecosystems they were managing. Just in terms of fire policy, the result of such a decentralized system would have been experiments with a great variety of approaches. Residents of some watersheds probably would have adopted Pinchot's total suppression approach, others might have let fires burn, and still others might have used controlled burns. Learning from one another's successes and failures, local managers of western watersheds almost certainly would have found their way to sound and sustainable fire policies much sooner and at much less cost of every kind than the gyrations in national policy have produced.

What might have been is not so much the point, however, as

what might now be. We are where we are. Western forests are in a generally unhealthy state because of a century of misguided fire and timber management policies, and there is now no clear path to forest health. The next chapter in this story can be told in terms of either a new round of national policies or a round of locally devised and implemented policies. This is true not only of fire policy but also of road policy, timber policy, dam and grazing, recreation and mining, wolf and salmon policy. If, through either pilot projects or compacts, westerners succeed in creating exercises in genuine watershed democracy, one side effect will almost certainly be a dawning recognition that these forests never really were "national forests." They were always northern Rocky Mountain forests or Cascade Range forests or Sierra Nevada forests. Their sustainability is inseparable from their particularity. Pinchot himself recognized this, and today's Forest Service is almost desperate to find a way to implement this understanding. Those efforts may yet succeed after a century of concerted failure, but in the meantime it seems the better part of wisdom to allow some fundamental questions to be raised about what it really means to call these "national forests" or about what Americans gain (as opposed to what they so obviously lose) by trying to manage them nationally.

Historical responsiveness is lost whenever the assumption is made that a given set of institutional arrangements are their own warrant—that they are legitimate because they exist. We see a hint of that kind of unquestioning rigidity in the tendency to equate public ownership of western lands with national ownership. "The public lands are public," George Coggins says, and no one can disagree with that. But he continues then, as if simply unfolding the implications of the public lands' being public: "They are the property of all of the people, not just those who live in their immediate vicinity. They are national assets."[24] Coggins writes as if the beginning of this little argument and the end said exactly the same thing. "The public lands are public. . . . They are national assets." But to be public and to be national are, of course, not the same thing. In this case, they happen to be the same thing: these public lands happen to be nationally owned at this point in history. But it is a logical mistake to assume that they can remain public only by remaining national, and it is a historical mistake to assume that because they have been nationalized, they must always remain so. The reservation of so much of the West in national ownership was no more a matter of manifest destiny than was the conquest of the West. Things might have been otherwise, and they might yet be otherwise.

In 1776, Thomas Paine brought the issue of sovereignty to a head with his pamphlet titled *Common Sense*. In it, he spoke in terms that might well be applied to today's unresolved issues of sovereignty in the West:

> As to government matters, 'tis not in the power of Britain to do this continent justice: the business of it will soon be too weighty and intricate to be managed with any tolerable degree of convenience, by a power so distant from us, and so very ignorant of us; for if they cannot conquer us, they cannot govern us. To be always running three or four thousand miles with a tale or a petition . . . will in a few years be looked upon as folly and childishness. There was a time when it was proper, and there is a proper time for it to cease.[25]

If there was a time when the national domination of the West was proper, there may also be a proper time for it to cease. There is nothing more fundamentally democratic—indeed, nothing more fundamentally American—than for Americans to ask whether the governing forms they inherited any longer serve their interests. In the West, the old and still deepening resentment of a fundamentally paternalistic and increasingly dysfunctional public lands system, combined with the vitalizing energies of cross-ideological cooperation now spreading across the region, make this the likeliest place in America to question in a profoundly Jeffersonian, democratic, and American way a system of governance that is steadily losing both its effectiveness and its legitimacy. Can westerners rise to the occasion? The next chapter suggests how that might happen.

How the West Might Govern the West

"I want to present to you what I believe to be ultimately the political system which you have got to adopt in this country, and which the United States will be compelled sooner or later ultimately to recognize. I think each drainage basin in the arid land must ultimately become the practical unit of organization, and it would be wise if you could immediately adopt a county system which would be convenient with drainage basins. . . . The government of the United States should cede all of the lands of that drainage basin to the people who live in that basin."
—John Wesley Powell

If the West now occupies a uniquely promising historical moment, it can realize that promise only by thinking broadly and expansively about western issues and institutions—by thinking and eventually acting at the scale of these broad and expansive western landscapes. To its credit, the region has managed to keep alive the memory of one man who did just that.

In 1878, Major John Wesley Powell published his *Report on the Lands of the Arid Region of the United States*, in which he set forth a remarkably broad and complex set of interlocking recommendations about public policy for the interior West. Focusing on aridity as the defining characteristic of the region, Powell proposed that a series of policies be shaped to fit the reality of western landscapes. The 1862 Homestead Act, for example, worked fine on well-watered landscapes, where the 160 acres the act allotted per homestead was actually enough in most instances to support a family. But Powell knew that in the West, 160 acres was either too much or, most often, far too little. Powell argued that land that could not be irrigated could be made productive only in much larger tracts, and he recommended that the acreage limit be raised to 2,560 acres—four full sections—on those forbidding landscapes. Conversely, he recommended that on irrigable land, the allotment be reduced to 80 acres. He proposed that on parcels of both sizes, the straight-line, square-cornered grid system so familiar on eastern landscapes be replaced by surveys based on topography, letting farms be as irregular in shape as they had to be in order to give everyone access to water.[1] Moreover, he maintained that on both arid and irrigated lands, these individual homesteads would be much more likely to prosper if they joined together within their watersheds to form grazing and irrigation cooperatives.

These two seemingly unrelated elements—cooperation and watershed organization—appeared in tandem repeatedly throughout Powell's work. Sometimes he seemed to intimate that organizing both private landownership and political jurisdictions according to watersheds and subdrainages would itself make cooperative behavior more likely. But regardless of where cooperation came from, Powell was convinced that these arid western landscapes could not be inhabited (or at least could not be inhabited in what we would now call a sustainable way) without a high level of cooperation among the inhabitants—just as he was convinced that where water was at such a premium, societies, economies, and policies would have to be organized according to the way water flowed. It was this crucial combination of cooperation and watershed organization to which Powell looked as the foundation of sound policy regarding not only private holdings but also the public domain. He put all the pieces together in his 1889 speech to the Montana Constitutional Convention in Helena. In his introductory statements, Powell remarked to the assembled convention:

> You are under peculiar conditions. In the eastern half of the United States we have settled governments . . . adapted to the physical condition of their country; but in the western half of America, the local, the state, the territorial, [and the] county governments . . . the regulations and the national government are in no sense adapted to the physical conditions of the country.
>
> I want to present to you what I believe to be ultimately the political system which you have got to adopt in this country, and which the United States will be compelled sooner or later ultimately to recognize. I think each drainage basin in the arid land must ultimately become the practical unit of organization, and it would be wise if you could immediately adopt a county system which would be convenient with drainage basins. . . . The government of the United States should cede all of the lands of that drainage basin to the people who live in that basin. . . . I believe that the people who live along every valley in this country should be the people who control three things besides the land on which they live: they should have control of the water[,] they should have control of the

common or pasturage lands, and they should have
control of the timber lands.[2]

Wallace Stegner summarized and paraphrased Powell's proposal as follows: "If it chose, Montana could organize itself and
set a pattern for all the still-forming states of the West."[3] Powell knew that what he was proposing was both radical and right.
He meant it when he said that if Montana—if the West—chose
to organize itself on the terms its own landscapes dictated, the
national government would eventually have to go along with it.
This was indeed hard-headed thinking about policies to match
the challenges of the western landscape, but it was also thinking
at a scale to match the grandeur of that landscape. Environmental historian Donald Worster, in an essay titled "The Legacy of
John Wesley Powell," commented, "To a greater extent than any
of his predecessors in western exploration, Powell tried to ask
comprehensive questions about the whole of the place, about
how it came to be what it was and how it was still taking form
before his eyes."[4] His was a call to westerners to exercise political initiative and courage of a variety that, had they responded in
kind, could have made the region proud of its boldness and fore-
sight for generations to come. But Powell was, in 1889, truly a
voice crying in the wilderness. As Worster explained, "it was
mainly western politicians who blocked Powell's reforms,
because they would have prevented private interests from getting control of resources and forced people into a collective pattern of settlement."[5] But the avarice of western politicians
merely echoed a corresponding national ethos. "The nation did
not give [Powell's recommendations] much thought at all,"
Worster wrote, "perhaps because they flew in the face of well-
established institutions, and more seriously, in the face of a
national culture of economic individualism."[6]

In any event, Powell's recommendations were utterly

ignored. There was no handing over of the public domain to local watershed democracies; there was in fact no watershed organization of any significant kind. And there was—throughout the West—precious little cooperation. What is amazing is that Powell, having been so thoroughly ignored, has not been forgotten altogether. But in fact he is not likely to be forgotten anytime soon, largely because his twin themes of watershed organization and cooperation are now coming so insistently and so conjointly into the West and its political culture. Even if that were not true, though, Powell would be worth remembering and revisiting simply because of the breadth and scope of his vision. It is still true, as Donald Worster insisted, that "we have not yet invented all the institutions we will ever need in order to live in the place. That is why Powell is still worth heeding."[7]

Is there any reason to believe that the West may be ready at last to begin inventing institutions suited to its uniqueness? There are many solid indications that it is. In particular, the two strands of thought so often wound together in Powell's work—the strands of cooperation and watershed organization—have now acquired such a momentum throughout the region that they have begun to emerge as an incipient alternative form of governance. Watershed councils and other mechanisms of western collaboration have become both increasingly effective and increasingly incompatible with the prevailing centralized and adversarial decision-making structures on the one hand and with the region's arbitrarily bounded political jurisdictions on the other. The West may soon be prepared to recognize how consistently those old structures prevent the region from determining its own fate on its own terms. That recognition may in turn enable the West to begin inventing institutions appropriate to a democratic people inhabiting a unique landscape.

There is no way to foresee every element that could eventually contribute to those new western institutions, but the West has now changed and matured enough to provide a few safe guesses about some of the elements. It seems all but inevitable, for example, that a major component of the evolution of these new institutions will be the development of various river basin governing structures. Often, at the heart of these arrangements will be a second element of the new western institutions: a renewed appreciation of and responsiveness to the sovereignty of the Indian tribes that play such a dominant role in many western landscapes. Finally, tying these two elements together, formal compacts among states or between states and tribes will often be the legal mechanism by which new institutions will be created in the West. These are among the key elements with which the West might begin to claim the self-governing sovereignty over its own landscape that John Wesley Powell saw as "the political system which you have got to adopt in this country."

More than a century later, nothing has vindicated Powell's analysis more thoroughly than the steady, insistent emergence across the West of watershed-oriented thinking and increasingly potent forms of watershed organization. Speaking at a 1999 conference in the Colorado River basin, law professor David Getches recalled Powell's exploration of the Colorado and concluded: "The key is going back to Powell's wisdom that this river and this watershed can be a unifying device, socially and culturally, for the West. If we look at it that way, we will be led to some kind of different institutional arrangements."[8] Following Getches' line of argument, a number of Colorado River basin stakeholders have proposed the formation of a new interstate compact for the region. Unlike the badly outdated 1922 Colorado River Compact, the new management entity created by such a compact would include representatives from Indian tribes and the federal government as well as the states in the basin.

The tripartite structure proposed for the Colorado basin was similar to a proposal that was already receiving serious attention in the Columbia River basin. As salmon populations have continued to decline in the dam-clogged Columbia and its tributaries and as more and more species have been listed under the Endangered Species Act, the prospect of a whole new layer of national control over the Pacific Northwest has sent tremors through the body politic of the region. One response has been to try to fashion new ways of governing the basin. The boldest proposal has been for a Three Sovereigns Forum, which would include the Columbia basin's four governors, one leader from each of the thirteen Indian tribes in the basin, and one federal representative. This combination of state, tribal, and federal representatives would have real authority to coordinate salmon recovery from the Rocky Mountains to the Pacific Ocean. Oregon's governor, John Kitzhaber, has played a leading role in this effort to create what he calls "a new regional governance structure for the Columbia Basin."[9]

Kitzhaber is one westerner who has demonstrated what it would mean to think at the scale these issues require. He speaks passionately and persuasively of the necessity for "bold, decisive action taken by the region as a whole" and asserts that "without changes of this kind, we will cede control of the destiny of the Pacific Northwest to interests outside the region." That result, he says, with the self-determining assurance that the West must now steadily cultivate, "is simply not acceptable to me." What is so refreshing about Kitzhaber's way of speaking is that it rises so far above the parochial demagoguery in which the West has too often been willing to indulge. Insisting that nothing positive can happen "unless we look for solutions that unite the region rather than divide it," Kitzhaber aims for "a victory of regionalism over parochialism."[10]

Kitzhaber's approach bridges the first two elements most likely to contribute to new governing institutions in the West.

His proposal is all about river basins, but it is also about sovereignty. What is in fact unique about the Three Sovereigns proposal (and what will almost certainly prevent it from being implemented anytime soon) is that as its name implies, it squarely addresses the now inescapable issue of sovereignty. In effect, it would elevate various forms of local or regional sovereignty—and, crucially, tribal sovereignty—to a place of equality with, if not preeminence over, national control. Whether or not this particular proposal is ever enacted, the serious consideration it has received is evidence of the increasingly inescapable fact that the old, centralized regime can no longer govern the West. At the very least, this bold proposal should serve as an inspiration to westerners and all who care about the West to begin imagining a new, far less centralized structure of sovereignty over western landscapes.

The Three Sovereigns proposal is intriguing in part because it puts western sovereignty over western landscapes squarely on the table, in part because it recognizes straightforwardly the central role tribal sovereignty must play in any such framework, and in part because it recognizes the emerging sovereignty concerns of non-Indian westerners, who have a foot in each world, sharing both imperial and native perspectives.

As these issues of sovereignty continue to present themselves in watershed and other western contexts, compacts are likely to be among the most effective vehicles for exploring and implementing any fundamental realignment of sovereignty. By their nature, compacts imply a particular kind of equality or parity among the compacting parties. These are necessarily agreements among sovereigns, and as such they offer both a proven and a promising vehicle for addressing some of the issues of sovereignty that have challenged the West for a century or more.

In terms of long-term policy implications, the most significant compacts have been those quantifying tribal water rights.

Those rights, recognized and secured by the United States Supreme Court in the 1908 case of *Winters v. United States*,[11] are both substantial in quantity and senior in priority to almost all nontribal rights. Through a combination of legislation and court decisions, states had established the authority to quantify tribal water rights within the context of statewide water adjudication or quantification processes, but they were still required to recognize the full extent of any given tribe's "Winters Doctrine" rights or risk having the federal courts quantify and enforce those rights. A number of western states have used compacts as an alternative approach to litigation. Montana took the lead in this field when it established the Reserved Water Rights Compact Commission in 1979 to negotiate compacts to quantify and secure tribal water rights. These water compacts are subject to state legislative, tribal, and congressional approval before they are finalized. At century's end, the Chippewa Cree tribe of the Rocky Boy's Reservation had achieved a congressionally approved, finalized compact. The compact with the Assiniboine and Sioux tribes of the Fort Peck Reservation was the first of these Montana compacts to gain state and tribal approval, but congressional approval was blocked by objections from some downstream states. Significantly, the state and the tribes have not allowed the lack of congressional approval to prevent them from using their compact to resolve their own upper basin issues.

Water rights are by no means the only issue now being addressed through compacts between states and tribes. The hundreds of tribal–state compacts now in existence address a diverse set of issues, including social service delivery, resource protection, law enforcement, zoning, and property rights. The 1988 Indian Gaming Regulatory Act spurred a new round of compact negotiations concerning the establishment and regulation of gaming activities on reservations.[12]

Against this backdrop, it is not surprising that as westerners begin to remember John Wesley Powell's advice about river basin governance, they would look to compacts as the vehicle of choice to create the new institutions the region must have to remain self-determining. Regardless of what becomes of the Three Sovereigns proposal in the Columbia basin, regardless of whether states, tribes, and the national government negotiate any new compacts on the Colorado, the use of compacts to reshape structures of sovereignty in the West is more likely to gain than to lose momentum in the coming years. Compacts are certainly not the only way to do this, but they do create opportunities to address the increasingly inescapable fact that the current framework of sovereignty can no longer adequately resolve a wide range of key western issues. The one pivotal western issue that has not yet been addressed or even widely discussed within the compact framework is the issue of the public lands. But given the fact that sovereignty has always been so central to the public lands debate, and given the increasing use of compacts to address (and redress) other issues of western sovereignty, there is good reason to begin thinking about how compacts could be used to address public lands issues in the West.

If the national government continues to lose ground in terms of its ability to manage so much of the West, and if westerners continue to gain ground in terms of their ability to work together across interest and ideological lines on public lands issues, it will make more and more sense to begin thinking about realigning sovereignty to give westerners more control over the public lands, not in order to exploit and ruin them but for the long-term sustainability of western ecosystems and communities. It is impossible to know in advance exactly what form this shift in sovereignty will assume. It may well (as in the case of the Three Sovereigns proposal) grow out of the emergence of new watershed-governing structures negotiated to address particular endangered species or other issues in specific drainages or ecosystems. Without exception, though, negotiations about those western issues will always have to entail the public lands, simply because the national government owns and manages land in every substantial western watershed.

In some basins, it might work to negotiate a compact in which the national landlord is simply given a seat at the table as the sovereign with jurisdiction over those particular stretches of real estate. Whether on the Columbia or elsewhere, this model is certain to be tried, and should be tried. But as with collaborative pilot projects, so also with compacts: westerners must now be open and adaptable to all possibilities. It may be that arrangements such as the Three Sovereigns proposal—in which the national government as landowner and regulator is one of the contracting sovereigns within the river basin—may work. But it may also be that history has by now moved beyond the point at which such shared sovereignty is either feasible or genuinely adaptive. It may be that the "irrepressible conflict" between national sovereignty and local collaboration will render anything like the Three Sovereigns proposal unworkable. Or it may simply be that the federal land management agencies will continue to lose governing legitimacy, and that some watershed somewhere will decide that the only way to govern that watershed effectively and sustainably is to challenge the assumption that what are now federal lands must forever remain federal lands.

While giving arrangements like the Three Sovereigns proposal every chance to prove themselves, then, westerners should also begin thinking their way into the increasingly likely scenario in which some western watershed at last decides to follow John Wesley Powell's advice to the 1889 Montana Constitutional Convention. The first watershed to do so may be a large one like the Columbia or Colorado basin or, perhaps more likely, a small one like the Henry's Fork River basin in Idaho or the San Pedro River basin in Arizona. Whatever the size of the watershed, what seems likely to happen sooner or later is that the diverse groups within it, who have worked together effectively for a few years but have repeatedly been frustrated by the federal land management system, will, as Powell suggested, propose that "the government of the United States should cede all of the lands of that drainage basin to the people who live in that basin."

How might this work? Specifically, how might it work within the framework of a compact? To explore the issue most fruitfully, assume that the drainage is one that encompasses one or more Indian reservations, two or more states, and some substantial amount of Forest Service or BLM land. The Snake River might serve as a useful hypothetical example for this exercise. While most portions of the Snake's watershed lie in Idaho, the river also drains small parts of Utah and Nevada and a larger part of Wyoming, and after leaving Idaho, it cuts across northeastern Oregon and empties into the Columbia River in Washington. There are three Indian reservations—Fort Hall, Duck Valley, and Nez Perce—on which members of the Shoshone, Paiute, Bannock, and Nez Perce tribes live. Within the Snake drainage, approximately 80 percent of the land is managed by either the Forest Service or the BLM. The BLM districts contained within the watershed are the Upper Columbia–Salmon/Clearwater River District, the Upper Snake River District, and the Lower Snake River District. The national forests drained by the Snake are the Clearwater, Nez Perce, Payette, Wallowa-Whitman, Salmon, Boise, Sawtooth, Challis, Targhee, Caribou, Humboldt, and Umatilla. Two national parks—Grand Teton and Yellowstone—are drained in part by the Snake, as are Craters of the Moon National Monument, in Idaho, and Hells Canyon National Recreation Area, which straddles the Oregon–Idaho border. The U.S. Army Corps of Engineers owns several dams in the watershed, most notably the Ice Harbor, Lower Monumental, Little Goose, and Lower Granite on the lower Snake, four dams that have been proposed for removal because of their adverse effect on Snake River salmon populations. To complete the picture, the Department of Defense operates Saylor Creek Air Force Range, the Department of Energy operates both the Idaho National Engineering and Environmental Laboratory (formerly the National Reactor Testing Station), and the Department of Agriculture operates the Dubois Experimental Station within the drainage.

How, then, might this complex basin create a new system of sovereignty? Assume first that the Three Sovereigns proposal for the Columbia basin as a whole stalls, in one of the number of ways it may indeed stall, but that the various interests along the Snake decide that enough key issues in their drainage simply are not being satisfactorily resolved by the existing system and that they should try to negotiate a new governing structure for their particular tributary of the Columbia. Assume that the major stakeholders in the basin work out, over a period of years (and no doubt hundreds of meetings), a vision for an ecologically and economically sustainable way of inhabiting the watershed, including new levels of cooperation among the sovereign tribes and their neighbors. Assume finally that the experience of all these stakeholders has persuaded them that the "irrepressible conflict" between centralized public lands management and place-based collaboration must be resolved if their vision is to have any chance of realizing itself. Not only must it be resolved, but now, they are convinced, it must be resolved in favor of watershed democracy. So they read Powell's speech once again, and then they persuade their governors, tribal councils, and congressional delegations to begin working on a Snake River Compact. Their message, which they ask their political leaders to convey to Washington for them, is roughly this:

Snake River Compact Proposal

We do not currently seek any change in the status of the properties of the Department of Defense and Department of Energy within the Snake River drainage, and while we expect the National Park Service to manage Yellowstone and Teton National Parks in ways that are responsive to the needs of the entire basin, we seek no devolution of authority over the parks. But in order to pursue in a consistent and effective way the ecologically and humanly sustainable vision we have developed, we seek control of all Bureau of Land Management and Forest Service lands in the basin. We are prepared to impose on those lands an enforceable public trust committing us to keep them public in perpetuity and to manage them for sustainable ecosystem health. We will create by the trust instrument a basinwide governing structure capable of fulfilling all these responsibilities. To give the trust ironclad enforceability, and at the same time to transfer title to the land in question to the trust, all six states and all three tribes will enter into an agreement under the Compact Clause of the United States Constitution, and we will work together to obtain from the rest of the country the congressional approval mandated by that clause.

Such a compact would, of course, be a very complex document, with a multitude of issues to be covered. The people in the basin, for example, might very well find it advantageous to retain the services of some or all of the BLM and Forest Service employees currently managing these districts, in which case there may need to be clauses in the compact concerning job or pension security or hiring preferences. The language about ecosystem health and sustainability would obviously be crucial for congressional approval. The compact might end up containing not only a guarantee that the land would remain public in perpetuity (except for land exchanges that would enhance the public estate), but also a guarantee that the land would be managed for ecosystem viability and sustainability, perhaps promising that each succeeding generation would inherit healthier ecosystems than the generation before.

The point in suggesting this hypothetical compact is not to fill in all the blanks or to anticipate even a small percentage of the objections that the very mention of such a possibility will certainly provoke. The purpose, rather, is to invite discussion and debate about the shifts in sovereignty over western public lands that Americans have ever greater reason to expect in the coming decades. The more open, thoughtful, and creative those discussions are, the more likely they will be to prove helpful when some watershed somewhere in the West does in fact begin to develop such a proposal.

Suppose, then, that something even vaguely similar to this hypothetical Snake River Compact were negotiated and approved for some western watershed. What then? Or, perhaps more helpfully, within what larger governing structure might such a self-governing watershed operate over the long term? Here, the level of uncertainty and speculation is at least as high as with the hypothetical compact, but here again there is value in beginning to think some way into the governing structures that might best fit this region for the foreseeable future.

One almost inevitable accompaniment to any site-specific watershed compact would be a West-wide regional coalescence. The first step in this direction might simply be a matter of political calculation. It is nearly inconceivable that anything like the Snake River Compact could ever gain congressional approval unless it was supported by a strongly united western congressional phalanx. The next chapter explores the political realignment that might make this possible. If western political leaders could indeed unite in support of any basin compact that included substantial devolution of authority over public lands, this would almost certainly set in motion a domino-like chain of events. Once regional political support had been mobilized for one such basin-specific compact, the same dynamics that had produced that agreement would almost certainly move even more quickly and smoothly to similar agreements in other western watersheds. At some point, this piecemeal dismantling of the centralized public lands system would begin noticeably to exacerbate the strains already afflicting that system. In other words, if watershed democracy ever gains a foothold in the West through something like a Snake River Compact, it will very likely spread from one basin to another, gaining momentum and legitimacy while casting into ever sharper relief the damaged legitimacy of the national system. This dual dynamic could be expected to lead in due course to a much more comprehensive West-wide proposal for wholesale devolution of public land governance.

The BLM in particular, with all its lands situated in the West, would be a natural candidate for a West-wide interstate compact to devolve ownership of all its lands to the kind of perpetual trust arrangements described in the Snake River basin example. Similar proposals for western Forest Service lands could not lag far behind. But even though such far-reaching proposals for public land devolution might come in the form of West-wide interstate compacts, they need not and should not be proposals to put the state governments themselves in charge. A better mechanism would be a regionwide compact very much along the lines of the hypothetical Snake River Compact. That is, the West-wide compact (which again would require congressional approval) would establish a thoroughly enforceable trust over the BLM and Forest Service lands not already devolved to basinwide trusts. The trust instrument would again guarantee that the lands would remain public in perpetuity, and the trustees would be bound to manage them for ecological sustainability. Consistent with the principle of entrusting responsibility to the people who know the land most intimately, the regionwide compact should contain provisions for further devolution to basin or bioregional trusts. In other words, at this point the West-wide trust, rather than Congress, would be the entity to which river basins or bioregions would make the case of their readiness to assume more localized control over the public lands in their area.

The further into the future we try to focus this picture, of course, the more difficult the effort becomes. In this sense, the story of emerging western sovereignty is very much like the story of grizzly bear reintroduction told in chapter 1. If grizzlies are ever brought back into the Selway-Bitterroot region, it will be possible to make some educated guesses about where they will go and what they will do. But precisely because these are sovereign creatures, there is no way their every movement can be controlled or predicted. Exactly the same is true of the West. The more sovereign it becomes over its own landscape, the more certain it will be to assert that sovereignty on its own terms—in terms only it can discover as it feels and thinks its way into its future.

When we try to imagine a western interstate compact to devolve control over the public lands, we run quickly into this veil of unpredictability. Still, it may be worthwhile to discern whatever emergent patterns may already be presenting themselves, because they are for now the best we can do in terms of glimpsing a trail through these woods. Two or three of those emergent patterns seem likely to hold up over time.

One is that the forces of globalism will continue to exert more and more pressure on the West—as they will on every other subcontinental region. What that means at a minimum is that the West as a region must position itself to take the greatest possible advantage of its comparative strengths within a global economy. These considerations will be crucial to any western proposal for devolution of the public lands. Many of the strongest opponents to any talk of devolution fear that the kind of global positioning the West would be inclined to do would be of the worst kind in terms of ecosystem protection. Certainly the past history of western efforts to decentralize control of the public lands gives weight to these fears, given that it has so often been resource extractors and users who have led the various versions of western resistance to centralized management. It would be naive to think that corporate exploiters are not still poised to take whatever advantage they can of any devolutionary proposal. But the fact is that the West's competitive advantage in the global economy does not center on exploitative resource extraction. In fact, quite the reverse is true. If there is one thing that distinguishes the West today—that makes it both unique and competitive among regions of the world—it is the fact that there are more relatively intact and thriving ecosystems there than anyplace else on earth. The West can secure its global niche only by recognizing that nurturing, protecting, expanding, and enhancing these ecosystems is a far better long-term competitive strategy for the region than would be any short-term exploitation of resources at the expense of ecosystem viability.

There are two ways in which the unique intactness of its ecosystems offers the West a competitive advantage. One is evident in the phenomenal in-migration into the region that has been taking place since the early 1990s. In the increasingly footloose postindustrial economy, more and more people can live and work wherever they choose, and given that choice, more and more people are choosing the West because of the attractiveness of its landscapes. There are still some western political leaders who remain oblivious to this competitive advantage, but as the next chapter argues, they are being increasingly marginalized, and they could not be the political center of gravity in a West that might make a serious and viable proposal for decentralizing sovereignty over western landscapes.

That center of gravity must rest with people who see not only that the West can attract and keep good workers and good businesses by protecting its environment and enhancing the health of its ecosystems, but also that such protection and enhancement is itself a globally significant economic activity. Every part of the world—and indeed the world itself—will be increasingly challenged in the coming decades by the necessity to figure out how human communities can thrive within sustainable and thriving ecosystems. The more pressing this challenge becomes, the more urgently the world will look for lessons and leadership from those places that have come closest to meeting that challenge. No place on earth is better positioned than the American West to serve as the world's classroom in sustainability. And the world will be willing to pay a good price for a good education if the West can coalesce around a regional strategy that puts this activity at the center of its global economic positioning.

This brings us to one more emergent trend to which the West will have to attend if it is to become sovereign over both its landscape and its future. That trend has to do with the growing awareness of the role of cities and city-regions in the global economy. One level down the fractal scale from the subcontinental region lies the metropolitan region, or city-state. Regional expert William R. Dodge, in his book *Regional Excellence*, argues that the metropolitan region "has emerged as the basic unit of competitiveness in the global economy," and goes on to characterize such regions as "the individual stalls in the farmer's market of global opportunities."[13] In *Citistates*, journalists Neal R. Peirce, Curtis W. Johnson, and John Stuart Hall put this phenomenon into historical perspective when they conclude that globalism "drives one to visualize our great cities, their suburbs, exurbs, and geographic realms of influence as citistates, entities that perform as critical actors, more on their own in the world economy than anyone would have dreamed since the birth of the nation-state in the 16th and 17th centuries."[14]

In the emerging global economy, certain North American city-states have already begun to consolidate the kind of competitive advantage that may precede a new form of political self-determination. In Puget Sound—the city-region centered on the Seattle metropolitan area, which in turn lies within the cross-border Cascadia subcontinental region—local brainpower is reshaping the regional economy, moving its center of gravity from aerospace to cyberspace. This puts Seattle and its larger region squarely within the matrix of the global economy and could threaten to turn the Puget Sound region into a place indistinguishable from any other place in the world. But in fact, the region's capacity to optimize its global role is dependent on its capacity to maintain a distinctive regional identity. The brainpower that makes the region so competitive at the global scale comes attached to individuals, who in their turn are attached to families, all with very high standards about the kind of place in which they choose to make their contributions to the global economy. And the very competitiveness of that economy is likely to push city-regions to develop effective structures of sovereignty. If the Puget Sound region, for example, cannot organize itself in such a way as to maintain a good and satisfying life for its new workforce, then eventually some other, more creative and effective region will edge it out.

Peirce, Johnson, and Hall analyzed the Puget Sound area in *Citistates*, concluding: "If the people of this region insist, they can have it all: exemplary environmental protection, shared economic progress, and design of true international distinction. But none of that will happen if they don't care, won't make decisions, won't accept some sacrifices." In 1993, Peirce and his coauthors predicted that "single-city solutions" would not be adequate to meet the region's challenges head-on: only a truly coordinated regional governing structure would do the job.[15] Although Seattle has not yet followed these authors' recommendation to consolidate responsibility and accountability in a regionwide popularly elected body, the Puget Sound Regional Council, formed in 1992 out of the ashes of the ineffective Puget Sound Council of Governments, has created a new and promising model for regional growth management and transportation planning.

Other metropolitan areas, particularly in America's interior West, have a long way to go before they can claim a comparable competitive advantage through their organization as true city-states. Within the West, city-regions are only beginning to understand that the competitiveness of the global economy requires them to operate as the real metropolitan economies they are while still recognizing the identity and autonomy of their component parts. Moreover, they are only barely beginning to sense how competitively damaging the old structures of sovereignty have become.

For an instructive example, take the case of Idaho. Fly north out of Salt Lake City, Utah, and you will see how that city serves as a hub for Ogden and Logan and for other settlements scattered across the floor of prehistoric Lake Bonneville. Then, before you know it, the settlements you are seeing, still manifestly lying within Salt Lake City's orbit, are in fact Idaho towns and cities. Pocatello clearly lies within that orbit, and in the increasingly fierce competitiveness of the global economy, Pocatello and Salt Lake City either will learn to think of their interests as operating within and being served by that city-region context or they will see those interests increasingly ill-served.

Meanwhile, far to the north in the Idaho panhandle sits Coeur d'Alene, separated from the state capital, Boise, by all but impassable mountain ranges. Coeur d'Alene bears no tangible economic connection to Boise, yet it is governed by Boise as if there were or ever could be such a thing as "the Idaho economy." The global economy merely laughs at such fictions. Its brutal disregard of them threatens to leave behind a place such as Spokane, Washington, because it is prevented by a state boundary from fully developing its natural connection to Coeur d'Alene, a mere thirty miles away within the easily and daily traversed valley of the Spokane River.

Finally, the highly entrepreneurial city of Boise does its best to position itself to play an effective global role, a role that has next to nothing to do with its being a state capital but everything to do with its serving as the hub of an economic region that reaches throughout the Snake River drainage. In these terms—which are the only terms that count anymore—Boise has vastly more reason to concern itself with Ontario, Oregon, situated where the Snake unwittingly crosses the Idaho–Oregon line, than it ever will have to concern itself with Coeur d'Alene. Yet the existing structures of sovereignty force Boise to meddle in Coeur d'Alene's affairs and prevent it from developing its natural relations with Ontario.

This state of affairs probably cannot last. The forces of globalism and continentalism will almost certainly lead a growing number of street-smart leaders in western cities to begin comparing notes about how damaging the existing structures of sovereignty are to their well-being. The West will move a step closer to being a globally significant and competitive player when farsighted business and civic leaders in Edmonton, Calgary, Spokane, Salt Lake City, Denver, and Albuquerque start thinking of their region not as a collection of arbitrarily bounded states and provinces but as a network of various mountain-defined city-regions and then start asking one another what global niche they might find themselves occupying together.

Chapter 5 suggested that for a variety of reasons, the West may be poised to play a leading role in the global emergence of more organic, land-conforming governing structures. If that is so, one type of change the West might well model is the use of old structures of sovereignty to shelter the emergence of newer, more viable forms. States and counties, not to mention nations, will certainly continue to function for some time in their existing format, but increasingly their role may be to serve as protective shells or incubators for the emergence of those more organic forms for which global competition is showing an ever stronger preference. How might this unfold in the West, and how might events within the region influence changes in governing forms elsewhere? One very likely change would be a revival of both the theory and practice of federalism.

Americans are so accustomed to calling the government of the United States a "federal" government that they have nearly forgotten what true federalism would look like: namely, a voluntary association of sovereigns in which the federated government has only the authority those internal sovereigns agree to give it. The government of the United States has become thoroughly national; it is not and has not since the Civil War been genuinely federal. But history never stands still, and the West, in pursuit of its own interests, may have no choice but to make the case for a renewal of federalism.

The hypothetical Snake River Compact provides a good starting point for imagining such emergent federal forms in the West. If a drainage like the Snake ever did succeed in becoming, by compact or otherwise, genuinely self-governing, it would create tremendous pressure on surrounding areas—especially, in the case of the Snake, on other Columbia basin subdrainages—to follow a similar course. City-regions and bioregions could be expected to follow this course in tandem. In the West, the two kinds of regions often coincide, just as Boise's city-region corresponds closely to the Snake River drainage. We can imagine, then, similar compacts and similar new governing structures up and down the Columbia basin—for example, on the Clark Fork River (the Missoula city-region), the Willamette River (Portland), or the Yakima River. Sooner or later, these self-governing subdrainages within the Columbia basin would almost certainly enter into compacts among themselves to create a Columbia governing structure capable of addressing basinwide issues. At that point, they would be back to the scale of the Three Sovereigns proposal—and they might then have a governing structure in place that could accomplish what the current public land management system has been almost totally unable to accomplish through the Interior Columbia Basin Ecosystem Management Project (ICBEMP).

This picture takes us so far beyond the current system of governance that it may begin to sound like science fiction. Yet it is science itself that encourages us to try to imagine the governing forms that will be appropriate to this new millennium.

In attempting to discern which forms are now most adaptive at the geopolitical level of life, complexity theorist Stuart Kauffman hypothesizes that the most viable structure for the new millennium will be "a federal system with partitioning into local semiautonomous regions."[16]

What Kauffman prescribes seems in fact to be occurring. From the global scale on down, the chief organizing principle of the postindustrial age seems to be that of natural, organic landforms related to one another in federal structures. The continental-scale federation of the European Union is one obvious example, but in many other places as well, new levels of organization are already tiering down, from continents to subcontinental regions to increasingly self-determining bioregions, watersheds, and city-states. The federal nature of this structure is still emerging, but what it implies everywhere is that at each level of organization, each naturally defined place will be sovereign in its own domain, with power to shape its own affairs up to the point at which its choices significantly affect neighboring places. Government power in this model would be apportioned according to an "ascending hierarchy," regionalist James Gardner suggests, "with regulatory authority vested in the lowest level at which it can be competently exercised."[17] Before long, we should expect to see the emergence of a genuinely federal form of governance even at the global scale. It will probably not be a federation of nations, which are becoming so painfully irrelevant to this emergent order, but it may well be a federation of autonomous continents.

We have a continental model for the kind of federalism that might emerge at the global scale in the late-twentieth-century metamorphosis of Europe's political economy, which also serves as a model for the kind of political leadership we should now watch for in a region such as the American West. Following World War II, continental Europe found itself so battered and torn that it seemed entirely likely to relinquish its proud tradition of world leadership and self-determination and sink into a position of vassalage to the world's two new superpowers. Against that threat, a handful of wise and visionary leaders, led by Jean Monnet, Robert Schuman, and Konrad Adenauer, decided that the only alternative to that unacceptable future lay along a path that to most observers seemed all but impassable. They concluded that the ancient, bitter intracontinental enmities, particularly that between France and Germany, must be subordinated to the common cause of strengthening Europe and positioning it to play an effective global role as a federated continent. Now, decades later, a truly federal continental government has been created. It is federal in the sense that the continental government has exactly as much authority as the subcontinental sovereigns have agreed to give it. Although this particular model of continental government is specific to its own setting, its federated structure seems likely to play out in different forms on other continents and, eventually, among continents at the scale of a federated global government, without which global capital cannot be held accountable to human and ecological concerns.

If, as Stuart Kauffman suggests, the world is sorting itself into "a federal system with partitioning into local semiautonomous regions," we should expect this emergent phenomenon to manifest itself at several different levels simultaneously. Chapter 5 argued that because of the dominance of landscape in the West and because of the region's unique relationship to the national government, the West may be at the forefront of Kauffman's "partitioning into local semiautonomous regions."

The time may not be so remote when leaders of city-regions and watersheds in the American West, like the visionary European leaders of the 1950s, will recognize their common interest, recognize how imperative it is in the global context that they act together, and begin asking how the real places they speak for can claim their own appropriate forms of self-government. They might then ask how those sovereign bioregions and city-regions can most effectively federate themselves into a larger, globally significant regional sovereignty, which might be called the Rocky Mountain West. Whether or not the region walks that path, it seems increasingly likely that in order to secure its natural global niche, the West may have no choice but to claim control over its own land base. But as the next chapter will discuss, the West can seize this opportunity only if it learns how to overcome the deep political divisions that until now have so seriously stunted the region's potential.

Chapter 9

Realigning
Western
Politics

"The West cannot carry what it has lifted."
—Wallace Stegner

Wallace Stegner's claim that the West had lifted more than it could carry[1] referred specifically to western water policy, but his evocative phrase might now be applied even more accurately to the region's public lands policy. For a century, westerners have begged, pleaded, and often demanded to be given jurisdiction over the public lands. In one way or another—whether through pilot projects or basin compacts or a West-wide compact—the region may well begin to see that wish fulfilled. The question then will be whether the West *can* carry what it has lifted— whether it can carry off in a responsible and sustainable way the management of its remarkable landscapes.

The question is not whether westerners are smart enough or experienced enough to do this work; clearly they are. The unresolved question is whether they can muster the political will—backed by the breadth of consensus—that will be required to convince the rest of the country that westerners should be entrusted with such a responsibility. The question, in other words, is at bottom a matter of politics.

Chapter 5 moved from Stegner's claim that "no place is a place until it has had a poet" to his claim that he had "pretty consistently despised [the West's] most powerful politicians and the general trend of their politics."[2] Here, it is time to confront seriously the question of whether the West can be a place, in the sense that it now needs to be a place, if its politics remain so widely despised—and if not, what kind of politics the West might be prepared to generate instead.

The West does in fact need a new politics. It is getting it, slowly, from the ground up, in the form of collaboration. This is where the transformation of western politics is most likely to come from. But how will this transformation play out in what we more commonly think of as politics—namely, partisan politics? As with the re-visioning of sovereignty, it is impossible to predict details of this political transformation with any confidence. Some form of political realignment is indispensable if the West is to break the old rebel-versus-empire standoff of its embedded politics. If such a realignment were to occur, it could come either in the reshaping of one or the other party, or both parties, or in the emergence of a new, openly regional party. The likelihoods diminish as we progress through that list, but it would be a mistake to rule out any of these options.

This book has more than once drawn historical parallels between America in the 1850s and the American West of a century and a half later. In terms of partisan politics, the 1850s were the period of greatest political upheaval in the nation's history. One old political party (the Whigs—the party of Abraham Lincoln at the beginning of the decade) disappeared altogether before the decade ended; several parties (including the Know-Nothings, or the American Party, and the Free-Soilers) appeared and disappeared over the course of the decade. One old party, the Democratic Party, survived, but only after being so seriously split along regional lines that it nominated two presidential candidates in 1860: John Breckinridge in the South and Stephen A. Douglas in the North and West. One new party, the Republican Party, rose from the detritus of all the turmoil, fashioned in six short years both the narrowest and the most overwhelmingly regional plurality in the country's history, and elected Abraham Lincoln president in 1860. The South, which was then and would remain for a century a Republican-free zone, immediately seceded.

The simple, pretty much incontestable historical lesson is that when regionalism becomes a powerful force, it can powerfully affect politics. It already has done so in the interior West, making the region at the beginning of the twenty-first century by far the most Republican section of the country. It is the old politics of the Old West that has created that picture. There is already a new politics emerging beneath the surface of that map, and it will soon, almost certainly, redraw the political map of the region. What it will then look like is as unpredictable as the political map of the country in 1860 would have been in 1850. But just as no one could understand the new politics of 1860 without understanding what had gone before (and what had gone awry), so it is that the place to start in the West is with the old politics that has become so deeply entrenched. For at least a decade before the turn of the century, the partisan politics of the West, at least regarding public land and natural resource issues, had fallen into a highly predictable pattern. It was a pattern that clearly gave the advantage to the Republicans within the region but often worked to the Democrats' advantage outside the West.

During the 1998 elections, I happened to be on the East

Coast, where I had the chance to hear a leading Democratic tactician analyze the election results and draw lessons for the 2000 election from them. Not surprisingly, one of the tactical thrusts had to do with consolidating and advancing the gains Democrats had made in what was threatening to become the solidly Republican South. Emboldened by this mention of regional politics, I asked whether there was any Democratic concern about the tightening Republican grip on the interior West. While I thought I knew the answer, I was not quite prepared for the brutal frankness with which it was delivered. "There isn't anybody there," this hard-boiled New Democrat replied. "There are fewer electoral votes in the interior West than in Pennsylvania. We have to concentrate our attention where the votes are." (It would actually take only six of the least populous public lands states—Alaska, Montana, Wyoming, Idaho, Utah, and New Mexico—to add up to Pennsylvania's twenty-three electoral votes. But the message is clear, and the point is taken—taken quite resentfully by westerners.)

The national Democratic Party's willingness to trade off votes from the "empty" (or at least nearly empty) West to garner support from the more coastal-based national environmental groups was dramatically exemplified by President Bill Clinton's designation of Grand Staircase–Escalante National Monument in 1996. The area covered by the new monument is rich in coal and minerals and therefore is seen as an economic resource for Utah. Clinton, who never had any chance of carrying Utah but might do better in Phoenix-dominated Arizona, chose to announce the creation of the Utah monument from the Arizona rim of the Grand Canyon. The voters of Utah quickly used the one means they had available to repudiate this action when they withdrew their support from the only Democrat then serving in the state's congressional delegation, Representative Bill Orton, and replaced him with Republican challenger

Christopher Cannon. Orton, who represented Utah's vast and sparsely populated Third District, covering the area where the new monument is located, tried to distance himself from the president's action by condemning it roundly. However, his southern Utah constituents were not moved and overwhelmingly voted for his Republican opponent. But from the national Democratic Party's perspective, the loss of this lone Democrat in the Utah delegation was a reasonable price to pay for the votes and support of the national environmental groups that saw the creation of the monument as a major victory. Undeniably, these actions have lost Democrats support among westerners. But then, these are the people who essentially do not exist in the tactical calculations of the national Democratic Party.

The relationship between national environmental and local western politics was exemplified at century's end in the proposal for a congressionally mandated "zero cut" policy on public lands. This campaign, which would halt all commercial logging in national forests, was originally coordinated by thirteen environmental groups, including the Sierra Club, the Native Forest Network, the John Muir Project, and the Inland Empire Public Lands Council. The National Forest Protection and Restoration Act, which proposed to end commercial logging on Forest Service and BLM lands and in national wildlife refuges, was introduced in 1997 by Representatives Cynthia McKinney, a Democrat from Georgia, and Jim Leach, a Republican from Iowa. In spite of its veneer of bipartisan sponsorship, this was a Democratic bill: of its thirty-one cosponsors, only two were Republicans. Not surprisingly, none of the sponsors was from the interior West or from any district dominated by public lands. In the West, where many small communities still depend on timber production from the public lands, this proposal is seen as just one more instance of nonwesterners (mostly Democrats) trying to exercise from afar a centralized dominion over western landscapes, with substantial adverse effects on the communities those westerners care so much about.

This kind of national approach to environmental issues still has great appeal to national environmental groups, which find in it not only a way to advance what they are convinced is good environmental policy but also an effective way to build membership around an emotionally appealing position. National environmental groups reward those congressional and presidential candidates (again, mostly Democrats) whose votes support the extension of the nationalist approach. This gains votes and contributions for Democrats outside the West, but within the region it has contributed to the party's steady decline. So far, the Democrats have found the trade-off acceptable, if not positively beneficial. This, then, is a snapshot of the Democratic side of the old western politics. We get a glimpse of the Republican approach from a different kind of story, which also enables us to see how these old western politics have been preventing the West from dealing creatively and adaptively with the historical forces now at work within and upon the region.

In June 1998, a report that *High Country News* called "perhaps the most far-sighted federal study of Western water since John Wesley Powell's visionary *Report on the Lands of the Arid Region of the United States*," was released.[3] The report was titled *Water in the West: The Challenge for the Next Century*. Its origins were impressive. The Western Water Policy Review Act of 1992 had directed the president of the United States to undertake a comprehensive review of activities in western states affecting the use and allocation of water.[4] The twenty-two-member Western Water Policy Review Advisory Commission (WWPRAC) was empowered and directed to conduct a study and produce a report on the state of water issues and policy in the West. The commission, which was officially chartered by Secretary of the Interior Bruce Babbitt in 1995, consisted of eight citizen members appointed by President Clinton, twelve members of Congress with jurisdiction over water programs, and the secretaries of the Department of the Interior and the Department of the Army.

Three years later, the commission completed its work and issued its report. A government press release declared the report's intention to be to "reorient federal programs so they further the sustainability of the West's people and environment" and asserted that all the commission's recommendations were made "within the context of an increased emphasis on watershed and basin management."[5] The report described what it called "troubling" trends in the West: a rapidly increasing population contributing to a loss of open space, degraded aquatic systems and water quality, pressing water supply problems, unrealized Indian water rights, a suffering agricultural economy, and increasing damage from both drought and floods.

In its broad analysis, the report validated and championed the recent upwelling of local watershed-level initiatives across the West. It called on the federal government to create links with existing watershed councils and "capitalize on the sense of ownership and obligation to others that exists foremost at the community level."[6] The report then went on to make sweeping recommendations for structural change that are indeed reminiscent of John Wesley Powell's recommendations: "We propose a change in the function and approach of the federal resource agencies to a 'nested' governance structure [that] reflects the hydrologic, social, legal, and political realities of the watershed."[7] This new governance structure for western river basins, the report stated, should not necessarily be implemented all at once but should be tested through a series of pilot projects. The report suggested that these pilot projects should focus on "experimentation and evolution," testing out a variety of approaches, including basin-level cooperative processes and mechanisms for securing and sustaining watershed-level funding.[8] The report's explicit reform message is contained in this excerpt from the executive summary:

> We anticipate that during the next century, the federal resources management agencies will undergo widespread realignment of their organizational and enforcement functions. Recognizing how slowly governmental institutions change, in this report we recommend a partial reorganization of functions which can be immediately implemented within the present governmental agency framework.[9]

It was not only the report itself that evoked memories of John Wesley Powell. The response to it was vividly reminiscent of the wall of opposition that eventually precluded enactment of any of the reforms Powell had suggested. Although the report asserted repeatedly that its goal was to empower watershed-level management entities and to acknowledge and incorporate "the successes that westerners are already bringing about to make government more responsive to local needs," critics argued that the essence of the report's final recommendation was nothing but "an imitation of the experiment in federally mandated river basin commissions that was tried and failed in the 1960s."[10] Although the report explicitly stated that the commission was not suggesting an expansion of federal power, some of the report's opponents insisted that it sought to dismantle states' authority in water allocation and management matters. The Western States Water Council contended, for example, that "the report's overall reliance on federal action and authority contrasts with existing interstate compacts and the growing recognition of the pivotal role states must play if we are to successfully deal with the complex challenges we face in water resources."[11] Patrick O'Toole, a Wyoming rancher and himself

a member of the commission, disagreed with the report's sin-
gling out of agriculture as the West's biggest polluter. In a dissenting letter, O'Toole spoke out against the proposed expansion of the federal Environmental Protection Agency's powers
and the diversion of water used for agriculture to other uses.

What western Republicans seemed most alert to in this situation was an opportunity to translate these criticisms of the
report into the particular form of anti-Washington rhetoric that
has contributed so substantially to Republican ascendancy in the
region. In this case, Alaska's all-Republican delegation took the
lead. Senator Frank Murkowski called the report "a thinly dis-
guised cover for the Administration's continuing assault on federalism and the primacy of State water law," while his Alaska
colleagues Ted Stevens and Don Young contended that the
report should not be issued at all because "it will only serve the
interests of a handful of activists who . . . seek to federalize water
in an effort to control and redistribute the resource."[12] With this
kind of criticism coming from the majority party in a steady bar-
rage, the work of the commission was practically guaranteed to
come to nothing. In fact, over the years western Republicans
had turned this kind of activity into a fine art. No matter how
benign any federal initiative might be, if it affected the West and
could be used to rouse the old western resentment of national
domination of the region, western Republicans could be
counted on to play that card.

This book has been built on the assumption that the future
of the West must involve a radical and permanent transcendence
of the region's embedded struggle between imperial-type environmentalism and Sagebrush Rebellion–type resistance. This
transcendence will in turn depend on a major political realignment in the West. What might that realignment look like? If in
fact the spread of collaboration across the West carries political
implications, those implications should start to play themselves

out in the language and positions of western politicians. Perhaps surprisingly, it will be easier to detect that change among western Republicans than among Democrats.

Ed Marston, publisher of *High Country News* and one of the West's most perceptive observers, provides one intriguing glimpse of this shift. In a February 2000 editorial titled "Craig versus Craig: May the Best Man Win," Marston began by characterizing Idaho senator Larry Craig as "the best friend the timber industry, the dam operators, and the dirt bikers ever had." Marston went on to call Craig "the Father of the Salvage Logging Rider—the West's most notorious law of the 1990s, which gave the timber industry yet another whack at public forests."

Craig had been, in fact, throughout the 1990s, exactly the kind of western representative to whom environmentalists could always point complacently when anyone suggested that the West should be given more control over the public lands. "So you want to turn them over to the kind of people westerners elect— people like Larry Craig," they would say with argument-clinching finality. And indeed, the West did seem to love to elect such people, with a regularity and enthusiasm that made it hard to see why such Republicans should ever abandon the anti-Washington stance that had turned the West into a one-party region. In the U.S. Senate alone, you could name Frank Murkowski of Alaska, Slade Gorton of Washington, Gordon Smith of Oregon, Orrin Hatch of Utah, Jon Kyl of Arizona, Wayne Allard of Colorado, Craig Thomas of Wyoming, and Conrad Burns of Montana and still leave plenty of other, similar western Republicans unnamed before circling back to Craig of Idaho, who, at least on national forest policy, set the pace and the tone for all of them.

Yet something was troubling Larry Craig; something was making him reexamine his party's position on public land issues, and Ed Marston was there to observe and report it. At a conference sponsored by the Center for the New West in Denver in

February 2000, Marston watched Craig display two different personas. One was the old Larry Craig, the "Father of the Salvage Logging Rider," whose banquet address Marston described in this way: "[Craig] warned against 'extreme environmentalists' and their dirty, low-down tricks and their attempts to destroy the West. It was one hell of a speech, and the Wyoming rancher next to me destroyed several tissues sopping up tears streaming down her face."[13] But Marston had also seen another Larry Craig at the conference—one who "listened attentively to the accounts of consensus efforts among loggers, miners, environmentalists and federal managers that dominated the conference."[14]

These two very different approaches led Marston, quite properly, to ask, "Which is the real McCoy: the conciliatory, compromise-seeking Craig, or the hell-and-damnation Craig?" The answer: "For the moment, both, as he tests the waters."[15] During the first months of the new century it was too early to tell, either in Craig's individual case or in the case of western Republicans in general, whether a genuine shift was afoot. But there were good reasons to believe that something new might be emerging within the western wing of the Republican Party. Craig's positive attentiveness to collaborative methods may have been new to him, but his junior Idaho colleague, Senator Mike Crapo, had long and enthusiastically embraced the collaborative approach, crediting the Henry's Fork Watershed Council in eastern Idaho with having taught him how promising such local, cross-ideological problem solving could be.

By the time Crapo joined Craig in the Idaho senate delegation in 1998, he was one of a growing number of western Republicans who, while remaining impeccably conservative on most fiscal and social issues, were making the western collaboration movement an integral part of their political platforms. Montana's hugely popular governor, Marc Racicot, for example, used collaborative processes aggressively in addressing such endangered species challenges as the bull trout, and he at least conditionally endorsed the collaboratively created Citizen Management Alternative for grizzly bear reintroduction along the Montana–Idaho border.

If there was Republican movement in this direction during the 1990s, and if there was leadership to that movement, the strongest and most visible leadership was provided by Utah's governor, Michael Leavitt. It was Leavitt who joined hands across party lines with Oregon's Democratic governor, John Kitzhaber, to create under the aegis of the Western Governors' Association the so-called Enlibra principles. The governors described these principles as a new "shared western doctrine for environmental management." According to the governors, "the doctrine speaks to greater participation and collaboration in decision making, focuses on outcomes rather than just programs, and recognizes the need for a variety of tools beyond regulation that will improve environmental and natural resource management."[16]

If Leavitt's sponsorship of the Enlibra principles signaled any kind of shift within the Republican Party in the West, it was a shift with deeply pragmatic roots. The pragmatism was reflected in the Enlibra principles themselves, especially in their reference to results-based evaluation of environmental benefits. One of the principles states, "Reward results, not programs—move to a performance-based system,"[17] which is about as pragmatic as a principle can be. But this pragmatism was more than a slogan for someone like Leavitt, and it would be difficult to comprehend any realignment that might be emerging within the Republican Party in the West without paying close attention to what lies behind this strand of pragmatism. The fact is that the Republicans, who have ridden their anti-Washington demagoguery to political dominance throughout the region, are beginning to recognize that winning every office in sight does not translate directly or easily into fulfilling the deepest desires of the people who put them in office. Winning office, in other words, is not the same thing as governing effectively. And although few Democrats would want to admit it, more and more western Republicans have been displaying a demonstrable concern with governing effectively.

Dirk Kempthorne of Idaho provided a telling example of this tension between acquiring office and getting something done. Kempthorne moved from the Boise mayor's office to the United States Senate in 1986. He served two terms in the Senate, where he was eventually joined by Larry Craig. Like Craig, he could readily have translated the tried-and-true anti-Washington Republican formula into as many terms as he might desire. But in 1998, Kempthorne left the Senate to return to Idaho and run for the office of governor. "Kempthorne attributes the move from senator to governor . . . to a desire to return home where the action is, now that the [1994] Republican revolution has returned power to the states," the *Idaho Post Register* reported. "It's a devolution of power Kempthorne prizes."[18]

Kempthorne's move from the Senate to the governorship might be understood as personally idiosyncratic, but in fact it reflects a discernible shift within the Republican Party in the West—a shift from ideological showmanship to pragmatic governing "where the action is." An unexpected component of that shift is a steadily stronger embrace by western Republicans of collaborative groups, processes, and techniques. In a sense, what this amounts to is the extrapolation of one of the key elements of collaboration to the realm of politics. By and large, people across the West who have spent decades fighting (and detesting) one another do not turn to collaboration out of kindheartedness or spiritual conversion. They do it because it works—because it solves problems that none of the existing political or administrative mechanisms has succeeded in solving. Larry Craig describes this as "an explosion of down-home creativity in solving public lands conflicts through consensus-based approaches throughout the West."[19] It is not surprising that pragmatic Republicans such as Leavitt, Racicot, and Crapo have embraced collaboration as one means of pursuing the hands-on, problem-solving, "get it done" governing that brought Dirk Kempthorne back to Idaho.

But the potential of the collaboration movement to nudge western Republicans in a new direction may not stop with the embrace of collaboration itself. Part of what so often makes collaboration work in local settings is the willingness of the ranchers or loggers or miners at the table to acknowledge the importance of the environmental values on which those on the other side of the table insist. That acknowledgment often sticks in the throats of people at those tables who believe that their communities and their livelihoods have been threatened by the top-down, "take it or leave it" way in which the old system has so often presented those environmental values. But at those local collaborative tables, it has repeatedly become clear that a more homegrown articulation of the importance of protecting ecosystems is a precondition to any collaborative solution that might sustain those communities and maintain those livelihoods. It may be, then, because so many of Larry Craig's rancher, logger, and miner supporters and constituents have sat at those tables and acknowledged those environmental values that Craig could say in late 1999, "We dare not abandon the national environmental ethic fostered through a long struggle by the laws passed by Congress during the 1960s and 1970s." "In my view," Craig went on, "this environmental ethic has been accepted and internalized to the point [that] it guides how we act and think. Most important, this ethic is a constant consideration in how we set public policy priorities."[20]

Does Craig mean this? Even if he does, can the Republican Party in the West adopt this environmental ethic as part of its standard operating framework? Only time will tell. Most Democrats who know the old Larry Craig and the old Republican Party in the West feel more or less smugly certain that such statements are only window dressing on Craig's part, or on the part of any Republican who might adopt a similar stance. But there is danger in such Democratic smugness, and Craig himself puts his finger squarely on that danger. He begins by acknowledging that for several years the resource interests and the accompanying Republican ideology were so powerful in the West that they could afford to ignore the forces of historical change:

> During the early 1980's, I found public land users— the timber, cattle and mining interests—defensive because of the previous 15 years of congressional action, which had ushered in a new framework of national environmental laws and a broader environmental ethic. Instead of embracing environmental awareness and responding to the need to create a sustainable balance, public land users elected to hang onto their previous vision of the world. They stood pat against all odds, even as natural resources managers in the Forest Service and Bureau of Land Management struggled to reflect these new statutory mandates and environmental ethic. In the end, this strong sense of denial among the public land users and those of us who represent them in the Congress overcame any instinct to seize the moment.[21]

Now, Craig is implying, as western Republicans embrace collaborative processes and incorporate from those local efforts their embrace of an environmental ethic, it is the Democrats and their national environmental allies who are in danger of being bypassed by history:

The national power structure today is as defensive as the structure that existed 20 years ago. Only now, it's the national environmental organizations who have replaced the national public lands user groups as the reigning establishment in Washington, D.C.

Nevertheless, the status quo is changing. Through local consensus based efforts, we have the capacity and resources to establish a responsible and inclusive sustainable balance between people and their land. Those unwilling to work together in this dynamic environment should consider themselves an endangered species. History suggests they will either adapt or disappear.[22]

It is not altogether clear why Senator Craig should warn key components of the Democratic Party about forces of history about to overwhelm them. It may be no more than a matter of delight in pointing out the error of the enemy's ways. But whether consciously or not, Craig may have been exercising an even more fundamental form of pragmatism than any that has yet been encountered. In the long run, no matter how powerful the Republican Party becomes or remains in the West, it cannot hope to accomplish anything substantial on the ground, especially on public lands issues, except on a bipartisan basis. No matter how weak Democrats are in the region, they can always, if pushed to it, enlist in defense of the current public lands system the support of nonwestern Democrats (and some nonwestern Republicans) backed by those national environmental groups Craig describes. Only a West capable of exercising an unaccustomed kind of bipartisan solidarity can hope to enact even a modest version of a western public lands agenda, let alone an agenda like the one described in chapter 8. No major river basin compact to create more decentralized structures of sovereignty, and certainly no regionwide compact to devolve authority over western public lands, could ever receive congressional approval in the absence of such a unified, bipartisan western approach.

What, then, would it take for western Democrats to play their part in that scenario? The change they would have to make is even more challenging than the one Republicans have already begun to make. In the case of the Democrats, it may be helpful to go back to the very origins of their very old party to get a perspective on that challenge. The 200th anniversary of the Democratic Party's rise to power with Thomas Jefferson's move into the White House in 1801 provides an unusual opportunity for all Democrats, but especially western Democrats, to remember why their party came into being in the first place, what has made it the world's most enduring political party, and what might enable it to play a constructive role in the emerging West.

For much of its long history, the Democratic Party was referred to by friend and foe alike simply as "the Democracy." It got that name because it vigorously and stubbornly espoused the cause of democracy in the face of very substantial segments of American society that had grave doubts about democracy as a way of ordering human affairs. The Democratic Party has survived so long not, finally, because it has served the interests of the poor or the downtrodden; still less, the interests of the middle class. It has not earned its place in history by forging a coalition of groups that see themselves as one or another kind of victim or by carefully calibrating its platform to what key swing voters enticed into focus groups say they care most about. What has earned the Democratic Party its place in history has been its commitment to and service of democracy itself.

Jefferson, who was a democrat in philosophy and orientation long before he founded the Democratic Party, was acutely aware that the enterprise of democracy—of people taking into their own hands the governing of their lives together—was a risky and vulnerable undertaking. Nothing in the world guaranteed its success; indeed, most of the world conspired against that success. Only constant vigilance, constant attention to and nurturing of the conditions that sustain democracy, could guarantee its perpetuation through time. Good constitutions and good systems of education were among the favorite Jeffersonian means of securing those conditions. But in the end, Jefferson became convinced that something more was needed: a political party whose central purpose would be to guard and advance the conditions under which democracy could flourish.

Over its 200-year history, the party Jefferson founded has often strayed from its central mission, sometimes disastrously, while other parties have occasionally fulfilled that mission in its stead. But the party has never completely eradicated from its institutional memory that fundamental commitment to democracy. The reason for having a democratic party is not to deliver the goods to some carefully calculated coalition of groups of individuals but to help democratic citizens maintain and extend the conditions that enable them to govern themselves, and to reap the satisfactions that come with self-government.

But this humanly enlarging dimension of democracy is always in danger of being lost, and it has in fact receded whenever some new way is found to take from people (or for people to hand over) the actual work of governing themselves. Jefferson knew this history; he knew this danger. If he could survey the American political system today, particularly from the perspective of the West, he would see a remote, often unresponsive, bought-and-sold decision-making system in which individual citizens have very little direct involvement, and therefore experience very little of the human satisfaction that comes from, taking direct hold of the world and shaping it as they and their neighbors think best.

If we go back to the first decade of the twentieth century,

when Herbert Croly published *The Promise of American Life*, we discover in one historical moment both the roots of the present-day philosophy of the Democratic Party and the roots of the party's current disastrous weakness in the West. Croly wrote his book in response to what he saw as a crisis in American democracy. That crisis centered on the question of how the American people could remain in control of their own lives and their own destiny in the face of the corporate economic forces that had come to dominate the country since the Civil War. For Croly, the crucial question was one of self-determination; it was a question of democracy and of how democracy could retain a vital presence in the face of those economic vectors. Croly's answer to that question required a departure from the old Jeffersonian mistrust of the national government. "Founded as the national government is, partly on a distrust of the democratic principle," Croly wrote, "it has always tended to make the democracy [i.e., the Jeffersonian party] somewhat suspicious of the national government."[23] "There is no reason," however, according to Croly, "why a democracy cannot trust its interests absolutely to the care of the national interest, and there is in particular every reason why the American democracy should become in sentiment and conviction frankly, unscrupulously, and loyally nationalist."[24]

It was the Democratic Party that finally took the path Croly had staked out, and in doing so, it did indeed abandon the Jeffersonian fear of big government. But this itself can be defended as a soundly Jeffersonian move, for Jefferson understood that one key to the perpetuation of democracy through time is that those who are committed to democracy must maintain a remarkable degree of responsiveness to changing circumstances. The very first clause of the Declaration of Independence, the greatest democratic manifesto in history, refers to the never-ending "course of human events," which periodically calls on a democratic people to question, radically, the way in which they are governed. Jefferson's later urging of "a little rebellion now and then" was just another way of making the same essential democratic point: if you are not putting seriously to the test the forms of government you have inherited, if you are not occasionally replacing them with something more suited to changing conditions, it is probably because your have lost your democratic edge.

It was this adaptive dimension of Jeffersonian democracy that Croly was invoking when he argued that the cause of democracy itself now required the abandonment of the old Jeffersonian fear of the national government. Surveying anew the "course of human events," especially the concentration of wealth and economic power that had occurred since the Civil War, Croly concluded that twentieth-century Americans could fulfill their democratic potential only by becoming much more self-consciously nationalist.

One of the earliest and purest manifestations of this New Nationalism was, as chapter 2 recounted, the creation and expansion of the National Forest System. The Forest Service got its start at precisely the same time that the national government was being reconfigured as a much more pervasive presence in American life than it had ever been before. The most visible actor on both fronts was, of course, Theodore Roosevelt, a Republican. It was during Roosevelt's presidency that the Forest Service was created, and it was during his presidency that, by his own (still accurate) words, "there was saved for public use in the National Forests more Government timberland than during all previous and succeeding years put together."[25]

In the end, the Republican Party proved deeply inhospitable to Roosevelt's New Nationalism. After his failed attempt to build a third party on that platform, the Democrats claimed and carried the nationalist banner. From Woodrow Wilson's Federal

Reserve System through Franklin Roosevelt's New Deal and Lyndon Johnson's civil rights legislation, Democrats have consistently turned to the national government to enact their agenda. The nationalizing of environmentalism, a major component of this agenda, has had a major effect on the West, and it has also played a major role in turning that region against the Democratic Party.

The overwhelming regional concentration of the public lands, more than any other factor, accounts for the turn-of-the-century Republican hegemony of the West. The Democratic Party is seen, correctly, as the party most supportive of the national government's domination of the West, whereas the Republican Party is perceived as committed to giving westerners some meaningful control over their beloved landscape. It is, in other words, their most fundamentally democratic instincts that make westerners vote so overwhelmingly Republican. Conversely, what makes the Democratic Party such a minority in the West is that it is widely and rightly perceived by westerners as fundamentally undemocratic. People who care deeply about the unique mountain, prairie, and desert landscapes they inhabit see a Democratic Party committed to policies they perceive as systematically preventing them from exercising meaningful democratic self-determination over their homeland. It is the Democratic Party that they most readily and angrily associate with a paternalistic attitude, which asserts that someone else always knows better than they how they should live their lives and organize their communities. If democracy implies trust in the people to manage their own affairs, the Democrats can only appear as the undemocratic party in the West because they seem never to tire of telling westerners, "We absolutely do not trust you to care for the place you have chosen to inhabit."

This is complicated, of course, by the fact that the Democrats have good reason to be proud of both their vigorous defense of the country's public lands and their environmental record. In fact, what makes the current crisis of the Democratic Party in the West so difficult to resolve is the fact that the party arrived at what has become to so many westerners an undemocratic position by following eminently sound democratic principles. Those most passionately supportive of the American system of public lands see two crucial democratic dimensions to those lands. One has to do with access: these lands, belonging to all citizens, may be entered and enjoyed by all; no one, out of personal greed or exclusiveness, can fence anyone out. Of equal importance is the fact that these lands, belonging to all, are subject to the control of all as a democratic people. Everyone decides what happens in the public forests and on the public grasslands. For many Americans, the public lands are among the noblest achievements of the national democracy. They stand for the farsighted wisdom and stewardship of which the nation is capable at its collective best. But many, if not most, westerners encounter the public lands system as anything but an empowering, democratic experience. Instead, their experience is often one of a frustrating, alienating bureaucratic paternalism.

On public lands issues, Democrats continue unquestioningly to adhere to the old, national democratic line. There may have been a time when this was good democratic practice, but it becomes a more questionable practice with every succeeding year, especially in the West. There are at least three things wrong with continuing the practice, and all should be of major concern to western Democrats. First is the fact that at this point, every new layer of national "democracy" spread across the West deepens the region's alienation. This is made all the more tragic by the second fact, which is that the national democracy, even though it might still have enough vitality to produce new levels of western frustration and resentment, is rarely any longer a living, humanly satisfying democratic force. Meanwhile, the third fact, the presence in the West of a genuine, vital democratic movement, is almost totally ignored, if not positively resisted, by the party whose mission it should be to feed and nurture that movement.

◆ ◆ ◆

There is something paradoxical about the fact that in the West, the region of the Democratic Party's greatest weakness, there should be such a vital, growing democratic movement and that it should be so thoroughly overlooked by the party. It is overlooked because of an assumption of the Democratic Party that no longer serves the party well anywhere, particularly in the West. It is the assumption that democracy is fundamentally about individuals—about finding out what individuals want as individuals and then figuring out how to give enough of them enough of what they want so that a crucial margin of them will vote for Democratic candidates. This individualistic premise makes the western collaboration movement either invisible or confounding to Democrats. But in fact, westerners might be in a position to remind the party about something fundamental to democracy itself. When Wallace Stegner spoke of the West learning that "cooperation, not rugged individualism, is the quality that most characterizes and preserves it,"[26] he echoed in western terms what Herbert Croly had meant when he insisted that "the people are not sovereign as individuals" but "only in so far as they succeed in reaching and expressing a collective purpose." This recognition of the essentially cooperative nature of democracy led Croly to proclaim:

> The really formative purpose [of democracy] is not exclusively a matter of individual liberty, although it must give individual liberty abundant scope. Neither is it a matter of equal rights alone, although it must

always cherish the social bond which that principle represents. The salutary and formative democratic purpose consists in using the democratic organization for the joint benefit of individual distinction and social improvement.[27]

By working together to solve social problems, Croly was saying, we elevate and expand ourselves as individuals. Jefferson also would remind us that democracy is not about asking people what they want as individuals and then putting together government programs to deliver just enough of what the narrowest possible slice of swing voters wants in order to secure one more electoral victory. Partisan politics at its worst may be about that, but democracy is about something entirely different. Westerners have begun to remember what that is, and they often seem to remember it better than "the Democracy" does. They remember it most vividly in collaborative settings.

When Democrats talk about democracy in public lands issues, they almost always assume the national democratic position that what legally belongs to all Americans should be governed by all Americans, which means that to give a few people in one place a special voice is inherently undemocratic. But such arguments now ring very strangely in more and more western ears. When westerners work hard together on issues that affect their homeland, it feels to them that what they are doing *is* democracy in the most fundamental, the most meaningful, the most enduring sense. When they balance their experience of joining with old enemies to solve hard problems together against the hidebound procedures of a national government and a national democracy that simply no longer seem to work, they feel that they are the real democrats.

The kind of work people have to do in these settings is different from anything else they encounter in public life. It requires them to think harder, better, more creatively; it requires them to reach beyond themselves, to transcend what they already know and comfortably believe; it requires them to listen closely and actively to people they have never liked or trusted, to see whether they can find in their adversaries' pervasive wrong-headedness some grain of insight that might open a pathway to a mutually beneficial solution. And the amazing thing is that it works.

There are failures, of course, and frustrating setbacks, but over and over again, people who push themselves beyond what they think they know find that together they can create something that can work, something that can last. But cooperation not only produces results on the ground; it also produces a unique satisfaction within its participants that they are then loath to let die. This cooperative or collaborative phenomenon has spread so fast because people who encounter it in one situation like both the results and the way the experience feels to them, and they take the first opportunity to replicate it in other settings. These feelings, these satisfactions, are fundamental to democracy as a human enterprise, and they are the core energy for any revitalization of "the Democracy."

At one point, Croly described the benefits of democratic citizenship in terms of "enveloping [the citizen] in an invigorating rather than an enervating moral and intellectual atmosphere."[28] What is so striking about the steadily multiplying instances of westerners coming together across ideological boundaries to solve public lands problems is precisely how invigorating the atmosphere of those settings proves to be, in contrast to the deeply enervating atmosphere of the national decision-making morass. But this problem-solving experience is invigorating in a specific way: it is democratically invigorating. It is precisely the solving of tough problems together that forces people to reach beyond their narrow selves, enabling them to discover together a wisdom they do not have as individuals and making them want to do more of this effective and humanly satisfying work. That is the absolute essence of being a democratic people.

If Democrats in the West could recover merely a glimmer of what it meant for the mission of their party and the cause of democracy to be wrapped together under the title of "the Democracy," they might perceive in the current situation both their own party's relentless contribution to the crisis of democracy in that region and the way in which a rededication of the party to the cause of self-government might in fact be very good politics—might be the best possible platform on which to rebuild the Democratic Party in the West. If the party is to return to its democratic roots, it will have to start paying attention to where westerners are actually practicing democracy and then begin asking what is getting in their way and what the party can do to help them. Part of the answer will be to put less of the party's faith in the centralized system of public land management and more faith in the capacity of westerners to manage their own landscapes. But western Democrats cannot do anything of the kind so long as they remain saddled with the prevailing approach of the national party to their remote region.

It is highly unlikely, though, that Democrats will be able to make the kind of shift proposed here unless Republicans simultaneously make one of nearly equal magnitude. It is impossible to imagine the environmentalists or other progressives who are so important to the Democratic Party trusting westerners with a greater say in running the West unless they could be shown that western control of the land would not be just a cover for corporate greed. Democrats, in other words, will not and probably should not abandon their essentially undemocratic attitude toward the West until Republicans and other conservatives agree to abandon their own most anti-conservative approaches to western issues.

The kind of bipartisanship that would now do the West the most good can come about only if western members of both parties make a fundamental shift—not toward the center but toward the true West. For Democrats, it would be a move toward democracy—toward trusting westerners to govern their own landscapes. For Republicans, it would be a move toward true conservatism—the kind of conservatism that made Theodore Roosevelt a Republican, a conservative, and a conservationist all at once. Those shifts are now within the reach of both parties, but both will need to let go of something that feels solid and safe and instead take hold of something less certain. Republicans must let go of a time-tested form of "just say no" anti-Washington demagoguery that still wins votes but solves no real western problems. Democrats must let go of dependable support on the part of environmentalists for centralized policies and proposals that do indeed deliver nonwestern votes but now rarely result in actual ecological protection for western landscapes.

If both western parties could more or less simultaneously let go of what no longer serves either them or the West, they might also each carry forward half of a new, broad-based and therefore politically potent western agenda. Democrats, drawing on those distant memories of "the Democracy," could give a new, bold, confident tone to that deep-seated western yearning for self-determination—a yearning that has until now sounded more like a high-pitched whine than a mature claiming of a well-earned sovereignty. Republicans, free at last to lay aside their resistance to sound ecological principles, could help articulate those principles on behalf of and in the voice of westerners who have come by their environmentalism from living on and loving well the landscapes they are now prepared to steward. While agreeing still to disagree on a broad array of subjects, then, western Democrats and Republicans could position themselves to stand shoulder to shoulder and, if not sing the same notes, at least harmonize their voices in support of a maturing western agenda.

The work facing western leaders in the first decade or two of the new century is to begin taking charge, one after another, of all the issues of greatest concern to the region. Those issues range from ensuring the survival and well-being of wolves, grizzlies, and salmon to guiding urban growth on western landscapes; from positioning the region to prosper sustainably in the global economy to fashioning new relationships between Indian tribes and their western neighbors; from dealing with dams and with water in general to fashioning new governing institutions for the public lands. Claiming and responsibly exercising western sovereignty over this range of issues will require a new form of leadership and will often require the development of a capacity for bipartisanship at every level of self-government. The western governors are already pursuing this form of regional bipartisanship, especially under the Enlibra banner. When Dirk Kempthorne left the U.S. Senate to run for the governorship of Idaho, he moved from an arena in which westerners still practiced the old politics of ideological posturing to one in which pragmatism was beginning to produce bipartisanship. But the West will not achieve real political maturity until its senators join its governors in developing a capacity for regional solidarity across party lines.

As the West develops a more robust, trans-ideological sense of its own direction and of the urgency of setting its own course, it will have to begin using its unique power in the U.S. Senate to bargain for control over its own land base and to set the stage for those other fundamental alterations in the geopolitical framework that the new global and continental orders are likely to require. The Senate has always lent itself to regionalism, often in a regressive way, but now its inherent regionalism might begin to emerge as a much more progressive force. The fact is that the Senate is the only American electoral institution from which land has not been deleted as a constitutional factor by the one-person, one-vote doctrine. As a result of the constitutional guarantee of two senators per state, the West has far more power in the Senate than its relatively small population would by itself warrant. In pursuing a western agenda by leveraging its senatorial power, it would be crucial for the interior West to forge political alliances with the other public lands states, especially Alaska and the Pacific Coast states, to consolidate the largest possible bloc of western votes in the Senate. Even then, of course, the region will not command a majority of votes in the Senate—but both constitutional provisions and Senate rules have always made the Senate an institution peculiarly susceptible to the actions of concerted minorities. A West united behind an agenda of ecologically responsible devolution of authority would be in a position to build alliances with nonwesterners across the political spectrum.

Only that kind of progressive, bipartisan, regional solidarity among western governors and within the Senate could make it possible to gain congressional approval for river basin compacts or for a West-wide compact to transfer responsibility for public lands to western institutions. Beyond such ambitious agendas, the West may well be called on to use its senatorial leverage to prepare the way for the kind of genuine federalism discussed in chapter 8. We can imagine a time when a bipartisan western political alignment will begin to make senatorial consent to United States Supreme Court appointments turn less on liberal or conservative versions of political correctness than on the appointee's commitment to genuine federalism. The Supreme Court, through two centuries of nationalizing decisions, has played a decisive role in the evolution of the nation's highly centralized constitutional structure. In the twenty-first century, the

Court and the Senate might well become the key bastions of a new, forward-looking federalism. If they do, it will almost certainly be because the West helped nudge them in that direction.

Perhaps the most urgent reason to reinvent federalism and revitalize democracy in a place like the American West is that the world itself must now acquire a capacity for self-government, which it has until now managed to get by without. Given the almost overwhelming economic, ecological, and social challenges now facing the entire world, it is at the global scale that the principle of self-government now faces its greatest challenge. The people of the earth have to take care of the earth—and of one another. Nothing less than global self-determination will do. There is no larger structure of sovereignty, no paternalistic system, that can protect the earth from its people. This means that humans must be developing everywhere the fundamental democratic faith that when people are given the opportunity and encouragement to deliberate together, they can indeed rise above their narrow self-interests and devise solutions that are smarter, sounder, more humane, and more sustainable than any undemocratic decision-making process could ever achieve.

But Americans cannot nurture democratic practice worldwide if they do not trust their own people to govern their own landscapes. If there was a time when national control of most of the West was the most democratic and the most ecologically sound approach, there is also a time when that approach must give way to a more vital, more human-scale, more grounded form of democracy. The time has come when westerners must be allowed to be in charge of the West.

Perhaps the question now facing America in general and the West in particular is whether Americans have enough resilient recollection of what Thomas Jefferson meant by "the course of human events" to recognize something new when something new is upon them. Nothing has been so essentially and eternally new in America as the West. The Rocky Mountains continued moving after the rest of the continent became sedentary, and now the Rocky Mountain West, for reasons largely beyond itself, may finally be prepared to help recall the nation to its deepest democratic roots.

Notes

Introduction: The Lay of the Land

1. Wallace Stegner, "Living Dry," in *Where the Bluebird Sings to the Lemonade Springs* (New York: Penguin Books, 1992), 60.
2. William Riebsame, ed., and James Robb, director of cartography (Center of the American West, University of Colorado), *Atlas of the New West* (New York: Norton, 1997), 62.
3. U.S. Census Bureau, Population Division, Population Estimates Program, *State Rankings of Population Change and Demographic Components of Population Change for the Period April 1, 1990, to July 1, 1999*, ST-99-5 (Washington, D.C.: U.S. Census Bureau, Population Division, Population Estimates Program, 2000).
4. U.S. Census Bureau, Population Division, Population Estimates Program, *Percentage Change in Metropolitan and Nonmetropolitan Populations, by Region and Division: 1990 to 1998* (Washington, D.C.: U.S. Census Bureau, Population Division, Population Estimates Program, 30 June 1999).

Chapter 1: The Lost Trail

1. Sherry Devlin, "Burns Takes a Shot at Griz Plan," *Missoulian*, 23 July 1997, A1, A12.
2. Ibid., A12.
3. William Kittredge, *Owning It All* (St. Paul, Minn.: Graywolf Press, 1987), 139.
4. Obituary, *Missoulian*, 29 July 1996.

5. Seth Diamond, "View Three of the Grizzly Bear Controversy: Seth Diamond," *High Country News* 28, no. 9 (13 May 1996): 15.

6. Phil Church, as quoted in Hank Fischer, "Bears and the Bitterroot," *Defenders* (Winter 1996–1997): 1–2.

7. Sherry Devlin, "Wise-Use Group Backs Griz Plan," *Missoulian*, 11 September 1997, A1, A11.

8. Sherry Devlin, "People for the West Disavowal of Article Favoring Re-introduction," *Missoulian*, 18 September 1997, A1, A10.

9. Sherry Devlin, "Grizzlies: For and Against," *Missoulian*, 7 November 1997, B1, B3.

10. Ibid.

11. Memorandum from Michael Dombeck, chief of the USDA Forest Service, to all employees, 30 October 1997.

12. U.S. Department of Agriculture, Forest Service, *USDA Forest Service Budget Summary, 1990–2000* (Available upon request from Forest Service Region #1).

13. Brian L. Horejsi, "Abdicating Duties to Local Group Subverts Interests of Bear, Nation," *Missoulian*, 16 October 1997.

Chapter 2: Imperial Origins

1. Wallace Stegner, *The Sound of Mountain Water* (New York: Doubleday, 1969), 37–38.

2. Willard Sterne Randall, *Thomas Jefferson: A Life* (New York: HarperCollins, 1994), 569.

3. Donald Jackson, ed., *The Letters of the Lewis & Clark Expedition with Related Documents, 1783–1854*, 2nd ed. (Urbana: University of Illinois Press, 1978), vol. 1, 63.

4. Ibid., 61.

5. Bernard De Voto, *The Course of Empire* (Lincoln: University of Nebraska Press, 1952), 411.

6. Thomas Jefferson to James Madison, 20 December 1787, in Julian P. Boyd, ed., *The Papers of Thomas Jefferson*, vol. 8 (Princeton, N.J.: Princeton University Press, 1953–1997), 426.

7. Theodore Roosevelt to Henry Davis Minot, 11 July 1877, in Elt-

ing Morison, ed., *The Letters of Theodore Roosevelt*, vol. 1 (Cambridge, Mass.: Harvard University Press, 1951), 29.

8. Theodore Roosevelt, *An Autobiography* (New York: Charles Scribner's Sons, 1946), 23.

9. Ibid., 24.

10. Edmund Morris, *The Rise of Theodore Roosevelt* (New York: Ballantine Books, 1979), 15.

11. Nicholas Murray Butler, *Across the Busy Years: Recollections and Reflections* (New York: Charles Scribner's Sons, 1939), 318.

12. Philip C. Jessup, *Elihu Root* (New York: Dodd, Mead, 1938), 404–405.

13. H. W. Brands, *T. R.: The Last Romantic* (New York: Basic Books, 1997), 488.

14. In 1905, Pinchot and Roosevelt transferred the forest reserves from the jurisdiction of the Department of the Interior to the Department of Agriculture, in which Roosevelt established the Forest Service as the managing agency.

15. Theodore Roosevelt, *Theodore Roosevelt: An Autobiography* (New York: Charles Scribner's Sons, 1946), 405.

16. M. Nelson McGeary, *Gifford Pinchot: Forester, Politician* (Princeton, N.J.: Princeton University Press, 1960), 79–80.

17. Roosevelt, *Autobiography*, 404.

18. Morison, *Letters of Theodore Roosevelt*, vol. 5, 603.

19. Roosevelt, *Autobiography*, 404–405.

20. McGeary, *Gifford Pinchot*, 83.

21. Michael J. Sandel, *Democracy's Discontent: America in Search of a Public Philosophy* (Cambridge, Mass.: Harvard University Press, Belknap Press, 1996), 217.

22. Sandel, *Democracy's Discontent*, 218.

23. Roosevelt, *Autobiography*, 36.

24. 42 U.S.C. Sec. 4331.

25. Ibid.

26. 16 U.S.C. Sec. 1531.

27. 16 U.S.C. Sec. 1131.

28. 16 U.S.C. Sec. 1600.

29. 42 U.S.C. Sec. 4332.

Chapter 3: A Century of Rebellion

1. George Mowry, *The Era of Theodore Roosevelt, 1900–1912* (New York: Harper and Brothers, 1958), 251.

2. William Robbins, *American Forestry: A History of National, State, and Private Cooperation* (Lincoln: University of Nebraska Press, 1985).

3. Paul Gates, *History of Public Land Law Development* (Washington, D.C.: Government Printing Office), 623.

4. Quoted in Ray Lyman Wilbur and Arthur Mastick Hyde, *The Hoover Policies* (New York: Charles Scribner's Sons, 1937), 230–231, from a message delivered to the meeting of western governors at Salt Lake City sent through Assistant Secretary Dixon on 26 August 1929.

5. Herbert Hoover, *The Memoirs of Herbert Hoover: The Cabinet and the Presidency, 1920–1933* (New York: Macmillan, 1952), 239.

6. Wilbur and Hyde, *The Hoover Policies*, 232–233.

7. Gates, *History of Public Land Law Development*, 524.

8. Wilbur and Hyde, *The Hoover Policies*, 232. President's announcement of 18 October 1929 in William Starr Myers, ed., *The State Papers and Other Public Writings of Herbert Hoover*, vol. 1 (Garden City, N.Y.: Doubleday, 1934), pp. 109, 110, 111.

9. Wilbur and Hyde, *The Hoover Policies*, 233.

10. Hoover, *Memoirs*, 240.

11. Gates, *History of Public Land Law Development*, 527–528.

12. From the foreword to the 1931 *Annual Report of the Secretary of the Interior*, quoted in Ray Lyman Wilbur, *The Memoirs of Ray Lyman Wilbur*, edited by Edgar Eugene Robinson and Paul Carroll Edwards (Stanford, Calif.: Stanford University Press, 1960), 413.

13. Hoover, *Memoirs*, 240.

14. U.S. Department of the Interior, *Taylor Grazing Act* (Washington, D.C.: Government Printing Office, 1934), 1.

15. Ibid., 1a.

16. Gates, *History of Public Land Law Development*, 611.

17. Ibid., 610–612.

18. Ibid., 614.

19. Ibid., 619. *Congressional Record*, 76th Congress, 3rd session, 24 May 1940, p. 6797.

20. Gates, *History of Public Land Law Development*, 619.

21. Ibid., 623.

22. Bernard De Voto, "Sacred Cows and Public Lands," in *The Easy Chair* (Boston: Houghton Mifflin, 1955), 279–280.

23. Bernard De Voto, *The Easy Chair* (Boston: Houghton Mifflin, 1955), 355.

24. Bernard De Voto, "The West Against Itself," *Harper's* CXCIV (January 1947), p. 245.

25. Gladwin Hill, "Stakes Are High in the 'Sagebrush Rebellion.'" *New York Times*, 2 September 1979, E5.

26. Verne Hamre, "LASER: Rolling Out the Big Guns," *American Forests* 87, no. 3 (March 1981): 56.

27. A. Constandina Titus, "The Nevada 'Sagebrush Rebellion' Act: A Question of Constitutionality," *Arizona Law Review* 23, no. 1 (1981): 264.

28. "The Sagebrush Revolution: Westerners Fight Restrictions on Public Lands," *Washington Post*, 11 November 1979, B3.

29. Nancie G. Marzulla, "Property Rights Movement: How It Began and Where It Is Headed," in *A Wolf in the Garden: The Land Rights Movement and the New Environmental Debate*, edited by Philip D. Brick and R. McGreggor Cawley (Lanham, Md.: Rowman and Littlefield, 1996), 40.

30. Hamre, "LASER," 26.

31. Ibid.

32. Ibid.

33. Ibid., 27.

34. For a detailed look at these bills, see John G. Francis and Richard Ganzel, *Western Public Lands: The Management of Natural Resources in a Time of Declining Federalism* (Totowa, N.J.: Rowman and Allanheld, 1984), 32–33.

35. Bill Prochnan, "Out in the Sagebrush, Watt Still Rides High," *Washington Post*, 26 July 1981, A2.

36. Ibid., A2.

37. Marzulla, "Property Rights Movement," 40.

38. The phrase *custom and culture* appears throughout the Catron

County Plan, Catron County, New Mexico, Ordinance 004-91 (21 May 1991), as noted by Scott Reed in "The County Supremacy Movement: Mendacious Myth Marketing," *Idaho Law Review* 30, no. 3 (1993–1994): 530.

39. Anita Miller, "Private Rights in Public Lands: The Battle Intensifies," *Urban Lawyer* 27, no. 4 (Fall 1995): 889–896.
40. Anita Miller, "The Western Front Revisited," *Urban Lawyer* 26, no. 4 (Fall 1994): 853.
41. Erik Larson, "Unrest in the West," *Time*, 23 October 1995, 52–66.
42. Quoted in Jon Christensen, "Nevada's Ugly Tug-of-War: A Visit to the Heart of the Sagebrush Rebellion," *High Country News* 27, no. 20 (30 October 1995): 1.
43. Jim Woolf, "Feds Targeted by Louder Thunder from Below," *High Country News* 27, no. 1 (23 January 1995): 4.
44. Christopher Wood, "The War for Western Lands," *Washington Post*, 7 May 1995, C2.
45. Quoted in Miller, "Private Rights in Public Lands," 891–892.
46. *United States v. Nye County*, 920 F. Supp. 1108 (D. Nev. 1996).
47. Warren Bates, "County Movement Backers Call Settlement Political Win," *Las Vegas Review-Journal*, 20 April 1997.
48. Chris Fotheringham, "Judge Orders Mediation in Road Dispute," *Elko Daily Free Press*, 26 October 1999.
49. Jon Christensen, "Nevadans Drive Out Forest Supervisor," *High Country News* 31, no. 22 (22 November 1999): 3.
50. Sherry Devlin, "Shovels of Solidarity," *Missoulian*, 5 January 2000.
51. Sherry Devlin, "Shovels of Solidarity Passes through Missoula, *Missoulian*, 28 January 2000.
52. Editorial, *Elko Daily Free Press*, 27 January 2000.
53. Glen Tenney, "At the Margin: The Multiple Meanings of the Shovels," *Elko Daily Free Press*, 30 January 2000.
54. Michael Jamison, "Anti-government Fervor to Spill into Libby Streets," *Missoulian*, 15 March 2000.
55. Editorial, *Missoulian*, 16 March 2000.
56. Jamison, "Anti-government Fervor," 15 March 2000.

57. Michael Jamison, "Rhetoric Drives Rights Speaker from Libby Talk," *Missoulian*, 18 March 2000.
58. Sandra Chereb, "Low Grade Insurrection Begins by Tossing 'Government Waste,'" *Missoulian*, 5 July 2000.

Chapter 4: The Decline of the Empire

1. Kenichi Ohmae, *The End of the Nation State: The Rise of Regional Economies* (London: HarperCollins, 1995), 12.
2. Benjamin Barber, *Jihad vs. McWorld* (New York: Random House, 1995), 39.
3. Andrew Hurrell, "A Crisis of Ecological Viability? Global Environmental Change and the Nation State," *Political Studies* 42 (1994): 146–165.
4. *BLM Interactive Town Hall Meeting Remarks by Secretary Bruce Babbitt, Phoenix, Arizona, March 24, 2000*, available on-line at http://www.blm.gov/nhp/news/speeches/pages/2000/sp000324 babbitt_allemployees.htm (1 January 2001).
5. Deborah Moore, Sue Miller, and Max Benitz Jr., "Local Interests Should Help Manage the Hanford Reach," *Spokesman Review*, 12 June 2000.
6. Jack Ward Thomas, "What Happened to the Forest Service?" *Chronicle of Community* 3, no. 1 (Autumn 1998): 17; Donald Snow et al., "The Lubrecht Conversations," *Chronicle of Community* 3, no. 1 (Autumn 1998): 7.
7. Paul Hirt, *A Conspiracy of Optimism* (Lincoln: University of Nebraska Press, 1994), 284.
8. Todd Wilkinson, "Forest Service Seeks a New (Roadless) Road to the Future," *High Country News* 30, no. 8 (27 April 1998): 8.
9. Forest Options Group, *Second Century Options for the Forest Service: A Report to the American People by the Forest Options Group* (Bandon, Oreg.: Thoreau Institute, 1999), 2.
10. Hirt, *Conspiracy*, xliii.
11. V. Alaric Sample, "Restoring the National Balance," *Chronicle of Community* 3, no. 1 (Autumn 1998): 22–23.
12. Hirt, *Conspiracy*, xxxix.
13. Pat Williams, "Congressional Politics in the Management of the

National Forests," *Rocky Mountain West's Changing Landscapes* 1, no. 1 (Summer 1999): 15.

14. Sample, "Restoring the National Balance," 23.

15. Forest Options Group, *Second Century Options*, 4.

16. Hirt, *Conspiracy*, xxxix.

17. Snow et al., "Lubrecht Conversations," 8.

18. Peter Chilson, "An Era Ends: Old Industries Face Reality," *High Country News* 30, no. 8 (27 April 1998): 12.

19. General Accounting Office, *Report to the Congress: Congress Needs Better Information on Forest Service's Below Cost Timber Sales*, GAO/RCED-84-96 (Washington, D.C.: Government Printing Office, 28 June 1984), 11.

20. Letter to Michael Dombeck from Frank Murkowski, Larry Craig, Don Young, and Helen Chenoweth-Hage, 20 February 1998, 4.

21. Ibid., 1.

22. Williams, "Congressional Politics," 15.

23. Sherry Devlin, "Plan Targets Columbia River Basin," *Missoulian*, 20 April 2000.

24. Jeff Selle, "Forest Plan Could Mean More Logging, Fewer Suits," *Coeur d'Alene Press*, 1 May 2000.

25. John Hughes, "U.S. Land-Use Plan of 63 Million Acres Is Biggest One Ever," *Seattle Times*, 8 May 2000.

26. Devlin, "Plan Targets Columbia River Basin."

27. Snow et al., "Lubrecht Conversations," 15.

28. Sample, "Restoring the National Balance," 23.

29. Thomas L. Friedman, *The Lexus and the Olive Tree: Understanding Globalization* (New York: Farrar, Straus & Giroux: 1999), 7–8.

Chapter 5: A Maturing Region

1. James Gardner, "Mastering Chaos at History's Frontier: The Geopolitics of Complexity," *Complexity* (journal of the Santa Fe Institute) 3, no. 2 (1997): 28–32.

2. Stuart Kauffman, *At Home in the Universe: The Search for the Laws*

of Self-Organization and Complexity (New York: Oxford University Press, 1995), 26.

3. Ibid.

4. Michael Sandel, "America's Search for a New Public Philosophy," *Atlantic Monthly* (March 1996): 74.

5. Strobe Talbot, "America Abroad: The Birth of a Global Nation," *Time,* 20 July 1992, 71.

6. Robert Kaplan, *An Empire Wilderness: Travel's into America's Future* (New York: Random House, 1998), 304.

7. Joel Garreau, *The Nine Nations of North America* (Boston: Houghton Mifflin, 1981).

8. Kaplan, *An Empire Wilderness,* 322–323. Kaplan cites the creation of the Cascadia Planning Group, the Pacific Northwest Legislative Leadership Forum, and the business-oriented Pacific Corridor Enterprise Council.

9. Frank Zoretich, "Southwest Shall Secede from U.S., Professor Predicts," *Albuquerque Tribune,* 1 February 2000.

10. Stephen Maly, "Global Positioning: Rediscovering the Natural Orientation of the Rocky Mountain West," *Rocky Mountain West's Changing Landscape* 1, no. 1 (Summer 1999): 42.

11. Garreau, *Nine Nations,* 311.

12. Wallace Stegner, *The Uneasy Chair: A Biography of Bernard De Voto* (Garden City, N.Y.: Doubleday, 1974), 117.

13. Ibid., 315.

14. David Wrobel, "Beyond the Frontier–Region Dichotomy," *Pacific Historical Review* 65, no. 3 (August 1996): 401.

15. Morris E. Garnsey, "The Rise of Regionalism in the Rocky Mountain States," *The Nation, Special Western Supplement* (21 September 1946): 18–21.

16. Ibid., 18.

17. Ibid.

18. Wallace Stegner, "The Sense of Place," in *Where the Bluebird Sings to the Lemonade Springs* (New York: Penguin Books, 1992), 205.

19. Peter Berg and Raymond F. Dasmann, "Afterword: Reinhabiting California," in *Reinhabiting a Separate Country: A Bioregional*

Anthology of Northern California, edited by Peter Berg (San Francisco: Planet Drum Foundation, 1978), 217.

20. Stegner, "Sense of Place," 201.
21. Robert Frost, "The Gift Outright," in *Selected Poems of Robert Frost* (New York: Holt, Rinehart and Winston, 1966), 299.
22. Wallace Stegner, "Living Dry," in *Where the Bluebird Sings to the Lemonade Springs* (New York: Penguin Books, 1992), 58.

Chapter 6: A Homegrown Western Democracy

1. Wallace Stegner, *The Sound of Mountain Water* (New York: Doubleday, 1969), 37–38.
2. Western Governors' Association, *Policy Resolution 99-013: Principles for Environmental Management in the West, June 15, 1999*, available on-line at http://www.westgov.org/wga/policy/99/99013.htm (1 January 2001).
3. Dan Dagget, "Getting Out of the Cow Business: Nevada's Sagebrush Rebels Shift Gears," *Chronicle of Community* 1, no. 2 (Winter 1997): 7.
4. Ibid., 9.
5. Ibid., 10.
6. Sarah Van de Wetering, "Doing It the Moab Way: A Public Land Partnership at Sand Flats," *Chronicle of Community* 1, no. 1 (Autumn 1996): 7.
7. Ibid., 10.
8. Michael Smith, personal communication.
9. Julia M. Wondolleck and Steven L. Yaffee, *Making Collaboration Work: Lessons from Innovation in Natural Resource Management* (Washington, D.C.: Island Press, 2000), 32.
10. Donald Snow, "Coming Home," *Chronicle of Community* 1, no. 1 (Autumn 1996): 41.
11. Donald Snow, "What Are We Talking About?" *Chronicle of Community* 3, no. 3 (Spring 1999): 35.
12. Theodore Lowi, *The End of Liberalism: The Second Republic of the United States* (New York: Norton, 1979).
13. Michael Sandel, "The Procedural Republic and the Unencumbered Self," *Political Theory* 12 (February 1984): 81–96.

14. Paul Hirt, *A Conspiracy of Optimism* (Lincoln: University of Nebraska Press, 1994), 284.

15. Snow, "Coming Home," 41.

16. Introduction, *Chronicle of Community* 1, no. 1 (Autumn 1996).

17. Barb Cestero, *Beyond the Hundredth Meeting: A Field Guide to Collaborative Conservation of the West's Public Lands* (Tucson, Ariz.: Sonoran Institute, 1999).

18. *Sustaining the Health of the Land through Collaborative Stewardship: Message to All Forest Service Employees from Mike Dombeck on His First Day as Chief, January 6, 1997*, available on-line at http://www.fs.fed.us/intro/speech/speech.htm (1 January 2001).

19. Mike Dombeck, chief, USDA Forest Service, "Regarding the Release of the Forest Service's Proposed Planning Regulations," 30 September 1999. Available online at http://svinet2.fs.fed.us/forum/nepa/rule/glickman.html.

20. George Cameron Coggins, "Of Californicators, Quislings, and Crazies: Some Perils of Devolved Collaboration," *Chronicle of Community* 2, no. 2 (Winter 1998): 27–33.

21. Brett KenCairn, "The Partnership Phenomenon," *Chronicle of Community* 1, no. 3 (Spring 1997): 38.

22. Ibid.

23. Ibid., 38–39.

24. Ibid., 39.

25. Michael Preston and Carla Garrison, *The Ponderosa Pine Forest Partnership: Community Stewardship in Southwestern Colorado* (Cortez, Colo.: Montezuma County Federal Lands Program, 1999), 4.

26. Ibid., 10.

27. Ibid., 43.

28. Steve Shelly, "Making a Difference on the Ground," *Chronicle of Community* 3, no. 1 (Autumn 1998): 39.

29. Preston and Garrison, *Ponderosa Pine Forest Partnership*, 42.

30. Ibid., 1.

31. Ibid., 42.

32. Janet D. Fiero, "Surviving and Thriving Ecologically: The Story of Two Regional Environmental Organizations Integrating Structuration, Autopoietic, and Social Construction Theories" (Ph.D. diss., Fielding Institute, 2000).

33. Grand Canyon Trust, *Restoring Forest Ecosystems*, available on-line at http://www.grandcanyontrust.org/restore_health.htm (1 January 2001).

34. Fiero, "Surviving and Thriving."

35. Brad Ack, telephone interview with Caitlin DeSilvey, 16 May 2000. Notes on file at the Center for the Rocky Mountain West, University of Montana, Missoula.

36. Ed Marston, "The Timber Wars Evolve into a Divisive Attempt at Peace," *High Country News* 29, no. 18 (29 September 1997): 10.

37. Ibid.

38. Ibid., 9.

39. National Headquarters, USDA Forest Service, commentary at the Third Land Stewardship Contracting Conference, Missoula, Montana, 23–24 May 2000. Meeting notes.

40. Ibid.

41. Ibid.

42. *Reclaiming NEPA's Potential: Can Collaborative Processes Improve Environmental Decision Making?* (Missoula: University of Montana, Center for the Rocky Mountain West, March 2000), 58.

43. Ibid., iii.

44. Ibid., 58.

45. Randal O'Toole, interview with Lisa Dix, 13 April 2000.

46. Donald Snow et al., "The Lubrecht Conversations," *Chronicle of Community* 3, no. 1 (Autumn 1998): 15.

47. Ibid., 16.

48. Douglas Kenney, *Arguing about Consensus: Examining the Case against Western Watershed Initiatives and Other Collaborative Groups Active in Natural Resources Management* (Boulder: University of Colorado School of Law, Natural Resources Law Center, 2000), vi, vii.

49. Ibid., ix.

Chapter 7: An Irrepressible Conflict

1. George Cameron Coggins, "'Devolution' in Federal and Land Law: Abdication by Any Other Name," *Hastings West-Northwest Journal of Environmental Law* 3 (Winter 1996): 211.

2. Ibid., 212–213.
3. George Cameron Coggins, "Of Californicators, Quislings, and Crazies: Some Perils of Devolved Collaboration," *Chronicle of Community* 2, no. 2 (Winter 1998): 30.
4. Coggins, "'Devolution' in Federal and Land Law," 213.
5. Emily Miller, "Trouble for Grizzly Bear Recovery Plan," *High Country News*, 29, no. 14 (4 August 1997) http://hcn.org/servlets/hcn.article?articleid=3499
6. Sherry Devlin, "Grizzlies: For and Against," *Missoulian*, 7 November 1997, B1, B3.
7. Brian L. Horejsi, "Abdicating Duties to Local Group Subverts Interests of a Bear, Nation," op-ed article, *Missoulian*, 16 October 1997.
8. Michael McCloskey, memorandum to Sierra Club's board of directors, reprinted in *High Country News* 28, no. 9 (13 May 1996): 7.
9. Ibid.
10. Stephen A. Douglas, speech given in Chicago on 9 July 1859, quoted in Robert W. Johannsen, *Stephen A. Douglas* (Urbana: University of Illinois Press, 1997), 641.
11. David Herbert Donald, *Lincoln* (New York: Simon & Schuster, 1995), 206.
12. William Seward, "The Irrepressible Conflict," speech given in Rochester, New York, on 25 October 1858, available on-line at http://douglass.speech.nwu.edu/sewa_b20.htm (1 January 2001).
13. Ibid. (emphasis added).
14. Bernard De Voto, *The Course of Empire* (Boston: Houghton Mifflin, 1998), 401.
15. Ibid., 402 (De Voto's emphasis).
16. Ibid., 403.
17. Ibid.
18. Donald, *Lincoln*, 398.
19. Coggins, "'Devolution' in Federal and Land Law," 212–213.
20. Kate Shatzkin, "A New Future? Reading between the Lines of the Puyallup Settlement," *Seattle Times*, 15 February 1990, 8.
21. "Intergovernmental Compacts in Native American Law: Models for Expanded Usage," *Harvard Law Review* 112, no. 4 (February

1999): 925 (no author noted), citing David H. Getches, "Negotiated Sovereignty: Intergovernmental Agreements with American Indian Tribes as Models for Expanding Self-Government," *Review of Constitutional Studies* 1 (1993): 120, 121.

22. Ibid., 923.

23. Michael Jamison, "Reclaiming Destiny," *Missoulian*, 27 February 2000. http://www.missoulian.com.archives/index.inn?loc=detail &doc=/2000/February/27-287-life1.txt

24. Coggins, "'Devolution' in Federal and Land Law," 213.

25. Thomas Paine, *Common Sense*, 1776, Quoted in Thomas Paine and Thomas Jefferson, *Paine and Jefferson on Liberty*, edited by Lloyd S. Kramer (New York: Frederick Ungar, 1994), 52–53.

Chapter 8: How the West Might Govern the West

1. John Wesley Powell, *Report on the Lands of the Arid Region of the United States*, edited by Wallace Stegner (Cambridge, Mass.: Harvard University Press, Belknap Press, 1962), 38–57.

2. John Wesley Powell, speech given at the Montana Constitutional Convention in Helena, Montana, 1889. Proceedings and Debate of the Constitutional Convention [Montana] 920–923.

3. Wallace Stegner, *Beyond the Hundredth Meridian: John Wesley Powell and the Second Opening of the West* (New York: Penguin Books, 1992), 315–316.

4. Donald Worster, "The Legacy of John Wesley Powell," in *An Unsettled Country* (Albuquerque: University of New Mexico Press, 1994), 8.

5. Ibid., 23.

6. Ibid., 18.

7. Ibid., 30.

8. Cited in Sue McClurg, "Managing the Colorado River," *Western Water* (November–December 1999): 13.

9. Oregon governor John Kitzhaber, comments to the Seattle City Club, 17 September 1999.

10. Ibid.

11. *Winters v. United States*, 207 U.S. 564 (1908).

12. "Intergovernmental Compacts in Native American Law: Models

for Expanded Usage," *Harvard Law Review* 112, no. 4 (February 1999): 925 (no author noted), citing David H. Getches, "Negotiated Sovereignty: Intergovernmental Agreements with American Indian Tribes as Models for Expanding Self-Government," *Review of Constitutional Studies* 1 (1993): 120, 121.

13. William R. Dodge, *Regional Excellence: Governing Together to Compete Globally and Flourish Locally* (Washington, D.C.: National League of Cities, 1996), 35.

14. Neal R. Peirce, Curtis W. Johnson, and John Stuart Hall, *Citistates: How Urban America Can Prosper in a Competitive World* (Washington, D.C.: Seven Locks Press, 1993), x.

15. Ibid., 90, 98.

16. Stuart Kauffman, *At Home in the Universe: The Search for the Laws of Self-Organization and Complexity* (New York: Oxford University Press, 1995), 271.

17. James Gardner, "Global Regionalism," keynote speech given at the Twelfth Annual US–Mexico Border Governors' Conference, Phoenix, Arizona, 26 May 1994.

Chapter 9: Realigning Western Politics

1. Wallace Stegner, "Water in the West: Growing beyond Nature's Limits," *Los Angeles Times*, 29 December 1985, 3.

2. Wallace Stegner, "The Sense of Place," in *Where the Bluebird Sings to the Lemonade Springs* (New York: Penguin Books, 1992), 205; Stegner, "Living Dry," in *Where the Bluebird Sings*, 58.

3. Tom Knudson, "Western Water: Why It's Dirty and in Short Supply," *High Country News* 30, no. 12 (22 June 1998): 1.

4. Pub. L. No. 102-575, Title XXX. Oct. 30, 1992, 106 Stat. 4693.

5. http://www.den.doi.gov/wwprac/reports/release.htm

6. Western Water Policy Review Advisory Commission, *Water in the West: The Challenge for the Next Century* (Denver: Western Water Policy Review Advisory Commission, June 1998), xxx.

7. Ibid., xvi.

8. Ibid., 6.

9. Ibid., xvi.

10. David Getches, "Some Irreverent Questions about Watershed-Based Efforts," *Chronicle of Community* 2, no. 3 (spring 1998): 33.
11. Gordon W. Fassett, chair, Western States Water Council, *Response re: Western Water Policy Review Advisory Commission Report*, 14 November 1997, available on-line at http://www.west-gov.org/wswc/resp-wwp.html (1 January 2001).
12. Western Water Policy Review Advisory Commission, *Dissenting Views to the Report of the WWPRAC*. Western Water Policy Review Advisory Commission, *Water in the West: The Challenge for the Next Century*. Denver: Western Water Policy Review Advisory Commission (June 1998), Appendix B: Commission Member Comments on Final Report "Dissenting Views to the Report of WWPRAC."
13. Ed Marston, "Craig vs. Craig: May the Best Man Win" (22 February 2000) Writers on the Range, op-ed syndication service of *High Country News*, www.hcn.org
14. Ibid.
15. Ibid.
16. Western Governors' Association, *Enlibra*, available on-line at http://www.westgov.org/wga/initiatives/enlibra/default.htm (1 January 2001).
17. Western Governors' Association, *Policy Resolution 99-013: Principles for Environmental Management in the West, June 15, 1999*, available on-line at http://www.westgov.org/wga/policy/99/99013.htm (1 January 2001).
18. Gene Fadness, "Kempthorne Wants to Return Home Where the Action Is," *Idaho Post-Register*, 16 October 1998.
19. U.S. senator Larry Craig, "Down-Home Mediation Solves Conflicts," *Denver Post Online*, 31 October 1999, available on-line at http://www.denverpost.com/opinion/pers1031b.htm (1 January 2001).
20. Ibid.
21. Ibid.
22. Ibid.
23. Herbert Croly, *The Promise of American Life* (New Brunswick, N.J.: Transaction, 1993), 33.
24. Ibid., 267.

25. Theodore Roosevelt, *Theodore Roosevelt: An Autobiography* (New York: Charles Scribner's Sons, 1946), 405.

26. Wallace Stegner, *The Sound of Mountain Water* (New York: Doubleday, 1969), 37–38.

27. Croly, *Promise of American Life*, 207.

28. Ibid., 409.

Index

253